Studying Disability

Studying Disability
Multiple Theories and Responses

Elizabeth DePoy
Stephen French Gilson
University of Maine, Orono

Los Angeles | London | New Delhi
Singapore | Washington DC

For information:

SAGE Publications, Inc.
2455 Teller Road
Thousand Oaks,
    California 91320
E-mail: order@sagepub.com

SAGE Publications Ltd.
1 Oliver's Yard
55 City Road
London EC1Y 1SP
United Kingdom

SAGE Publications India Pvt. Ltd.
B 1/I 1 Mohan Cooperative
    Industrial Area
Mathura Road, New Delhi 110 044
India

SAGE Publications
    Asia-Pacific Pte. Ltd.
33 Pekin Street #02-01
Far East Square
Singapore 048763

Printed in the United States of America

Library of Congress Cataloging-in-Publication Data

DePoy, Elizabeth.
Studying disability : multiple theories and responses / Elizabeth DePoy, Stephen French Gilson.
    p. cm.
Includes bibliographical references and index.
ISBN 978-1-4129-7576-6 (pbk.)
    1. Disability studies. I. Gilson, Stephen French. II. Title.

HV1568.2.D467 2011
362.4—dc22   2010005923

This book is printed on acid-free paper.

10   11   12   13   14   10   9   8   7   6   5   4   3   2   1

Acquisitions Editor:	Kassie Graves
Editorial Assistant:	Veronica K. Novak
Production Editor:	Libby Larson
Copy Editor:	Heidi Crossman
Typesetter:	C&M Digitals (P) Ltd.
Proofreader:	Susan Schon
Indexer:	Wendy Allex
Cover Designer:	Candice Harman
Marketing Manager:	Stephanie Adams

Contents

Preface   vii

Acknowledgments   ix

PART I. Foundations

Chapter 1: Foundations   3

Chapter 2: Looking Back: Ancient Greece Through
    the 19th Century   9

Chapter 3: Disability in the 20th and 21st Centuries:
    Medical Condition, Construction, or Commodity   25

PART II. Description and Explanation: Building on
    Explanatory Legitimacy

Chapter 4: The Descriptive Element of Explanatory
    Legitimacy Theory   45

Chapter 5: Explanations Introduced   55

Chapter 6: Longitudinal Explanations   67

Chapter 7: Environmental Explanations   77

Chapter 8: Categorical Explanations   91

Chapter 9: Systems Explanations   103

Chapter 10: Contemporary and Emerging Explanations   115

PART III. Legitimacy

Chapter 11: Legitimacy—What Is It?   141

Chapter 12: Who Is a Legitimate Category Member?   147

Chapter 13: Legitimate Humanities Responses   161

Chapter 14: Legitimate Social Science Responses   169

Chapter 15: Legitimate Professional Responses   175

PART IV. Fashioning Communities

Chapter 16: Integrative Academic-Professional Stance Through
        Disjuncture Theory   191

Chapter 17: A Model of Community Legitimacy: Creating
        Human-Environment Juncture   203

References   215

Index   235

About the Authors   247

Preface

Writing this book has been a gift for us. Over the past five years, since the publication of our last book on disability, *Rethinking Disability*, we have read widely and have heard and had exchanges with many scholars in Disability Studies and other fields that are relevant to the study of disability, and of course with our students. Our main purpose in writing this book was to continue our commitment to building on the excellent work of current scholars and to advancing well-informed, progressive theory of disability with an eye toward its application to human rights.

In this work, we have considered and integrated many viewpoints, research studies, and epistemic and axiological positions. Looking backward in history and broadly across the globe has brought us to the marriage of disciplines and ideas that, until now, have not been considered complimentary or relevant to disability. For example, our reading in economics, business, and commerce have stimulated us to consider the power of marketing and branding as definitive of disability as well as a powerful change agent.

As we read, teach, inquire, and engage with colleagues, we experience the paradox of thinking more broadly yet more sharply focused. In the 21st century context in which we are virtually connected and electronically befriended, we would suggest that this seeming paradox is essential and timely for the progressive thinking necessary to cull and bring diverse knowledge to bear on redefining and responding to disability as part of the larger context of human experience.

The book is organized into three major sections. The first part, Foundations, provides a historical backdrop and explores the current contextual trends that have been important in shaping perspectives of and responses to disability. We reintroduce our conceptual framework, Explanatory Legitimacy, in this section to provide the reader with a systematic, logical structure through which to analyze the large body of knowledge that we then tackle in the second section. Part II delves into theoretical descriptions and explanations of disability, from classical longitudinal views that prescribe desirable human experience to emerging conceptual frameworks that scramble and then reorder the intellectual universe and thus the study of disability. Parts III and IV put the theory horse to work for us, applying multiple viewpoints to our ultimate ideological aim of creating a world in which all bodies not only fit but also are welcomed with comfort and tolerance.

Who should read this book? We believe that everyone who is concerned with human rights and diverse bodies should read this work. The ideas are gently provocative in hopes that reading will stimulate rethinking disability as a natural and inherent part of human experience in which fit between bodies and environments needs to be improved. Allowing ourselves to accept a pluralistic understanding of disability can be followed with creative responses that span acceptance to dramatic change.

Acknowledgments

We have many to thank for supporting this work. First, we acknowledge the students who have contributed to our thinking, those who studied with us prior to this writing as well as to the students who read this manuscript and offered critical and constructive feedback.

Of particular note are three of our colleagues who reviewed and provided detailed and valued criticism: Allison Carey, Kristine Mulhorne, and Stephen Marson. Family and friends as well as our colleagues around the world have also been great supports to us.

Our involvement in scholarly organizations such as the Society for Disability Studies, the Disability Section of the American Public Health Association, and the Disability Studies Issues element of the Association on University Centers of Excellence on Disabilities has provided the opportunity to present ideas as works in progress and receive informed scholarly feedback from our colleagues.

Our dear colleague and friend, Noomi Katz, in providing the opportunity for us to share our ideas in Israel, influenced us to make our work global and accessible to other national and linguistic cultures.

Finally, Sandi Oliver has been a model for this book. Her dream, Someday Farms, exists today in Hermon, Maine, and is the epitome of juncture. The equine-human community that she creates at Someday Farms welcomes diverse beings and bodies. Excellence and commitment not only are encouraged for some but also are expectations for all. Sandi has given us the gift of seeing our vision in action.

Thank you.

SAGE gratefully acknowledges the contributions of the following reviewers:

Brenda Jo Brueggemann, *Ohio State University*
Allison C. Carrey, *Shippensburg University*
Denise De La Garza, *University of Texas at Austin*
Stephen M. Marson, *University of North Carolina*
Kristine A. Mulhorn, *Drexel University*
Nancy Hancock Sharby, *Northeastern University*

PART I

Foundations

1

Foundations

The Merriam-Webster Online Dictionary (2010c) defines *foundations* as structures, principles, tenets, or axioms on which to build. Because strong foundations create sound scaffolding for the development of thinking and theory, the chapters in Section 1 look back in history to provide a chronological set of ideas and structures on which to ground current analyses of disability. However, foundations are not static or monistic. The theoretical lenses through which we look back influence not only what we see but also how we interpret and then use our observations to make sense of knowledge and to guide how we apply learning to diverse contexts.

In this chapter, we briefly introduce you to the language and theory through which we analyze disability past, present, and future: Explanatory Legitimacy Theory. This theory is embedded within and builds on the genre of legitimacy theories, which have a long, interdisciplinary history. According to Morris Zelditch (2001), legitimacy theories can be traced as far back as the writings of Thucydides in 423 BCE, in which questions were posed and answered about the moral correctness of power and its muscled acquisition. Although legitimacy theory was birthed by political theory, questions of legitimation have been asked of numerous domains, including but not limited to social norms and rules, distributive justice, and psychology. And while there are differences in the application of legitimacy theories to diverse substantive questions, what all have in common is their search for credibility and normative acceptance. That is to say, legitimacy theory examines the basis on which a phenomenon is seen as genuine or authentic.

Legitimacy theories have posited a range of factors that determine the authenticity or acceptability of laws, rules, or determinations. These elements can be explicit, such as public consensus about genuineness, or tacit, such as efforts to obscure power brokering (Zelditch, 2001). Among legitimacy theorists, Weber (1958) is perhaps best recognized for his assertion that social order inherent in values, norms, and beliefs cannot be maintained without acceptance of this order as valid. Applied to group interaction, legitimacy theory has the potential to denude the normative beliefs that underpin hierarchies, power relationships, and categorization and to expose the values that imbue category status and acceptable responses.

In the tradition of legitimacy theories, Explanatory Legitimacy Theory seeks to analyze, detangle, and clarify categorization and response by focusing on the source of authentification and valuation of explanations for category membership. Rather than political power as its object and subject, Explanatory Legitimacy Theory is concerned with the credibility, value, and acceptance of causal theories which parse and assign humans into groups and then fashion responses to group members.

Moreover, drawing on the work of Shilling (2008), Explanatory Legitimacy synthesizes pragmatism within its foundation in legitimacy, providing the analytic framework for looking at purpose to frame how and why values are applied to explanations and responses to specific groups.

Given the debates about the nature of disability, Explanatory Legitimacy provokes thought and analysis of diverse perspectives and has the potential to validate the use of each within different purposive contexts. Capitalizing on the clarity of seminal legitimacy thinkers such as Habermas (2003) and Parsons (1956), the Explanatory Legitimacy framework clarifies theory types so that each can be compared to those similar in structure and subject.

As we will discuss in Chapters 2 and 3, numerous definitions and models of disability have been advanced and published within the latter part of the 20th and early 21st centuries. The dynamic presence in which models and approaches advance, recede, coexist, or conflict suggests the pluralistic boundaries and influences on the term and its usage and response to it. Explanatory Legitimacy lays bare the axiological context for each model, critically evaluting each for use on its own or in concert with others.

Disability: Description, Explanation, Legitimacy

We present the key principles and language of Explanatory Legitimacy Theory here only to frame our presentation of foundations. Once the foundations have been explored through the lens of the theory, the chronological bedrock will be set on which contemporary trends can be located, analyzed, and prodded for future directions.

In Explanatory Legitimacy Theory, we build on historical and current analyses and debates by defining disability as a human phenomenon comprised of the three interactive elements: description, explanation, and legitimacy. Parsing and distinguishing dialogue into these three divisions enhances the clarity of discussions and comparative analysis by labeling the level at which conversations about human characteristics take place.

Description encompasses the full range of human activity (what people do and do not do and how they do what they do), appearance, and experience. Three intersecting dimensions of description—typical/atypical, observable/reportable, and diversity patina/diversity depth—are germane to the discussion of disability. The typical/atypical dimension is a dynamic categorical system of norms and standards of human activity, appearance, and experience. Typical involves activity, appearance, and experience as most frequently occurring and expected in a specified context. Atypical refers to activity, appearance, and experience outside of what is considered typical. For example, typical walking for an adult would consist of a two-legged gait that follows the alternating advancement of each leg with heel strike preceding toe strike. Atypical walking might involve the use of crutches for ambulation.

The observable/reportable axis speaks to the degree of abstraction and inference that is brought to description. Observable phenomena include activity and appearance and fall under the rubric of those that can be sensed and agreed on, while reportable phenomena, which we denote as experience, are known through inference or telling. An example of an observable phenomenon is walking, and an example of a reportable phenomenon is pain when walking. Identifying abstraction even at the point of description is critical to understanding how diverse views emerge and are reified. We address these points in detail in Chapter 4.

The diversity axis addresses human difference. It spans a continuum from what we refer to as *bodies and backgrounds* diversity patina to the diversity depth. Patina is defined as the surface appearance of a material as a result of exposure (e.g., silver patina; Farlex, 2010d). While it is unique to each object, patina articulates with its exterior environment and thus divulges only a shallow, public appearance. Encased in this part of the axis are the current identity dialogues that refer to race, culture, gender, ethnicity, sexual orientation, and more recently disability (DePoy & Gilson, 2004) and age. Diversity depth, at the other extreme, comprises ideas and individuality that cannot be nomothetically coagulated and essentialized.

The second element of Explanatory Legitimacy leading to the categorization of disability is the set of explanations for doing, appearance, and experience. Different from description, which answers "what" questions, explanation engages with the "whys" of human description. Following with our example of walking, a medical explanation for pain in ambulation might be the diagnosis of arthritis, while an explanation in the exterior environment might be the presence of stairs as barriers that require ambulatory activity that causes pain.

The third definitional element of disability is legitimacy. It is not until this element that humans are purposively situated in categories to which group responses are attributed. Legitimacy is therefore divided into subelements: judgment and response. Judgment refers to axiological assessment of groups and/or individuals (sometimes competing) regarding whether what one does (and thus what one does not do) throughout life, how one looks, and the degree to which one's experiences fit within what is typical and have valid and acceptable explanations that authenticate group membership. Responses are the legitimate actions (both negative and positive) that are deemed credible and appropriate by those rendering the value judgments about legitimacy of group membership. Legitimacy is embedded within a purposive contextual backdrop.

We have selected the term *legitimacy* to explicate the primacy of judgment about acceptability and worth in shaping differential definitions of disability and in determining community, social, and policy responses to those who fit within diverse disability classifications. As we will see in subsequent chapters, many complex factors come to bear on legitimacy. Only some of these factors have been identified in the current literature. They include social values, economic benefit, cultural beliefs, and power structures (Jost & Major, 2002).

To briefly illustrate, let us return to our walking example and consider two people, Ann and Barbara, both of whom walk with a clumsy gait (observable) and are unable to navigate an escalator or stairs to access the second floor of a public building. The descriptive element in this example refers to the limitations experienced by Ann and Barbara in their mobility and access to the second story. Further, because these gaits are out of the ordinary, both walking and access are atypical. Descriptively, then, what both individuals do (walk) and do not do (ascend stairs or an escalator) are atypical and observable.

The next element is explanation. From a medical explanatory perspective, Ann's atypical gait and lack of access are attributed to a diagnosis of cerebral palsy and Barbara's to alcohol dependence. If, however, the environment is seen as the explanatory locus, the presence of the escalator and stairs and social conventions are explanations for limited access, not the atypical walking due to a diagnostic condition. Note that we still have not identified either person as disabled.

Now we come to the determination element of our theory: legitimacy. Because we assert that disability is a judgment about authenticity and worth, legitimate membership in the disability category is determined by who makes the judgment, in what context, and under what set of rules. In this case, both Ann and Barbara name themselves disabled not because of their diagnostic conditions but because of the environment. Ann sees the escalator and stairs as the disabling environmental factors, while Barbara identifies social pressures and nonacceptance as the disabling elements in her life. If we look at the medical community, Ann and Barbara are also considered disabled since both have enduring medical-diagnostic conditions that interfere with their "typical functioning." However, if we now look at eligibility criteria for public assistance, Ann is disabled but Barbara is not. The judgment is rendered on the explanation, not on the description. Further, the legitimate response differs. Ann can obtain public safety net support, and Barbara cannot. In determining who is worthy of public support, the legitimacy or adequacy of the explanation for atypical activity is a function of social, economic, and cultural value. Implicit in the denial of disability status for Barbara is the notion that she is responsible for her own circumstance, is not authentically disabled, and thus is not deserving of a support response.

Before looking back in time, we highlight a major issue in theory and analysis: applying contemporary language to historical discussion. We address this point in detail in Chapters 2 and 3. In these chapters, we draw attention to the term *body*. Although popular vernacular implies that the body is limited to the flesh container and its organic contents, reference to the body throughout this work refers not only to one's organic anatomy and physiology but also to the range of human phenomena that derive from bodies in action, thought, belief, and experience (Baudrillard, 1995; DePoy & Gilson, 2007). This definition is potent in integrating the multiple elements of *embodied* human experience and thus in conceptualizing diversity beyond observed patina characteristics of the organic body. Thus the body and its function include but are not limited to physiology and anatomy. Rather, the body is comprised of the sensory body, the emotional body, the spiritual body, the economic body, the productive body, the expressive body, the body of ideas and meanings, and the body in multiple garb and spaces.

We are now ready to visit the history of earlier civilizations, always keeping the theoretical tools of Explanatory Legitimacy intact and poised for analysis.

2

Looking Back

Ancient Greece
Through the 19th Century

As early as ancient civilizations (Chahira, 2006), there is documentation of a range of responses to "the atypical human" from fascination to revulsion (Barrett, n.d.; Longmore & Umansky, 2001a). Examining images and text historically is always an interpretative practice; thus, we urge the reader to consider that our interpretations are made on the interpretations of others. However, the benefit of looking at history without assuming its truth value gives us a two-way, opaque, but important window on how civilizations responded to embodied difference and how our own interpretation of that response foregrounds the values and prejudices that undergird our 21st-century stance (Cohen & Weiss, 2003; Rose, 2003). In this chapter, we visit diverse notions of and approaches to atypical bodies through chronological and varied geographic contexts up through the end of the 19th century as the basis for understanding the evolution and roots of current definitions of and responses to disability. An investigation of historical text directly or indirectly focusing on disability reveals the following commonalities:

1. What is atypical differs according to context.

2. In each era there have been several potential, assumed, and accepted explanations for a single atypical human characteristic.

3. These explanations form the basis for legitimate categorization and subsequent response to category members.

4. The responses proffered provide an analytic window on the beliefs, values, politics, economics, intellectual trends, and level of technological development of the times, as well as a reflective platform on how current definitions of disability influence how we interpret history (Rose, 2003).

A Lexical Lens and Disability

Historical scholars such as Olyan (2008), Chahira (2006), and Rose (2003) have analyzed text, image, and artifact as the basis for cobbling together historical events and their meanings. Given the evidentiary primacy and availability of text (Clapton & Fitzgerald, 1997), we therefore enter our history through a linguistic portal as this symbolic element of social and cultural groups is critical and often the central data source through which to interpret contextually embedded values and meaning (Baudrillard, 1995; Belsey, 2002).

Looking through a lexical lens, the term *disability* has only recently become a signifier for the grand category of atypical bodies. Early Islamic literature does not contain a single term for embodied conditions, but rather tethers what would be considered today as disabled to illness of the body and heart (Rispler-Chiam, 2007). In the Western world, disability's predecessor, *handicap*, was alleged to have emerged from the cap-in-hand proclamation, in which Henry VII in 1504 CE, recognizing the plight of injured soldiers, formally allowed these worthy citizens to beg in the streets as a means to their own subsistence. More broadly, the recognized use of the term handicap is an equalizing scoring system in which less competent or accomplished persons are artificially advantaged to increase the likelihood of their success when positioned against a superior opponent. In the early part of the 20th century, the term handicap was apprehended by medicine and ascribed to individuals with bodily differences that ostensibly placed them at a disadvantage. Ultimately the word *handicap* in this sense came to mean a specific embodied condition such as a physical or mental handicap. Given the current pejorative notion of bodily inferiority, it is no surprise that a euphemistic term to replace *handicap* was sought to describe bodies that did not conform to the "typical." It is curious that the term *disability* was selected as a respectful replacement for handicap, given that the prefix *dis* emerged from DIS, the name given by ancient civilizations to the ruler of Hades, or the underworld. DIS was portrayed as punishing mortals by extracting their health, well-being, and capacity to function in their environments.

Unfortunately, that we must approach history with current language creates conceptual confusion, and thus we ask you to bear with us and consider

Rose's (2003) dilemma. As she indicated, the nascence of medicine, the historical absence of diagnostic categories, and the critical differences in how economic, cultural, political, religious, social, military, and technological elements of environments were configured and played out over history, which renders the lexical term but not the phenomenon of disability, irrelevant to times before the 20th century. But how does one communicate to a contemporary audience for the purposes of historical analysis without naming the entity under scrutiny with familiar contemporary parlance? Naming disability as the object and subject of study presupposes that it existed and was recognized, albeit differently. We have attempted to partially resolve the quagmire by using the terms typical and atypical to denote a full range of frequency of behavior and appearance, from most to least respectively. As we discuss in detail in other chapters, we have selected this terminology rather than normal/abnormal or able-bodied/disabled to circumvent the value judgments that are embedded in them and to reflect the absence of both of these binaries in historical data (Rose, 2003). With that clarification, let us now gaze back to antiquity.

Early Civilizations

Ancient Greece has caught the intellectual attention of disability history scholars for several reasons. First, there is a fertile body of recorded text and imagery that portrays what we refer to today as impaired bodies. Second, the thinking of Greek philosophers is considered timeless as ancient thinkers have advanced ideas that remain relevant and potent in the 21st century (Thiher, 2002). Third, Ancient Greece provides a complex historical tapestry from which threads of current attitudes and practices toward human difference continue to be respun into new cloths. Fourth, the Greeks were technologically and intellectually sophisticated and thus have great relevance to contemporary times.

A prevalent belief expressed in disability studies literature about the Ancient Greeks was their antipathy toward those with bodies that were at the extreme ends of the atypical range. Responses were ostensibly the expulsion of these bodies from Greek communities, resulting in death (Braddock & Parish, 2001). However, Rose (2003) cautions us to eschew such simplistic and monistic analyses of disability history in Ancient Greece given the complicating factors of geographic expansiveness and naturally circumscribed cultural diversity. So when we speak of Ancient Greece we are referring to the *Greeces* that encompass the multiple elements of Greek culture.

It is curious that the present use of the prefix DIS is consistent with the recorded devaluation of atypical bodies in Ancient Greece reflected in classic myths such as the *Iliad and the Odyssey* (Rose, 2003). Similar in role and function to our art and media today, these and other myths reciprocally depict and enshrine value (Harrison, 2006). From analysis of these texts and other symbols, it appears that those who were mildly atypical experienced a range of support and inclusion in community life from none to full but that in many areas, extreme deviations from the typical were considered inhuman (Braddock & Parish, 2001; Martin & Volkmar, 2007; Rose, 2003), particularly in newborns. As we noted above, there is significant disagreement among scholars regarding the interpretation of legitimate responses to atypical bodies in Ancient Greek civilizations. Rose asserts the inaccuracy of the prevailing view of Greeks as murderers of deformed neonates who were allegedly labeled as monstrosities and expelled from communities to die. She does not deny this practice but claims its limited occurrence across the Greeces. Rather, analysis of myth and symbol reveal the historical common denominator of multiple explanations and responses to atypical bodies and minds on the basis of why the atypical had occurred, its frequency, and whether it could be cured (Rose, 2003; Thiher, 2002). For example, baldness, a typical referent that was conceptually located adjacent to weakness, incompleteness, and other conditions that were explained as imperfections, was tolerated but not valued (Rose, 2003). Supporting Rose's assertion about the pluralistic responses to atypical bodies, Hephaestus, the god of fire, was portrayed as mobility-impaired but with extraordinary power that immortalized him in Greek mythology as magical (Yong, 2007).

Curiously, inferior intelligence was ascribed to the descriptive condition of the inability to hear (DePoy & Gilson, 2004; Rose, 2003). Note the similarities of our contemporary "diagnostic" practice of labeling those whose performance is inadequate on IQ tests as cognitively impaired. Similar to the Greeks, intelligence is used as a grand abstract term that is inferred as a set of capacities and skills and then tautologically reified through observation of those definitional elements. A primary difference between the Greeks and contemporary Western cultures in assessing intelligence lies in the asserted indicators of the construct. As we examine throughout chronological time, because explanation is an inference, multiple inferences such as one's level of intelligence, goodness, or moral judgment have been inductively theorized, ascribed to human behaviors and indicators, and then counted to ensconce these theories as truth (Baxter, 2007).

While the explanation for human variation in activity in ancient civilizations did not meet the criteria for viable science according to contemporary positivist models, Aristotle's early scientific studies and systematic description of the observable world provided a means to identify what was "natural," through what we would consider empirical or logical methods. At the same time, Hippocrates development of medicine and the application of empirical knowledge to treating illness placed rational thought somewhat in opposition to previous mystical explanations of atypical activity. The permeable boundaries between philosophy, literature, and science created a fertile ground for defining, observing, and metaphorically depicting the natural as its opposite, alterity (Thiher, 2002).

When atypical activity was explained in immoral terms, the community, not surprisingly, was not amenable to providing support. However, when atypical performance resulted from war injury—where the explanation was known and considered to be heroic—some cities maintained a pension fund to be made available. (To what extent funds were disbursed to women is not known; however, women were not allowed citizenship status and likely were not eligible for funds.) Thus, as far back as ancient civilizations, variations of the human condition were identified in contrast to what was typical, and some explanations for extreme variation were met with legitimate acceptance and supportive responses while others were not tolerated (DePoy & Gilson, 2004).

Table 2.1 identifies the values and contextual factors of the ancient Greeces that were important in shaping views of what was typical and atypical—how those activities, appearances, and experiences were explained and what values legitimated who was considered human, subhuman, and/or superhuman.

Table 2.1   Contextual Factors in Ancient Greeces

Context	Contextual Factors
Dominant social values	Emphasis on beauty, perfection of form, loyalty to the state, hard work for the benefit of Greece
Geographic/natural	Southern Europe isolated from surrounding area by mountains; maritime travel still primitive
Economic	Agricultural sufficiency supported city dwellers; trade routes established across the Mediterranean
Political	Greek world organized into city-states; highly effective fighting techniques established them as leaders in war; earliest democracies provided one vote/one man for all citizens of the state (male landowners); social organization promoted through rhetorical public debate
Religious	Polytheism; knowledge of the gods transmitted through story; divination
Intellectual	Organization of knowledge by Aristotle; development and standardization of education; medical studies by Hippocrates; spiritual and supernatural hegemony

Spotlighting different histories, we turn our attention to literature from early Jewish, Christian, and Muslim civilizations. With the exception of some human differences such as short stature (Chahira, 2006), atypicality was not a popular or seminal topic of discussion in existing texts and documents. However, text from the Hebrew Bible, early Christian and Muslim documents, and images of the times are rife with symbolic referents to diverse atypical human conditions, appearances, and behaviors. Analysis of these precious snippets reveals four major themes relevant to atypical bodies (Clapton & Fitzgerald, 1997; Olyan, 2008; Yong, 2007):

1. There is no grand category of disability discussed in the Bible or other theological documents examined.

2. Categories of specific "defects" are aligned with devaluated, stigmatized, and excluded status.

3. The Hebrew Bible is replete with binaries such as ugly/beautiful and lame/not lame, and the devalued category of the binary is most frequently linked to terms depicting descriptors that might be included in contemporary disability definitions (e.g., ugliness linked to lameness).

4. While specific disease and defect are treated somewhat differently, most are residents of the "undesirable neighborhood." Some imprisoned there more than others.

5. Responses to people with embodied differences are diverse.

From textual analysis, it appeared as if Islam was more extreme in its marginalization of "defects" than the Hebrews, but both shared a metaphoric and textual disdain for atypical bodies and behaviors. According to Rispler-Chiam (2007), Islam viewed specific embodied conditions as "illness of the heart" (p. 9) yet the writings about atypical conditions, illness, and incapacity are complex and contradictory. The extent to which "illness" is caused by Allah is uncertain, given the internal inconsistency of the text. However, the term *unbelievers* emerges in many of the writings related to illness, providing the opportunity for cure if the afflicted become legitimate believers (Rispler-Chiam, 2007).

In the early Jewish theological texts, those who were "blemished" were prohibited from joining the Jewish priesthood because of spiritual beliefs that only priestly perfection should link God and the earth (Abrams, 1998). However, congregation members did not carry those same expectations for earthly matters; thus, those with atypical appearance were permitted to be full participants in spiritual activity. Even with the permission to worship, those who were atypical in Jewish communities were in large part viewed as punished by God. The explanation for atypical appearance and activity was therefore spiritual and moral reprehensibility. As we will see in the next chapter, the beliefs and attitudes of these so-called primitive early civilizations continue to inhere in current thought and praxis. Curiously, in Egypt, representation of individuals with short stature suggested that this group was well integrated into Egyptian society providing that functional deficits were not present (Chahira, 2006).

The references to disability in early Japan differ according to religion. Shinto texts suggest that a disabled offspring was caused by impurity of the parents (Nakamura, 2006). The metaphoric story of the Leech child is curious in that the disabled infant is excluded but returns as a deity, revealing the complexity of embodied difference (Nakamura, 2006).

Buddhists looked to bad Karma from previous lives as the causal element of atypical conditions. Yet the centrality of compassion in Buddhism rendered obligatory responses of care. Confucianism situates responsibility for embodied difference within a royal hierarchy, with the emperor at the accountability helm. Those who were least able to work were most devalued.

Middle Ages

There is limited knowledge of disability in the Middle Ages, with the majority of the literature focusing on Western civilizations. This part of our historical journey, while taking some short voyages beyond Europe, is therefore lexically and analytically situated mainly in Judeo-Christian civilizations and interpretations. According to Metzler (2006), who concentrated her inquiry on Europe, the negative stigma currently held about the Middle Ages as intellectually vacant both limited scholarly investigation of disability in this era and further glazed the analysis with pejorative and inaccurate assertions of disability being exclusively linked to sin and punishment. Evidence from accounts of miracle healings, theological literature, the scant medical writings of the era, and images in art indeed reveal that the typical Western European tapestry against which the atypical emerged was frayed and threadbare, characterized by pervasive poverty and deprivation (Farmer, 2002; Metzler, 2006). Although there were variations circumscribed by diverse geographies, cultures, and beliefs (Green, 2006), human conditions such as blindness, deafness, and lameness associated with impoverished living conditions were woven into daily life and image (DePoy & Gilson, 2004; DePoy & MacDuffie, 2004; Green, 2006). As discussed above, terms such as disability, impairment, and illness were not part of the lexicon of the Middle Ages. Rather, Latin words such as *imbecillis, deformans,* and *defectus* were used to describe embodied phenomena (Metzler, 2006; Yong, 2007). Curiously, because of their association with extreme poverty, these conditions and others such as blindness or lameness were typical and thus were not central to aberrant identities (Green, 2006). As we noted, there is significant disagreement on the extent to which supernatural and divine explanations were ascribed to impairments. Different from Braddock and Parish (2001) and Winzer (1993), Metzler suggested that as the Middle Ages unfolded, the emergence of medicalization, albeit unlike contemporary medical thinking and practice, started to unseat sin and divinity as the major legitimate explanations for and responses to disabling conditions. The importance of the church in the Middle Ages cannot be diminished however. Embodied difference in appearance, behavior, and experience spanned the theological explanatory range from monster to miracle, and according to Yong (2007) was interpreted as a concrete sign of God's creativity.

Among historical accounts of disability in Islamic nations, Rispler-Chiam (2007) notes that there is disagreement among scholars regarding the degree of tolerance toward individuals with atypical appearance and behavior in the Middle Ages. Because of the variety of explanations for the occurrences of extreme difference in activity, appearance, and experience (from sin to supernatural and natural causes), treatment and community responses were diverse across the globe (Green, 2006).

Of particular note was the growth of institutional and charity approaches to individuals who were atypical, particularly for those who were not embedded within strong kinship systems of their own (Farmer, 2002; Green, 2006). The seeds of faith-based hospitals were sewn in the Middle Ages, as it was not unusual to find members of the clergy in the Christian religions, Islamic societies (Barrett, n.d.), and Buddhist Monks in the Far East (Nakamura, 2006) providing medical treatment to those who were considered ill. The role of faith in healing also has its roots in the Middle Ages. People who could not see or think as most others did, among other human differences, were often the objects of faith healing, a practice that provided concrete evidence of God's love, presence, and power (Finucane, 1995).

Charity in the form of service and almsgiving exonerated the giver in the eyes of God, once again providing a purposive explanation for the extremes of human difference. Through the work of St. Francis of Assisi, the suffering of the poor and sick (particularly individuals with leprosy) gave a moral role to the recipients of care as well as those providing care. Faith-based care for those who approximated the low end of worth was born and now serves as the archetype of contemporary secular charities and institutions (DePoy & Gilson, 2004).

Consistent with Metzler's (2006) claims about the unrecognized richness of the Middle Ages, Braddock and Parish (2001) refer to evidence of some town support for people with atypical thinking and other forms of activity. However, because of the extreme poverty of the population at large, they note that many families would not have been able to provide long-term support, and so it was not unusual to find atypical individuals ultimately turning to begging for survival. This phenomenon is reflected in the literature and artwork of the times, in which beggars are often depicted as individuals who are blind and lame (DePoy & Gilson, 2005/2006; Farmer, 2002).

Not all differences were tolerated even if they were attributed to or associated with poverty. In areas where the population believed in demonic explanations for aberrant bodies, those who behaved in ways that were described as "mad" were feared and persecuted as witches. Increasing social disorder in part was attributed to such individuals, and their murders therefore served as a rallying point for the masses (Stiker, 2000).

Table 2.2 summarizes the seminal contextual factors that shaped explanations of and responses to atypical bodies during the Middle Ages in Western Europe.

Table 2.2   Contextual Factors in the Middle Ages

Context	Contextual Factors
Dominant social values	Catholicism, charity, homogeneity
Geographic/natural	Bubonic Plague killed nearly half the population in Europe in the mid-1300s CE
Economic	The population initially engaged primarily in rural farming through feudalistic arrangement; labor shortages pressured wages upward; monetary system developed; urban centers developed; technological advances improved agricultural production; medicalization emerged
Political	Manorial lords held power over serfs through landownership in exchange for military service; Catholic Church sponsored the Crusades; professional guilds controlled membership and production standards as towns developed
Religious	Primacy of Catholicism throughout England and the rest of Europe initially, challenged by Luther and Calvin in the 1500s CE; waning power of the Catholic Church, especially in England, resulted in the Reformation, a time of persecution for Protestants and other heretics
Intellectual	Intellectual advances were primarily in the area of religion, as reconciliation was attempted between the existence of hardship, mishap, and monstrosity on the one hand and belief in an all-knowing, loving God on the other

The Enlightenment

Moving forward in chronology, as the complexity and differences around the globe became known to civilizations, history outgrew its boundaries as a single narrative of one's own people. However, similar to our discussion of the Middle Ages, the majority of analyses of disability during this era occur through a Western European lens.

In Western Europe and traveling across the Atlantic Ocean to the fledgling United States, an amalgam of both enlightenment and religious thinking prevailed. As the belief in the supernatural was slowly being dethroned by science at the end of the Middle Ages, views of difference were being drastically altered. Advances in scientific knowledge about the anatomy and physiology of the human body contributed to a growing sense that illness and differences in human activity could be explained by observations in the physical world (Stiker, 2000). These views are reflected in the literature and art of the Renaissance period (McClellan & Dorn, 2006; Thiher, 2002). For example, Francis Bacon was particularly important in advancing the systematic study of these observable phenomena (Michalko, 2002; Weller & Wolff, 2005). In 1605 CE, Bacon published *The Advancement of Learning, Divine and Human,* in which he refuted the notion of moral punishment as the cause for behavior that was considered "mad." Humanism in art, emphasizing actual knowledge of underlying physical form, also emerged at this time, depicting detailed and accurate representations of the human body (Nauert, 2006).

Central to shaping notions of the desirable human form were Leonardo da Vinci's creations. Despite Herculean male proportions, da Vinci's Vitruvian Man became the gold standard on which architecture hung and still hangs its form and function hats (DePoy & Gilson, 2007; Margolin, 2002). Moreover, the separation of mind and body with the mind characterized as logical and triumphant over and controlling of the flesh (Michalko, 2002) located disability within the weakened body, opening it up for scrutiny and cure. The power of this perspective slowly became globalized in non-Westernized, nondeveloped countries during Renaissance colonialism (Livingston, 2005). Yet, as noted by Livingston (2006), the divergent perspectives on the nature of humans between Western and non-Westernized cultures were in conflict limiting the application of rationale individualism that formed the basis for embodied notions of disability to understanding disability in African civilizations.

In the West, moral explanations of difference in human activity, appearance, and experience did not disappear as philosophers, clergy, playwrights, artists, and others continued to illustrate the metaphoric use of atypical bodies and minds to communicate diverse meanings (Mitchell & Snyder, 2000;

Thiher, 2002). Thiher points to the centrality of Shakespeare and Cervantes in shaping contextual notions of madness that still prevail today.

Explanations for the distinction between atypical birth-based and acquired human characteristics were developed during this time (Stiker, 2000) and served as platforms for value distinctions as well. For example, some birth-based failures in activities necessary for typical growth were explained as "monstrosities," while differences in what individuals did that resulted from observable explanations such as injury were regarded as natural (Stiker, 2000). Distinctions were drawn between activity, appearance, and experience that were consistent with what today would be referred to as mental illness and mental retardation (McClellan & Dorn, 2006; Thiher, 2002; Yong, 2007).

As in early civilizations, the legitimate response to people who behaved in atypical ways was in large part influenced by how these behaviors were explained and how the explanations were valued. Moving forward in the Enlightenment era, however, brought increasingly complex explanations for all human activity, appearance, and experience, including the atypical. Particularly of note in Westernized developed countries, as religious hegemonic explanations gave way to philosophical and systematic intellectual rationales (McClellan & Dorn, 2006), the interplay of economics and social factors in influencing analysis of all human experience emerged and influenced explanations of the atypical as well.

For example, the population of the poor often contained a disproportionate number of individuals who exhibited atypical activity and appearance. As evidenced by the English Poor Laws, social explanations for these differences were met with resources, while explanation seated in individual blame was not (Scanlon, 2008). Even with the assertion of objectivity (Durant, 1991), the social bias toward self-discipline was therefore apparent in legitimate responses early in the history of Western civilization as well as in some, but not all, non-Western regions (Nakamura, 2006; Olyan, 2008). As example, in civilizations such as Botswana, a highly social context, individualism did not fit conceptually with indigenous beliefs and practices, and thus a colonialized view of disability as restricted to individual body was not useful to advance analysis of atypical explanation and response in these environments (Livingston, 2006).

With economics now embedded within the European explanatory canon, the differential role of individual wealth in response to the atypical could be interrogated and postulated. Not unlike current times, those with resources were not necessarily governed by the legitimacy criteria that shaped the response to poor individuals. Treatments for the atypical with medical explanations did exist and were available to those who could pay (Metzler, 2006). Although it is likely that economic status had always played a role in judgment and response, prior to the Enlightenment the primacy of religion in shaping values and legitimate responses obfuscated or overshadowed other influences.

In the Enlightenment, the recession of religion as explanatory for natural phenomena, the emergence of epistemologies which created a foundation for the social science of economics, and the emphasis on systematic production made it possible to identify the role of economic status in creating different legitimacy criteria for the poor and the rich (Kaul, 2008).

Based in large part on Cartesian and positivist thinking, institutions for those who behaved in ways that were observed and classified as mad developed and flourished during the 17th century. These served to remove irrational thinkers from public view rather than as a means to change behavior (Thiher, 2002). This era also saw the proliferation of poorhouses, punitive institutional settings for the poverty-stricken, many of whom could not work due to embodied conditions (Wagner, 2005). Although some whose most basic needs could not be met outside of institutional settings sought solace and home in these edifices (Weller & Wolff, 2005), institutions primarily were characterized by harsh conditions (DePoy & Gilson, 2004), clearly indicating the devaluation of institutional residents.

In colonial America, explanations for frailty that were based in illness and aging were valued as worthy of care. Thus, in small communities with no other resources, the care of frail elders was provided by families, women in particular (Green, 2006). The ethnic, cultural, and religious homogeneity of early colonial America fostered acceptance of poor, ill, and elderly members who were not seen as blameworthy (Axinn & Stern, 2000). Further, atypical activity, appearance, and experience that were explained by poverty were not always distinguished from those explained by illness, and so informal arrangements for the care of the poor were not necessarily different from those provided to individuals whose atypical characteristics were explained by illness (see Table 2.3). This phenomenon is not surprising, given the infancy of medical thinking about human activity.

The Victorian Era

Proceeding into the Victorian era, values of continental Europe, England, the newly colonized America, and less developed countries began to take divergent courses, as did conceptualization and legitimate judgment and response to the atypical. According to Holmes (2004), the works of Victorian authors such as Dickens illuminate the atypical in Western Europe as melodrama, a cultural stage so to speak in which the atypical is showcased as anomaly, failure, or unfortunate freak. From her analyses, Holmes further induces a forward thinking definition of disability as those conditions for which European cultures were not prepared. It is curious to note the appearance of this perspective in Victorian literature given the asserted ownership and dating of

Table 2.3 Contextual Factors in the Enlightenment Era

Context	Contextual Factors
Dominant social values	Poor distinguished as *worthy* or *unworthy*; in America, small communities that were ethnically, culturally, and religiously homogeneous cared for their own poor
Geographic/natural	Expansion of Western civilization to the *New World*
Economic	Beginning of industrialization: mass production and cost minimization; science of economics began; businesses of printing and journalism develop; banks established; profit motive developed
Political	Money is equated with power; English Poor Law of 1601 legislated financial relief in the community, especially for workhouses
Religious	America: homogeneous Puritanism
Intellectual	Rationalism; Bacon publishes *The Advancement of Learning, Divine and Human* in 1605 and refutes sin as the cause of madness; systematic thought extended to economics and society; literacy level increases

the "social model" as emerging in the United Kingdom in the 1970s. Further supporting Holmes's definition is the growth of the Victorian asylum (Wright, 2001; Yong, 2007), which continued the Medieval creation of segregated, incarcerating environments for "imbeciles" and "lunatics." Such institutions removed atypicals from public spaces as well as unburdened the women who had been responsible for providing care. Collecting atypical individuals under a single roof so to speak facilitated the medicalization of these two groups, as they became an easily accessed object for scientific scrutiny (Yong, 2007).

In the United States, of particular consequence to legitimate definitions of and responses to difference is the growth of the American economy rooted in large part in the uninvited procurement of land on which American Indians lived and on the importation of slave and immigrant labor from other countries (Axinn & Stern, 2000; Holstein & Cole, 1996). The existing system of poor relief in colonial America that was based in communal values and shared beliefs was ultimately challenged by the influx of people from diverse geographic regions of the world and by indigenous people (Wagner, 2005). The juxtaposition of indigenous and immigrant people peppered with economic prosperity and increasing economic concern created a complex backdrop for understanding responses to atypical bodies. The rationale for inclusion and in-home responses to the atypical that were apparent in early colonial America were breaking down and quickly became unseated by contemporary "medical" explanations (Axinn & Stern, 2000), feathering the nest for medical and ultimately broader professional colonization and ownership of the "atypical body and mind" (DePoy & MacDuffie, 2004; Mink, Solinger, & Piven, 2003; Teghtsoonian, Moss, & Teghtsoonian, 2008).

Despite the appearance of medicine, morality and social circumstance were still dominant explanations for unusual behavior, experience, and appearance in the United States. Moreover, with the vast resources available to *everyman* in the New World, tolerance (and thus acceptance of poverty as a legitimate explanation for the atypical) and charitable responses quickly degenerated. Poverty was assumed to be a self-imposed condition resulting from intrinsic laziness in an environment that was rich and in which economic productivity was becoming a paramount value (Axinn & Stern, 2000; Wagner, 2005).

In response to the increasing social costs and disapproval of poverty, the towns and cities began to build poorhouses for the poor of all ages, the sick, and those behaving in a manner consistent with what today would be categorized as intellectually impaired, mentally ill, or socially deviant (Wagner, 2005; Yong, 2007). These categories of people held dependence and lack of productivity in common. Circumstances within the poorhouse were particularly and intentionally harsh to encourage families to support their members at all costs rather than abandon them to the care, and thus the expense, of the local government. The elderly were increasingly represented among the population in poorhouses as attitudes toward the unproductive frailty of old age grew increasingly unfavorable and illegitimate for sound community response (Wagner, 2005). Those who aged well were considered morally "worthy," and those who did not were "unworthy" of comfort and support.

As noted by Holstein and Cole (1996), the life of a 19th century immigrant was not often conducive to aging well, and thus emergent categories of legitimate worthiness were in large part a function of poverty of racial and ethnic groups. Recognizing this trend, disabled immigrants were often expelled from the United States at entry points such as Ellis Island (O'Brien, 2004). While poverty, illness, and morality had been the primary explanations until now, observable diversity categories, including race, ethnicity, and other intrinsic human differences, were all thrown into the "explanation stew" without the public recognition that poverty and economic circumstance of these groups were underlying factors in explaining the atypical.

Of particular historical importance to understanding contemporary disability theory and practice responses were the abstract creations of Quetelet (1969) who invented the mathematical constructs of the normal or bell-shaped curve and measures of central tendency. These two ideas form the foundation of contemporary empirical knowledge and fabricated the dissection of humanity into the two categories of "normal" and "abnormal" (DePoy & Gilson, 2007). Applying the bell-shaped curve to human variation, Quetelet (1969) extrapolated the concept of "the normal man," who was considered to be both physically and morally normal. Synthesizing probability theory with the "normal man" construct, normal was not only interpreted as the most frequently occurring phenomenon but also morphed in translation to what "should be." Observation therefore turned to prescription, and anyone with observed phenomena on the tail ends of the curve was categorized as "abnormal." Fields of study and professions (with medicine in the lead) which espoused and reified these positivist approaches to inquiry as truth (such as normal and abnormal psychology, medicine, special education, social work, and so forth) all distinguished between normal and abnormal and claimed the "abnormal" as their epistemic and ontological property as well as their axiological obligation (DePoy & Gilson, 2004, 2007).

What sense do we make of all this in Western cultures? Consider the hallmark of the industrial era: mass production. Mechanization and production standards were based on statistical projections of what an average worker should "normally" accomplish within a given set of parameters, at minimum. Efficiency experts, such as Fredrick Taylor (Kanigel, 1999), aimed to study and increase the rate of normal production as a basis for economic growth.

As industrialization advanced and associated economic productivity with legitimate goodness, links between standardized expectations, moral judgment, unemployment, and disproportionate poverty among people with activity, appearance, and/or experiential differences further located legitimacy of explanations in terms of productivity. The attribution of "not" normal activity, appearance, and experience to assumed productivity limitation was and remains an important determination of current disability legitimacy.

Legitimate support responses to abnormal individuals, as expected, followed value judgments about who was worthy and who was not. Poverty in and of itself was no longer considered a legitimate explanation for atypical activity or need for supports or services, and thus the poor were not treated well (Axinn & Stern, 2000; Stone, 1986; Wagner, 2005; Yong, 2007). Those who could not compete were unable to find jobs to generate income and thus fell into the ranks of the morally reprehensible to be met with the legitimate response of incarceration in poorhouses. What made people legitimately "good" was the capacity to earn (Longmore & Umansky, 2001b; Scotch & Schriner, 1997). As presented in Table 2.4, complexity of contextual factors increased during the Victorian era, setting the stage for the dominance of economic resources in shaping notions of typicality, explanations for atypicality, the criteria for legitimately acceptable explanations, and legitimate rationale for community response.

Table 2.4 Contextual Factors in the Victorian Era

Context	Contextual Factors
Dominant social values	Increasing diversity in ethnicity, values, and customs across the population; productivity; profit
Geographic/natural	Immigration from diverse parts of the world
Economic	Industrialization; economic expansion across the country using slave labor; global markets available even for produce after the development of steamships and refrigeration
Political	Democracy with two-party system (Republicans and Democrats)
Religious	Mainly Christian, but diverse across slave and Asian populations
Intellectual	Quetelet (invention of statistics and the concept of normative thinking); Locke (ideas are not innate); Hume (knowledge depends on a series of perceptions); behaviors are based in "habits" of thinking; utilitarianism (virtue is the greatest good for the greatest number of people)

It is curious to note that the term *disability* in the early 20th century did not include medical diagnostic conditions, as revealed in the 1906 edition of the *Standard Dictionary of the English Language* (2010) that proffered:

Lack of ability of some sort

Impotence

The state of being disabled

A crippled condition

Lack of competent means

Inability (the disabilities of poverty)

Legal incapacity or the inability to act (the disability of lunatics and infants)

Note that these definitions are both expansive and progressive in that they do not delimit disability to specific diagnostic explanatory conditions or exclusively embodied phenomena but rather approach disability from a broad descriptive stance not entwined with explanation.

3

Disability in the
20th and 21st Centuries

Medical Condition,
Construction, or Commodity

In Chapter 2, we looked back at the history of disability from early civilizations through the beginning of the 20th century. We noted the linguistic friction caused by referring to past phenomena with contemporary terms (Nancy, 2008). While disability lexicon in the 20th and 21st centuries in the United States becomes somewhat more familiar to us, we find a new challenge brought about by global diversity of language and conceptualizations of difference. And so we continue to ask you to bear with us as we analyze and discuss disability using contemporary intellectual and linguistic tools from Western civilizations.

As we enter the 20th century, the medicalization of embodied difference is not yet complete. The preeminent social, moral, spiritual, and most recently economic explanations were fading but not yet eclipsed. It is curious to note that even in the presence of historical accounts, the scholars of the late 20th century who resurrected these explanations as new and original models neglected to indicate their predominance over deficit explanations throughout most of our written history.

Since writing our last disability book in 2004, there has been a tremendous growth in disability history scholarship. Rather than reiterate the excellent work that has already been produced, we use Explanatory Legitimacy as a lens through which to analyze important trends and to address issues that have escaped significant scrutiny.

Through this stance we foreground the influence of contextual factors on value judgments (not on human activity, appearance, experience, or even the explanations attributed to human phenomena) as the key to understanding categorization, the legitimate hierarchical system which locates embodied otherness into categories (Clapton & Fitzgerald, 1997), and the responses that are deemed legitimate for members. We now turn our analytic attention to the trends that have shaped contemporary understandings of and responses to disability since the turn of the 20th century. Before we begin our analysis, we remind you that while global notions of disability are becoming engorged with Westernized notions of atypical and typical embodiment, civilizations differ widely in their perspectives and lexicon. In this chapter, we therefore examine four primary contextual factors that have coalesced in the 20th century in developed nations to inform contemporary Disability Studies: (a) science, technology, and professional authority; (b) industrialization, standardization, and the advancing primacy of a global market economy; (c) human diversity; and (d) reconstituting the fragmented body. We turn to a discussion of each of these now.

Science, Technology, and Professional Authority

The advancement of science and technology has been a crucial factor in reshaping conceptualizations of disability and responses to it across the globe (Warschauer, 2004). As we saw in the last chapter, Enlightenment thinking provided the foundation for the growth of medical science and for the emergence of medical explanations for embodied difference in the mid-19th century. However, while scientism was an important intellectual and epistemic European and US trend at the turn of the century, it operated in the background and thus shaped the interface among typical and atypical people (Tregaskis, 2004).

Professionalization of medicine, not the scientific knowledge itself, was the element that positioned physicians as dominant in characterizing and claiming disability as their expertise and work (Nancy, 2008). Thus, because physicians were able to assert professional authority, the atypical was colonized and then owned by medical explanations (Friedson, 1980). To a large extent, disability in the 21st century still is synonymous with long-term or medical conditions despite efforts to rebrand it and relocate disability outside the body (DePoy & Gilson, 2008).

Thus, the increasing sophistication in knowledge and technology not only shaped disability as primarily medical but also ensconced the medical and health professions as guardians and gatekeepers in many aspects of the lives of people with legitimate diagnoses. We provide additional detail on this important point later in the chapter when we examine the central role that medical and health professionals play in how disability ethics and legislation have been formulated and enacted (Gleeson, 1997).

The love affair and continued waltz between medicine and technology further reified disability as an embodied medical condition and gave life to the disability industry (DePoy & Gilson, 2008; Gill, 1992). Central to this industry are pharmaceutical corporations, diagnostic entities, profitable treatment techniques, manufacturers and retailers of durable medical equipment and assistive technology, and proprietary training. Great advantages of this industry are that it has made it possible for people not only to survive with frailty and illness but also to have significantly extended the life span and participation of the typical and atypical person. But the industry is a multi-edged sword (Livingston, 2005; Tregaskis, 2004; Yong, 2007).

Claimed ownership of advancing technology and scientific knowledge created the foundation for the development of professional education as well as the need for the newly minted role of *expert*. In order to occupy this role, extended education had to be completed and certified. While education ostensibly ensures a high standard of knowledge acquisition and use, this practice sets the scene for restrictive licensure designed to maintain the knowledge in the hands of a few legitimate experts on whom those who were not legitimate members of this elite group became dependent (DePoy & Gilson, 2004; Riley, 2006). This dependency, in a context of capitalist dominance, provided an excellent opportunity for economic advantage exercised by health professionals, physicians in particular, who were held in high esteem and paid accordingly. So as we can see, the advancement of scientific knowledge and technology was important in lifesaving and enhancing strategies as well as in the creation of an elite group of professionals who exchanged specialized knowledge and skill for status and economic benefit (Seldon, Bartholomew, & Myddelton, 2007).

As the 20th century unfolded, the explosion in science, coupled with the desirability of health professional status, was influential in the proliferation of specializations within medicine and in the development of health professions, including medicine, which named and crafted responses to individuals and groups with atypical bodies (Friedson, 1980). Included among these fields were nursing, psychology, social work, and the rehabilitation professions (e.g., physical therapy, occupational therapy, speech and language pathology, and vocational rehabilitation).

It is interesting to note that as these professions grew and became competitive, the team approach over other possible collaboration strategies was selected and espoused as the best method for determining and responding to disability. In this framework, professionals theoretically pool their expertise to make decisions about how best to work with, treat, or assist disabled individuals and groups. Many models of teamwork have been posited, all based on communication and the assumption that mutually exclusive expertise will be combined to achieve the most desirable intervention results. However, the team approach, in which multiple professionals, sometimes with competitive value and ethical professional codes, each charge for service, has provided the opportunity and justification for another layer of intervention: managed care (Kongstvedt, 2003). Under managed care and similar approaches, individuals with atypical bodies (Strasser et al., 2005) who receive services from multiple providers are assigned to an individual who orchestrates both services and payment for those services.

Thus, while technology (Warschauer, 2004), professional knowledge, and social status have brought major opportunity for providers, these factors have also created limiting conditions in that the increasing cost of technology has elicited managed-care control and has forced providers from small practices into large global corporations that can purchase and maintain costly technologically based research and practice (Stone, 2001).

The confluence of professional hegemony, diagnostic views of disability, and technology has not only had a significant influence on direct treatment and practice but has also erected a medicalized context for ethics, values, and policy related to embodied conditions. Debates about the meaning of embodied anomaly of 20th and early 21st century technologies such as prenatal testing, mapping the human genome, robotics, and so forth have remanded, and to a large extent contained, disability ethics within the domain of bioethics. We discuss this issue in greater detail later in the book.

So far, we have located technology adjacent to medicine and professional hegemony. However, the important role of technology is not restricted exclusively to the professional arena. Technology has evoked profound differences in the lives of individuals with disabilities, how they interact with others and one another, the erosion of theorized dependency by technological solutions, and so forth (Warschauer, 2004). Of particular importance in the technological arena is the growth of electronic communications with their potential to paint, materialize, and market images (Longmore & Umansky, 2001a; Riley, 2005). "Whether by better or for worse, the metamorphoses of a person's image are controlled by the image maker" (Riley, 2005, p. 2). As technology has changed, so have images, their method of presentation, and the venue. In developed nations, the portrayal of disability in film and electronic media has provoked debates about numerous issues including but not limited to identity and who should control image, the purposive use of embodied difference, and so forth.

Of course, no history of disability in the 20th century would be complete without discussing computer technology. The extent to which computers have been increasingly embedded into daily life in the 20th and early 21st centuries is obvious at the points of direct interface between humans and machine, and less so as the interaction becomes more abstract and obfuscated. Given the largesse and complexity of technology and disability, we devote more detailed attention to it in Chapter 10 and throughout the book.

Industrialization, Standardization, and the Advancing Primacy of a Global Market Economy

There are numerous theories and definitions of the market economy, each with an emphasis on different essential elements of a system of producing products and services and exchanging resources for consumption. In this chapter, we define the market economy as a system of exchange in which production is divided into diverse labor groups and products and services are, for the most part, self-regulating according to supply and demand. Although market economies to a greater or lesser extent are manipulated and controlled by government, they have free trade as their philosophical foundation (Rivoli, 2009). Given this definition, it is clear that the development of the global market economy has been and continues to be a critical factor in how disability has been conceptualized, defined, and treated in the 20th and 21st centuries. On many levels, economics, productivity, and profit have been primary in shaping our current views of legitimate disability and our responses to these views (Riley, 2006).

Three points related to the historical development of the market economy are important in our discussion in this chapter. First is the rise of industrialization and mass production at the turn of the 20th century in Europe and the United States. This phenomenon was responsible in large part for poverty to be jettisoned as a legitimate, worthy explanation for the atypical. That is not to say that poverty did not exist. To the contrary, many were poor as market-based modes of production became increasingly institutionalized in Western Europe and the United States in particular and influenced parts of the globe that were not as timely in their adoption of these production structures.

However, despite the recognition that poverty has negative consequences for all domains of human activity, its legitimacy as explanatory and worthy of adequate responses diminished at the turn of the 20th century (Axinn & Stern, 2000). Only in the latter part of the 20th century was the relationship between poverty and disability once again foregrounded and rhetorically asserted through disparity agendas. Capitalizing on the civil rights movements of the 1960s, these conversations primarily highlighted economic differences in opportunity and access to resources associated with disability category membership but even now have not proceeded to a sufficiently complex analysis of distributive processes and structures that have the potential to decrease significant chasms in resource equity (Michaels, 2006). As example, health care disparities between nondisabled and disabled groups in access to health care, work opportunity, and essential resources have been increasingly recognized and attended to in the literature and in some respects in response. However, the vagueness of advantage and disadvantage as well as the range of distributive diversity among disability category membership is only nascent in its consideration. That is not to say that poverty does not remain disproportionately high among groups labeled as disabled. However, the complexity of analysis necessary to unpack the morass of cause and consequence and to inform relevant and adequate responses is underdeveloped (Harris & Associates, 2000).

Related to poverty is the historical centrality of the importance and nature of work in the 20th and early 21st centuries. At the latter part of the 20th century, the location and characteristics of the workplace shifted and have become more flexible with the potential of technology to expand the work location even to mobile computing and communicating from one's easy chair. However, going to work at a physical location outside of one's home remains the dominant paradigm even now and defines one's worth as a contributor to the market economy. Thus, the capacity to work has been a primary marker of one's social value.

As such, the early, small, private nursing homes that provided safety and care for disabled family members were replaced with larger institutions with tripartite concern for releasing family caregivers to economic production, removing the atypical from public view, and maximizing the profit potential of institutional care (Foundation Aiding the Elderly, n.d.). It is important to note the gender role in caregiving. Although not extensively explored and addressed in research and analysis until the women's liberation movement and a shift in gender equity, gender was a critical factor both in culturally and in economically influencing who legitimately could receive care, by whom, and of what nature (Stone, 2001). Because traditional gender roles did not position women in remunerative employment until the latter half of the 20th century, they were default caregivers mostly for men who became incapacitated (Kane & Kane, 1998).

Curiously, in institutions for those with mental and intellectual explanations for atypical description (and thus without physical restrictions), the market economy was integral in shaping policy and practices. Institutions isolated individuals from the community, removing the burden of care from those who were employable or who needed to care for nondisabled children. Furthermore, during the Great Depression, administrators developed operating strategies for employing patients as an unpaid workforce (Foundation Aiding the Elderly, n.d.; Stiker, 2000). These practices, asserted to be therapeutic, perpetuated the economic survival and growth of institutional care in times of economic scarcity and set a precedent for the future economic exploitation of individuals with mental and cognitive diagnostic explanations for atypical activity, appearance, and experience (Braddock & Parish, 2001). When institutional care was deemed too costly, deinstitutionalization was initiated, with the rhetorical justification of community inclusion. Unfortunately, the services and resources that would be needed to assist these individuals to successfully adjust to life in an environment that had social and behavioral standards for which institutional residents were unprepared were not sufficient.

A second point regarding the market economy is the development of what we refer to as the disability industry (DePoy & Gilson, 2009). Remember that above we noted the professionalization of disability and the claiming and possession of disability by the health care industry. Not unexpectedly, health care was not the only group that sought to derive significant economic benefit from direct and tangential involvement with disability. For example, regardless of how nursing homes were originally conceptualized, care systems grew into a multi-billion-dollar industry in which economic stakeholding and profit were and continue to be driving forces (Davis, 1997; Gill, 1992; Gleeson, 1997). As we indicated earlier, increasing costs of technology and insurance also paved the way for the proliferation of global provider corporations whose focus is on maximizing profit through engaging in the disability industry (Riley, 2006).

Third, there is an increasing shift from the charitable not-for-profit to the profit sector in many parts of the disability industry, highlighting the recognition on the part of disabled individuals and the industry that disability has the potential to create new and important consumer markets (DePoy & Gilson, 2009; Riley, 2006).

Of critical importance and clearly related to the growth of the market economy is the role of mass production. Although mass production originated before the 20th century (Tate Museum, n.d.), its primacy as a mode of product development emerged in the United States and England around the turn of the century. Mass production allowed the fabrication of large quantities compared to the individual crafting of one object at a

time. Because of the automated mechanisms and division of labor, standard sizes and appearances became the hallmark of mass produced items, creating a profit-driven normative tail that in essence wagged the dogged notion of typical and desirable embodied dimensions, appearances, and behaviors. As we discuss in subsequent chapters on design, standards became codified and prescriptive of how bodies should look and function, and in contrast, how nonstandard bodies should be treated and homogenized into production standards. An extreme example was the Ugly Laws passed in numerous urban areas around the turn of the 20th century. The following text is representative and reveals the devaluation of individuals on the basis of their nonstandard appearance:

> No person who is diseased, maimed, mutilated, or in any way deformed so as to be an unsightly or disgusting object or improper person to be allowed in or on the public ways or other public places in this city, or shall therein or thereon expose himself to public view, under a penalty of not less than one dollar nor more than fifty dollars for each offense. (Grandquist, 2009)

Note that building on Quetelet's handiwork, *bodies* refers broadly to the cognitive and moral body as well as the physical body (Boyles, 2007).

Diversity

Before we contemplate how diversity influenced disability, we attend to and clarify the word *diversity*. Since the turn of the 20th century, it has shifted in meaning from *variety* to *difference* and then to *category membership*. In the 1913 edition of *Webster's Dictionary of the English Language*, diversity is defined as "dissimilitude, multiplicity of differences, variety." This definition is reflective of the chronological context in the United States when those with different appearances, languages, and other embodied phenomena became increasingly proximal to one another.

Illustrating the conceptual changes are the following current definitions of diversity: biological difference (Wilson & Lewiecki-Wilson, 1999), racial difference (Shiao, 2004), noticeable heterogeneity (Farlex, 2010a), and minority group membership (Basson, 2004; Healy, 2004). These definitions are typical of late 20th-century perspectives in which diversity has increasingly been equated with identified groups, specifically some but not all who have been the object of historical discrimination (Anderson & Middleton, 2005; DePoy & Gilson, 2004; Healy, 2004; Mackelprang & Salsgiver, 2009).

Relevant to disability history, the bifurcation of bodies into normal and abnormal emerged from large-scale screening and surveillance (Armstrong,

2002; Rosenfeld & Faircloth, 2006) with ascription of *diverse* only to embodied deviance. Philosophically consistent are chronological, ontological, and epistemological shifts of diversity from a characteristic belonging to all humans to one that names its owners as marginal (Thomas, 2001). Immigration trends, civil rights movements, policy changes, technology, and increasing globalism (Healy, 2004; Parillo, 2005) have been important influences on diversity conceptualization in the 20th and early 21st centuries. Thus disability, while somewhat dissimilar from nonpermeable diversity categories, increasingly has been located within the diversity discourse as the intellectual trends of the latter part of the 20th century became more complex and interdisciplinary.

In the mid- and even the waning of the 20th century, diversity patina (or what we have referred to as bodies and backgrounds diversity) was the primary basis for assigning the diversity label to bodies, perhaps because of its focus on observable differences in human appearance that coalesced with the new juxtaposition of ethnically, racially, and otherwise diverse groups resulting from 20th century immigration patterns, particularly in the United States. In the United States, immigrant populations settled in many cities, and African American descendants of slaves who had populated mainly the rural South began moving to urban centers to find work. The proximity of diverse groups, while idealized by some of the popular culture of the time, created friction and intolerance that played out in and affected the identification and care of those who appeared atypical due to legitimate medical explanations (Scotch, 2001). For example, in response to exclusion from agencies and services for Anglo-American whites, the African American community created its own self-help hospitals, homes for the aged, unemployment relief, and other similar services based on the values of kinship and mutual aid. Similarly, ethnic groups outside the mainstream of observable Anglo-American categorization, such as Jews, created their own systems of aid and support (Abrams, 1998).

As the 20th century proceeded, the number of groups included in diversity patina expanded. An increasing focus on integrationist multiculturalism (DePoy & Gilson, 2004; Goldberg, 1994) and cultural competency discourse have been omnipotent in the literature and rhetoric of the time, enlarging the diversity patina membership beyond race, ethnicity, and culture to include human differences together with, but not limited to, age, sexual orientation, health and illness, and ability. The move on the part of disability rights activists to position disability within the multicultural/human diversity discourse and to define a distinct disability cultural diversity patina have both benefited and limited people with medical explanations for atypical activity, appearance, or experience (Gilson & DePoy, 2005). Benefits have included increasing recognition and protective legislation to redress historical discrimination. However, we propose that the lack of diversity depth and the potential for this analysis to lead to more complex human rights responses has contributed to segregation masquerading as specialized policy and legislation, as we discuss in depth in Chapter 16 (Bassnett, 2001).

Consider, for example, the diagnostic explanation of Down syndrome. The designation of Down syndrome as a legitimate medical explanation has placed individuals with that label under protected status in several countries. Social action resulting from this status includes, but is not limited to, consent decrees forcing deinstitutionalization and supporting community inclusion. However, while civil rights have been asserted and progress has been made in this arena, individuals labeled with Down syndrome continue to be subject to stigma and to exclusion from community life and resources (Scotch & Schriner, 1997). Consider the individual who is able to work in competitive employment but because of discrimination is not given a chance despite his or her skills. This individual might not even have a choice of living environment or roommates.

Reconstituting the Fragmented Body

We see one overarching challenge and struggle of the 20th and 21st centuries circling around a major intellectual and praxis dilemma that we refer to as reconstituting the fragmented body. Let us examine what we mean by this term. As we have discussed, over the chronological, geographical, cultural, and social regions, the human body and its boundaries have been scrutinized, adorned, scorned, materialized, and manipulated through diverse agendas. With the legacy of the Enlightenment synthesized with the profitability of standardization, the body has been carved into fragments of organic and fabricated components (Butler & Parr, 1999) and cleaved by cultural, intellectual, and professional self-service. Superimposing the term *disability* on top of an already splintered definition of *bodies* has created a quagmire that has characterized discussions of disability in the late 20th and early 21st centuries. To conclude our visit with the past, we propose that contemporary history leaves us with the body in fragments and thus with the charge to reconstitute the body as the basis for expanding human environment fit, or what we have referred to as *full juncture*. (See Chapter 10.) Here, we briefly introduce nine slivers of embodiment that are relevant to defining and responding to disability:

The body as impaired or disabled

The atypical body as estranged

The prescriptive body

The political body

The included body as excluded

The euphemistic disabled body: wheel chairs, low vision, and hearing impairment

The politically correct body as subcategory

The linguistic body

The performing body

As we will see, Disability Studies grapples with which of these embodied or environment elements is the definitional seat of the construct as well as which should be the domain of response. Throughout the book, we look at these slivers, expanding them to their full size, immersing ourselves in their interrogation and analysis, and then situating them in applied response. The task that raised its presence and now looms for Disability Studies scholars is the reconstitution of the body and its location in environments that meet and provide comfort for a full range of human diversity.

The Impairment/Disability Binary

The impairment/disability binary was first proposed in the United Kingdom in the 1970s in efforts to clarify what is meant by embodied deficit and then to guide the concomitant responses to this condition. According to Henderson (2006), impairment is a corporeal condition which leaves a body aesthetically or functionally different and to a great extent inferior to the typical unimpaired body. Disability is distinguished from impairment as a social condition in which impaired bodies are met with discrimination and exclusion. In this nomenclature, terms such as physically or cognitively disabled do not make sense and should be supplanted by physical or cognitive impairment. From this distinction, the social model of disability emerged. Through this modular lens, the body is not indicted as the locus of disability at all. Disability is simply a discriminatory social response to an atypical body.

The Atypical Body as Estranged

Building on the social model, this sliver is embedded within the facet of discrimination. Estrangement ranges on a continuum from social ostracism to removal of civil and human rights on the basis of embodied difference. As example, until the passage of Public Law 94-142 in the United States, children with atypical bodies were excluded from public education (Mitchell &

Snyder, 2000). And in Japan, Hays (2006) found that despite legal prohibitions against discrimination, employers chose to pay hefty fines rather than hire employees with embodied differences.

The Prescriptive Body

As noted by many scholars of embodiment and Disability Studies (Mitchell & Snyder, 2000; Nancy, 2008; Siebers, 2008; Titchkosky, 2007), the construction of disability defines its opposite, *not disability*. The category of disability lies in the realm of alterity or otherness and thus, by its presence, prescribes what should be common, typical, and normal. Moreover, prescription lays the foundation and opens the floodgates for corrective strategies, which we now refer to as evidence-based practice. For example, Wolfensberger's 1972 work, *Normalization*, reified normal behavior and then prescribed how to produce it in those who did not comply to the normative model. Although contemporary, politically correct lexicon does not spotlight the concept of normal as prescriptive, Wolfensberger's ideas still live within revised verbiage, most recently referred to as "social role valorization" (Wolfensberger & Thomas, 2007). That universities still teach courses in abnormal psychology, pathology, and so forth removes the rhetorical camouflage from the prescriptive body. As we discuss throughout the book, the debate evoked by the prescriptive body as rejection of the atypical condition or outright intolerance of those whose bodies do not conform to prescription is frequent, incendiary, and fractious.

The Political Body

In 2004, Gilson and DePoy conducted a study in which they were attempting to ascertain differences in disability identity between those born with and those who acquired atypical, embodied conditions. Testing group differences in the nature of a construct assumes the existence of the phenomenon—in this case, disability identity. The findings revealing that only one informant asserted a disabled identity were curious until understood within a political context. The informant was part of a disability activist group in which identifying as "disabled and proud" (Hahn, 1991) was as much a political statement as a personal one. This research foregrounds the political body that emerged early in the 1970s as individuals with embodied differences sought political power to redress exclusion (Hahn, 1991, 1993). Media, legislative, intellectual, and even counterculture strategies have been and are currently being employed to assert the political body, or as Linton (2005) suggests the

Body Politic. We return to this embodied element that seeks political influence and power in subsequent chapters.

The Included Body as Excluded

This sliver refers to the rhetoric of inclusion that has been an increasing part of disability policy and praxis during the latter part of the 20th century. As built institutions have been dismantled, terms such as *mainstreaming* and *community integration* became popular in the latter half of the 20th century. These words were replaced with the term *inclusion* to denote the placement of atypical bodies in nondisabled geographies. We agree with Titchkosky (2007), who undresses inclusion to reveal a segregated and excluded body. The term *inclusion* itself is defined as the action of "taking one in" or containing (Merriam-Webster, 2010d). Thus the lexical definition of inclusion unmasks its actors and their agency with those already in the "mainstream neighborhood" in control of who they will both let in and contain. Titchkosky (2007) further reminds us of the oxymoronic nature of specialized inclusion programs. If special programs are needed to include people in a social, employment, or other context, these programs are created by those already situated comfortably, are bounded and different often with eligibility criteria, and thus maintain otherness, albeit in a more central location.

In one of our research inquiries, we traveled to a western state in the early 1990s to see the fabled, exemplary, community living sites for individuals with embodied differences. Our inquiry revealed a host of community living apartments in which previously institutionalized individuals resided. Examination suggested the analogy of meteorites that have been created by the combustion of a larger meteor, the institution. That is to say, these homes were just smaller, more dispersed versions of institutions, with the same staff, policies, and so forth. What had changed was simply size and location of these rhetorically inclusive programs. As we discuss in subsequent chapters, contemporary history has left us at the portal of a major challenge for civil rights scholars and activists to move beyond current models of excluded inclusion to meaningful redefinition and redesign of environments that are welcoming.

The Euphemistic Disabled Body:
Wheelchairs, Low Vision, and Hearing Impairment

This theme refers to the wheelchair, low vision, and hearing impairment as not only the symbols of disability but also the major response loci. Although some limited responses to bodies with other atypical characteristics have been part of the 20th and 21st centuries, a synthetic gander of visual culture exposes these three conditions as the penultimate symbols of disability. A significant part of environmental response is therefore devoted to the erection of ramps, enlarged doorways, elevators, lifts, Braille signage, captioning, and other built environment modifications and gizmos to allow wheelchair and communication access. Analysis of these images and what images are missing highlights *access* as euphemistic only for some, and further suggests who is considered as a member of the disability club for whom special accommodations will be made. Figure 3.1 presents the "access symbols" for public venues.

The Politically Correct Body as Subcategory

Reflected in this jagged sliver is the language used to respectfully discuss disability and disability type. First is the overarching, grand category of disability in which members of the group are referred to as persons with disabilities. This person-first vernacular was coined to affirm "personhood" before invoking

Figure 3.1   The Euphemistic Disabled Body: Wheelchairs, Low Vision, and Hearing Impairment

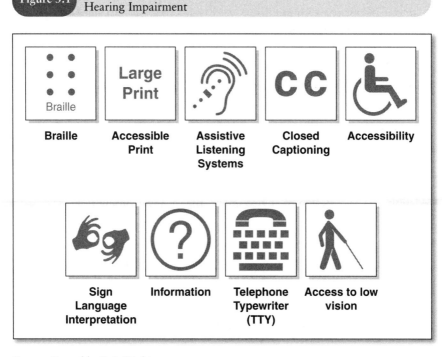

Source: Created by B. J. Kitchin.

the "d" word. Based on the rhetorical premise that people are not simply their disabilities, person-first language sought to replace human descriptors such as cripple, schizophrenic, handicapped, and so forth. The disabling subcategory, such as cognition, visual impairment, mobility impairment, and so forth remain in the "naming" of people as long as these words are moved behind the apron strings of "person." So in the United States and in other parts of the world as well, 20th-century public talk about what subcategory of one's body is disabled can occur with the use of politically correct monikers.

Although not popular in many regions, such as the United Kingdom, many entities in the United States vehemently argue in favor of this lexicon. We address this ongoing language policing in the contemporary history chapter because the focus on political correctness has been an important 20th and even 21st century trend in academic, government, and professional milieus. However, similar to Michaels (2007), we suggest that maintaining debate and argument on what language is most correct derails a larger and more profound needed change, that of equalizing resources, valuation, and respect. Moreover, as we have noted above, locating disability "with a person" reifies its embodiment and flies in the very face of the social model that person-first language is purported to espouse. Person-first language lays bare the devaluation of disability in contemporary US history as it is used only for certain conditions, disability being the major one. We have not heard anyone suggest that beauty, kindness, or even unkindness be located after personhood. We never refer to undesirables with terms such as murderer, misogynist, misanthrope, stingy, and so forth. How much disdain does a condition have to bear to be located after personhood is asserted?

Curiously, language is not simply restricted to what is apparent, explicit, and articulated, but also has the potential to wield its power in its negative spaces or what we refer to as the tyranny of the opposite, or what is *not* said. The words and phrases that comprise person-first language, while cobbled by committee (so to speak) for the purpose of political correctness, are often opaque in what is *not* spoken. That is to say, modifiers that are part of human experience (such as disabled, crippled, retarded, and so forth), rather than being reconceptualized as human diversity, remain *not* desirable; rather they are lexically relocated after personhood to obfuscate what is *not* desirable. Inherent and perhaps not effectively shrouded in these linguistic finaglings is the unworthiness of these modifiers and a hierarchy of worth and *not* worth on the basis of category membership.

The Linguistic Body

The linguistic body is a late 20th-century phenomenon in which the body is seen as a metaphor. Growing out of the embodiment literature and then expanded in literary criticism, this sliver foregrounds the role of language and image as meaning-maker. Through this lens, linguistic image defines the boundaries of bodies and reflects their comparative worth. The recent neuroscience lens that locates language within the neurology of the corpus has caught the embodied linguistic wave, probing the linguistic body for its uniqueness and evolutionary locus.

The Performing Body

Embedded within the postmodern intellect of the late 20th and 21st centuries is the view of the body as performance. Related to disability, scholars such as Mitchell and Snyder (2000), Fries (2007), and Siebers (2008) suggest that the disabled body is on show, the object of the public stare, and thus performs intentionally or more frequently unintentionally. From this vantage point, the disabled body performs its embedded roles, those of alterity and difference that then creates the body's nonexample: normalcy. Furthermore, the disabled body is evocative of performance from "normal bodies" who respond with several 20th century themes. Depending on the nature of performing disabled body, these responses may be charity, pity, awe, disdain, or aesthetic nervousness, among many other scripts.

So Where Does History Leave Us Now?

Although medical explanations remain primary in defining disability even now, and the body remains in fragments, the history of disability took an important turn in the latter half of the 20th century that has significantly influenced responses to it. Disability rights scholars and activists eschewed the medical explanation for disability, since such explanations of permanent deficit were impotent in advancing social justice, equality of opportunity, and rights as citizens for those who were members of the disability club (DePoy & Gilson, 2004; Nussbaum, 2006; Stein, 2006). Rather than accepting themselves as the "work" for the disability industry, disabled scholars looked externally to the body to explain disability. Early scholars such as Oliver (1997) and Linton (1998, 2005) proposed the intolerance and rigidity of social and built institutions rather than medical conditions as the explanation for disability. Words such as *inclusion, participation,* and *nondiscrimination* were introduced into the disability literature and parlance reflecting the notions that people who did not fit within the central tendencies of Quetelet's "normal curve" were disabled by stigma, prejudice, marginalization, segregation, and exclusion. Demands for equality of opportunity were anchored on theory and research, which documented the locus of disability within systems of oppression and discrimination rather than internal to the organic body. With the view of disability explained by external social, economic, and political factors and by marginalization, exclusion, and abrogation of human rights (Nussbaum, 2006; Stein, 2006)—rather than an internal medical condition, the locus for disability and thus for necessary responses has become a moving and complex target. We refer to these views under the umbrella of disability as constructed. Still, professions, policies, and theory, despite their assertions to look beyond the body, situate disability within the organic human domain, as evidenced by embodied eligibility criteria even for human rights and antidiscrimination legislation, and further exposed by oxymoronic terms such as physical, cognitive, learning, and mental disabilities. Because deficient bodies are the object of disability rights discourses and responses, this conceptual quagmire reveals the inherent hegemony of medical abnormality (Davis, 1995) that all but eclipses constructed perspectives in explaining the atypical and locating disability within the body, regardless of the narrative indicting systems of oppression rather than bodies as disabling factors.

As we note above, the early 21st century leaves many challenges for characterizing and responding to bodies that display embodied diversity, attract the gaze as the "other," and that frequently live in the underbelly of charity and inclusion. We have foregrounded two of these critical errands in this chapter: reconstituting the body and reconciling the medical-constructed binary. In subsequent chapters, we examine the epistemic and theoretical players on the disability field as the basis for understanding necessary to advance viable and relevant social change.

PART II

Description and Explanation

Building on Explanatory Legitimacy

4

The Descriptive Element of Explanatory Legitimacy Theory

In this chapter, we explore the descriptive element of Explanatory Legitimacy Theory. As we introduced in Chapter 1, description focuses its attention on what *is* and thus provides clarity about what is being discussed and debated with regard to defining disability. Three essentials—activity, appearance, and experience—comprise description. Because Explanatory Legitimacy seeks to provide a clear language for considering and debating equivalent concepts and principles, we have distinguished these three elements from one another to further disambiguate dialogue.

1. *Activity* is defined as performance or movement. It comprises what people do, how they do it, and conversely what they do not do throughout their lives. By *do not do* we refer to what is missing from expected activity, which thus may be considered as atypical. Some, but not all, theoretical lenses attribute pathology or abnormality to atypical, but we do not.

2. *Appearance* is defined as how people look to others and to themselves.

3. *Experience* is defined as one's personal and unique ways of being, articulating, and sensing. Experiences are not directly ascertainable and must be inferred or asserted by the "experiencer."

Although *description* may seem straightforward, let us look further to see how complex it is. By analytically examining and then building on relevant literature, we advance our organizational framework of description. We suggest that human activity, appearance, and experience span a full range of diversity and have been categorized along the three previously introduced axes: observable/reportable, typical/atypical, and diversity patina/diversity depth.

Foundations of Description

Human description provides the initial foundation on which to begin explanatory analyses, categorization, and legitimate responses to category members. It is not surprising that the questions of what people do, how they appear, and what they experience have been pondered and answered in many ways by philosophers, social scientists, theologians, and others. Current research methods reveal a logical hierarchy of abstraction, since seeking rationale for why something is occurring requires that one be clear on what the object of investigation and analysis is. Consider these epistemic approaches to illustrate. In search of common themes among all humans, anthropologists have observed people in their environments to discover the tacit and explicit factors that govern human description in groups (Ember & Ember, 2002). The key methods of inquiry in anthropological and related research (observation and interview) are consistent with the three elements of description that we have posited and seek to systematically characterize and ripen description for explanation (Gubrium & Holstein, 2009). Experimental-type inquiry begins with Level I, or descriptive questions, to establish existence before seeking further abstraction (DePoy & Gilson, 2005/2006). And historians have collected and analyzed information from years past on which to further advance current and predictive understanding of human behavior on the basis of what *was* (Thomas, 2001).

In short, description provides diverse maps or taxonomies as the basis of navigating the complexity of human phenomena. Descriptive elements provide perimeters for further inquiry and theorizing about the multiple views that can be applied to human activity, appearance, and experience.

We now detail and illustrate the three conceptual descriptive axes—observable/reportable, typical/atypical, and diversity patina/diversity depth—because of their critical importance to legitimate categorization.

Observable-Reportable Axis

Observable description, referred to as *observables*, is comprised of activity and appearance that can be ascertained directly through sense data and agreed on by more than one observer. By *sense data*, we mean data that can be understood through one or more of the five senses of hearing, touching (including feeling), smelling, seeing, or tasting. Most often, observable description results from hearing, touching, smelling, or seeing.

Reportable description, referred to as *reportables*, are indirect or inferred descriptors of human phenomena. The *observable-reportable axis* forms the basis for the other two axes because the knowledge obtained through senses, or sense data, is the least abstract of the descriptive data. Thus, we suggest that observable description is the unifying element of human behavior. That is to say, all people, no matter what their diversity characteristics are, engage in observable common activity that can be sensed by others, the most basic being survival behaviors such as eating, sleeping, and so forth (Watson & Schwartz, 2004). Because reportables are experiences that are not directly ascertainable and must be inferred or asserted, determination of human similarity and difference and typical/atypical is less clear when proceeding on reportable data.

The questions of what people do, how they appear, and what they experience have been approached and answered in many ways by philosophers, social scientists, theologians, and others. Although we cannot cover all the theories on human description, we draw your attention to the importance of theory in bounding and guiding description through the dense thicket of perspectives. So, although description is the most basic and least abstract unit of Explanatory Legitimacy, it is rife with disagreement depending on how observation and report are refracted by varied conceptual lenses. In Chapters 5–10, we present and apply multiple theoretical genres to description, and so in this chapter, we just introduce some basic ideas to ground our understanding of descriptive diversity as it applies to disability.

Longitudinal Theories

We begin with human development literature and developmental theories, or what we refer to as *longitudinal theory*. We have named them longitudinal to reflect the value on time foregrounded and used as descriptive as well as explanatory. Longitudinal theories have provided a prolific, influential body of knowledge with particular importance to the typical/atypical axis of human description and thus to the study of disability. These theories translate the typical/atypical axis into binaries of normal and not normal or abnormal over the span of a human life. Although there are numerous longitudinal theories that address all aspects of activity, appearance, and experience (as we detail in Chapter 6), what all have in common is the tenet that there are a set of typical observables and reportables that can and should be present as humans age.

Perhaps the most famous of the longitudinal theorists was Sigmund Freud (1938). Focusing on reportable psychosexual development, he and those who built on his theories posited that all individuals were intrinsically predetermined to unfold in typical ways through a series of normative stages. Deviations from those stages were a function of pathological family relations, or, for post-Freudian theorists, dysfunction in the interaction between the developing individual and his or her emotional-social context (Davis, 2002; Hutchison, 2007). Of course, only a small part of psychosexual theory is descriptive, but the descriptive element of this set of approaches creates the platform on which to determine if an individual fits within what is typical and desirable and for the subsequent application of explanatory analysis.

Theorists such as Piaget (1962, 1985) who addressed human thinking adopted similar deterministic approaches to diverse domains of human activity.

Initial developmental stage theories were built by conducting research on humans and using observations of human activity at specific ages across the life span to determine what was characteristic, frequent, and therefore normal (Davis, 2002). From these theories, based on observation or reportable inference of what is, norms were developed and translated into prescription or what should be. In essence, what is now asserted as desirable in human performance, appearance, and experience is based on what the majority of people did during systematic observation, or what was most typical. Deviance, or what was atypical, was therefore defined as outside the limits of normal (Davis, 2002; Hutchison, 2007).

Interestingly, Freud developed his theories of normal psychosexual development largely on the basis of data from his clinical practice (Freud, 1938), and Piaget (1962, 1985) theorized cognitive development on the basis of inferences about his observations of his own children (Mussen, 1983).

Environmental Theories

In large part, thinkers who perforated the significant role of inference in longitudinal description with the claim that its evidence base was untrustworthy looked away from descriptive chronology to what they considered as clear observable responses to environmental elements which could also be observed. As you can already see, theoretical spectacles magnify different parts of description such that description itself is not monistic.

As we discuss in more detail in Chapter 7, we have defined environment broadly as sets of conditions. Theories in this category place their emphasis on conditions, both within the body and external to it. *Interior environment theories* are concerned with observable and reportable conditions, structures, and processes that are embodied. While longitudinal and interior environment descriptors are not mutually exclusive, each shines its spotlight on a different set of descriptive performers. As will be discussed in Chapter 7, the interior environment lens focuses descriptive attention on biological, physiological, and psychological phenomena, many of which are based in biology and therefore seek to describe and visually create scientific observable conditions (Pauwels, 2005). Clearly, interior environment descriptors have become elevated and ensconced as primary in contemporary, medicalized discussions of disability.

Exterior environment theories target description of conditions that are external to bodies. Unfortunately, this boundary is not clear, particularly with principles of contemporary theories of embodiment. However, classical behavioral and learning theories do mate the distinction between internal and external conditions and thus are clear exemplars of exterior environment descriptive frameworks. Bringing the observable-reportable axis to the forefront and eschewing reportables, exterior environment behaviorists posited that theories inferred from abstract indicators of human description. That is to say, reportables were based on untrustworthy evidence. In response, they developed theories in which a direct or a mediated behavioral reaction to environmental stimuli was observed and recorded. As we will see in Chapter 7, these descriptive studies empirically preceded and gave rise to explanatory notions of human behavior as a response in total or in part to external conditions (Hutchison, 2007).

Longitudinal and environmental approaches to characterizing human description have formed the foundation for current views of what is typical and atypical even with the increasing attention to diversity correlates, including but not limited to the patina variables of race, ethnicity, geography, class, sexual orientation, and socioeconomic status. Moreover, as we discuss in detail, basic longitudinal (developmental) theories form the foundation for standardized testing that identifies acceptability and deviance in multiple domains of human activity, appearance, and experience (Aylward, 1994).

Cultural Theories

Anthropology has advanced another important way of looking at humans. Classical anthropological research relied on ethnographic inquiry to infer and then characterize typical practices and the explicit and tacit rules that governed them. Classical anthropologists immersed themselves in unknown groups that they named *cultures* to observe activity as the basis for discovering the boundaries and characteristics of that particular culture, including criteria for membership, kinship, roles, language, symbols, rituals, traditions, and rules of behavior (Wiseman, 2000). Ethnographic research methods and variations thereof have been applied more recently to characterize norms and expectations within familiar cultures, such as the teen culture and rural cultures in developed nations.

Although culture has multiple definitions, here we define it as a construct that attributes shared identity, language, tacit rules, symbols, rituals, and expectations to all members of a specific group. Ethnographic inquiry among other narrative and theory-building approaches has been instrumental in defining cultural norms and distinguishing culturally specific differences in what is considered typical among diverse groups. Feminist researchers have relied largely on theory-building strategies of inquiry to characterize gendered differences in all areas of human activity, appearance, and experience (Hanson, 2002).

Culturally sensitive approaches to examining human description from a diversity patina perspective specify cultural norms and membership rules and distinguish these from nonmembership or membership that is atypical (Liamputtong, 2008). Theory emerging from this type of inquiry has been influential in making the atypical typical. What we mean here is that phenomena considered atypical through the lens of traditional longitudinal theories have been investigated and aggregated into groups that share common characteristics. So within each atypical group, typical attributes are highlighted and become predictive of all members (DePoy & Gitlin, 2010).

Although diversity patina descriptions most commonly comprise the substance of diversity dialogue in developed nations, we caution you that the assumption of additional phenomena that are held in common by those with the single diversity patina characteristic without verification is as problematic as the application of any other theory in circumstances in which it is irrelevant or inaccurate. Gould (1996) illustrates in his classic book *The Mismeasure of Man* how diversity patina in the form-specific, observable characteristics of immigrants who came through Ellis Island (such as a protruding brow and dark eyebrows) was used as inferential evidence to signify limited intelligence. Thus, the mere presence of these characteristics was attributed to a meaning of cognitive deficiency and resulted in placement in state schools despite one's capacities.

Similarly, consider the exclusion of women from men's competitive sports. While it may be accurate to say that most women could not compete with men in professional football, using gender rather than skill as a means to make that decision illuminates how diversity patina can be used to exclude and even unintentionally discriminate.

Categorical Theories

While anthropological methodology is an important generator of descriptive diversity theory, it has been joined by many other fields in creating what we refer to as the genre of categorical theory. These approaches to description foreground the diversity patina/diversity depth axis and are concerned with describing the range of differences among groups and the individuals within them. Included in this large genre are abstractions attending to variations in human description related to age, race, ethnicity, gender, sexual orientation, culture, stereotypes, geographic diversity, and health, ability, and function (Harrison & Huntington, 2000). We give great attention to these theories throughout the text as disability description as human diversity patina fits best in this genre.

A major challenge in conceptualizing disability as categorical patina is to unscramble and clearly navigate the labyrinth of description and other inferences. Schneider (2004), in his seminal text on stereotype, refers to the failure to do so as *essentialist*. That is to say, if individuals or groups possess a characteristic considered to be essential, essentialist diversity patina thinking leads us to the false conclusion that the characteristic must indicate a greater meaning such as group membership or exclusion or to the assumption of a set of descriptive traits and qualities in all who possess that essential diversity patina characteristic (Davis, 1997; DePoy & Gilson, 2007).

Systems Theories

On the other end of the spectrum from biological elements and categorical patina descriptors, systems theory describes humans in context. The nature, size, scope, and predictability of the descriptors can vary greatly from systems within individual bodies, to universal, family, global, economic, political, and even virtual domains. Regardless of the reach, behavior, or nature of system boundaries and contents, all systems describe their parts as interactive. In classical systems theories—also referred to as predictable and deterministic (Sardar & Abrams, 2009)—within a system comprised of multiple variables, descriptive functions can be anticipated based on knowledge of other variables and their behavior. Dissimilar to classical linear systems, chaos theorists describe order in what appears on the patina surface as nonsystematic and random.

Emergent and Contemporary Theories

We have delimited the category of Emergent and Contemporary Theory to values, ideas, and principles that fit within the school of postmodernism. In general, theories that fall under this category are concerned with the context-bound and linguistically driven nature of description. In contrast to the monists, who believed that a single reality could be described through clearly defined systematic strategies, postmodern theorists identify description as a pluralistic perception, influenced by the social, cultural, linguistic, educational, gendered, and biological/physiological lenses through which each individual examines phenomena. As you can imagine, single sets of descriptors that are hallmarks of the other theories that we have briefly discussed above do not exist in postmodern theories. Rather than viewed as fixed and constant, constructs such as normalcy, beauty, function, health, and similar ideas are seen as variable, individualistic, and contrived functions of mass media and symbolism. We have located Explanatory Legitimacy Theory in this category, as it provides the framework for attribution of pluralistic explanations to descriptors, and even descriptors are seen as symbolic.

Of particular relevance to our analysis of disability, appearance has been interrogated extensively in diverse bodies of descriptive literature. The judgment regarding typical and atypical appearance of bodies, body parts, and mannerisms and adornments is proposed as context-bound and provides the photographic image for the negative of the atypical (Davis, 2002; Garland-Thomson, 1996; Mitchell & Snyder, 2000). Descriptive criteria for beauty, looking healthy, dressing appropriately, and so forth are specific to cultures, subgroups, and contexts and are normative (Davis, 2002). For example, consider the contextual changes in conceptions about healthy bodies, obesity, cleanliness, and even the health of specific body parts or systems, such as women's musculature (Mitchell & Snyder, 2000).

Professional knowledge, which informs assessment and treatment, begins with notions of typical and atypical descriptors from the collective and relevant theoretical literature. For example, occupational therapists who claim human activity as their domain of concern have foregrounded practice on literature from longitudinal, interior environment, and more recently the descriptive interaction between bodies and exterior environments (Kielhofner, 2004). Medicine and nursing rely heavily on interior environment descriptors.

Of particular relevance to our discussion of the descriptive element of Explanatory Legitimacy Theory is the International Classification of Functioning (ICF). The ICF is the most recent revision of the International Classification of Functioning and Disability (ICIDH-2) (Ustun et al., 2002), a classification system that uses activity descriptions to distinguish among health, illness, impairment, and disability. Until the most recent versions, the ICIDH was criticized for its negligence of exterior environment influences on health and disability. Recognizing the ill fit of this categorical assessment with increasingly diverse populations, the need for a multidimensional, universal approach to descriptive assessment was asserted and undertaken (Ustun et al., 2002).

Borrowing the work of DePoy and Gilson (2004) and building on current descriptive theory, Tables 4.1 and 4.2 present taxonomy of the universe of human description divided into observables and reportables. The taxonomy was synthesized from the activity categories from several seminal taxonomies, the ICF (World Health Organization [WHO], 2010), and activity classifications from the occupational performance framework posited by Kielhofner (2002).

As you can see by our descriptive categories, we make no judgment about what is typical or atypical, and we do not use the term *function* to describe our stance on human activity. We have tried to be exhaustive and as mutually exclusive as possible for clarity and ease of use.

Table 4.1 Observable Human Description

Self-care—Hygiene, toileting, feeding, and maintaining health and safety

Work—Preparing for or engaging in earning, economic, and in-kind contribution or production (including unpaid home care and child care)

Play—Recreation activity

Rest—Sleep, relaxation for the purpose of health maintenance

Transportation—Mobility activity with or without assistance, including moving in one's immediate environment or from one environment to another by car, bus, and so forth

Social relating—Interacting with others at all levels, including intimacy, family, and community

Worship—Attending or participating in spiritual activity

Citizenship—Civic activity distinguished from work, including volunteering, voting, and so forth

Table 4.2 Reportables

Sensing—Hearing, seeing, feeling (e.g., pain, well-being, moving through space, and touch), tasting, and smelling

Perceiving—Internally organizing sensory input

Emoting—Loving, hating, and so forth

Believing—Thinking that something is true

Thinking—Cognition

Knowing—Possessing information

Understanding—Agreeing with one or more individuals on the interpretation or meaning of a phenomenon

Segue

In this chapter, we have provided an overview of the scholarly pluralism in investigating and characterizing human activity, appearance, and experience. On the basis of the literature and building on current taxonomic organizations of human description, we proposed three descriptive axes. We then examined description broadly through the filter of four theory genres, each which will be discussed in detail in Chapters 5–10.

5

Explanations Introduced

In this chapter, we focus our attention on explanations for description that have been important in defining disability and responses to it both historically and contemporarily. As the second element of Explanatory Legitimacy Theory, the explanatory dimension provides the rationale for human description. It is this dimension, not description, on which value judgments regarding legitimacy, both of belonging in the disability category and of responses to those who are members, are made.

Multiple and often competing explanations for what people do, how they look, and what they experience have been posited in contemporary Disability Studies literature. In Chapter 3 on contemporary history, we introduced two overarching and competing explanatory genres: medical-diagnostic and constructed. In this chapter, we reknot and cast an even more expansive net. Moving beyond a cursory distinction between medical and social explanations of disability is critically important to understanding the perspectives both in themselves and as the basis for value judgment. Using the taxonomy of theory genres that we introduced in Chapter 1, we now discuss explanation as foundational to axiological decisions and set the conceptual stage for a detailed discussion of each in subsequent chapters.

Longitudinal Explanations

As we noted in Chapter 4, this category of theory explains human description as a function of individual, group, and even phylogenetic passage through time. Remember that this category includes a large range of theories that have more traditionally been referred to as predeterministic, life stage, life span, life phase, and related explanatory frameworks to theories which primarily focus on the factors that influence an individual's development over time. The common and valued element among explanatory longitudinal theories is that they account for each of the three descriptive axes—observable/reportable, typical/atypical, and diversity patina/diversity depth—not only as characteristics but also as caused primarily by one's maturation along a linear temporal continuum. In this class of theory, typical human description, that which we defined in Chapter 3 as most frequently occurring, is conceptualized as normal and desirable. The atypical, the descriptive locus of disability, is explained by a host of factors that occur at the "wrong time" in the unfolding chronology of a life span, and thus halt, decelerate, or deform standards of temporal growth.

For example, Piaget's (1959, 1962) longitudinal conceptual framework of cognitive development is still used as a primary foundation to structure public education in many countries. Similar to previous longitudinal theoreticians, Piaget was a predeterminist. That is to say, he asserted that descriptive, reportable, cognitive development occurs in a predetermined standard manner activated by biological maturation and normative observable activity. Thus, Piaget asserted that until an individual is biologically ready and physically performative, he or she cannot advance to an increasingly sophisticated level of cognitive performance. This explanatory theory, therefore, paves several pathways to legitimate disability membership. The direct route is age-inappropriate, cognitive performance. Less direct but fail-safe entries include atypical physical and sensory maturation. (See Chapter 3 for a full discussion of how disability is understood through the thoughts of Piaget and related theorists.)

Recently, longitudinal explanations, such as life phase theory, have been updated, to some extent, to reflect consideration of human diversity patina. However, a time-orientation to human growth and function still posits a set of standards and deviations within a *nomothetic* (group) context. For example, in response to claims that intelligence testing was culturally biased, theories of multiple intelligences have emerged. Some of these theories have renamed and redefined observables and reportables which had not previously been included under the rubric of cognition as cognitive skill (such as social interaction), thus expanding the notion of intelligence beyond the classical reasoning skills identified by Piaget and his successors (Gardner, 2000). Yet, within each of these intelligence categories, typical and desirable age-appropriate skills are explicitly or implicitly identified.

Longitudinal theories form one important theoretical root of medical diagnostic explanations for disability. First, conceptual frameworks are tested and verified through nomothetic research methods, those in which within-group commonalities and between-group differences are sought. Once reified through science, age-appropriate appearance and disappearance of observables is prescribed. If unanticipated description lurks in the shadows or parades in the spotlight, medical explorers seek to unearth the cause of the untimely intruders through the second major root of medical-diagnostic thinking, interior environment theory.

Environmental Explanations

Environmental explanatory theories attribute the cause of human description, primarily the observable of behavior, to the influence of human and nonhuman environmental conditions on individuals. The theories in this category range from explaining human description as a function of the interior environment to the view that human description is influenced by multiple proximal and distal conditions that are outside of one's body.

Interior environment theories, noted above as the second major root of medical diagnostic explanations of disability, rationalize human description as a function of biological, genetic, and inferred corporeal conditions, structures, and processes. In these approaches, body functions and structures are comparatively observed against standard healthy processes through a series of methods such as medical examination, analysis of body fluids, imaging, functioning, and so forth. Through interior environment explanations, the disabled body is the object of interest and, in essence, is one of pathography, or what Couser (1997) refers to as the narrative of the body that is ill or impaired. This narrative inheres in the sequence of examination, diagnosis, and treatment that comprises the interactive cycle among providers and the body seeking help. While observables are confirmatory, reportables also play an important role in the characterization of the "health" of the interior environment. As defined, reportables are inferred processes which precede artful assumptions and diagnoses about the interior environment (Groopman, 2007). For example, a diagnosis of autism relies on specific sets of predefined, atypical, social, communicative, sensory, and motor behaviors that signify interior environment disruption indicting neurological systemic malfunction. Consider this passage from Volkmar's (2007) recent book on autism. "These children might not be particularly responsive to the comings and goings of their parents, but be exquisitely sensitive to changes in the inanimate environment" (Volkmar, 2007, p. 2).

Interior environment theories have been major-league players in disability, not only in definition and response but also in creating a climate in which bioethical dilemmas germinate and thrive (Scully, 2008). We discuss this critical point in depth in Chapter 6.

Exterior environment theories explain human description as responsive to conditions external to the corpus. These theories span a huge scope, from examining the effect of the immediate environment on behavior to suggesting that distant and unknown variables are viable explanations for human description. Further, these approaches posit a range of perspectives, from the view that behavior results directly from environment stimuli to the notion of appearance, behavior, and experience resulting from environmental conditions mediated by interior environment observables and reportables such as intelligence, personality, power differentials, values, beliefs, and even genetics. Exemplary of new iterations and advances through this complex lens is the new initiative on the part of the National Institutes of Health in the United States to develop centers that will investigate how the interaction of genes and the environment influence children's health (Bock, 2009).

The behaviorists, who were seminal in establishing exterior environment theories early in the chronology of this genre, posited a linear causative relationship between observable environmental stimuli and observable behavior. You might recall the names of Skinner (1977) and Pavlov, (1928–1941, 1957), who deductively tested and verified direct observable behavioral changes when they experimented with negative and positive external environmental stimuli. An example operationalizing this theory genre in responding to disability is *applied behavioral analysis* (Keenan, Henderson, Kerr, & Green, 2006), a technique anchored on behavioral reductionism that is used and debated for its efficacy in provoking and sustaining acceptable social behaviors, particularly among youth who have been diagnosed through interior environment theory with autism.

Increasing the level of complexity to include more variables were the learning theorists such as Bandura (1977, 1986) who built on the work of the behaviorists by acknowledging the environmental influence on observable behavior. The summative effects of the interior and exterior environment suggested that variation on the interior environment had a mediating effect on both reported and observed descriptive responses to the exterior phenomena. This work has been influential in areas of interior environmental theory that attribute learning to the interaction of external cues with the neurological, sensory, and physiological conditions (David, 2005).

By expanding the exterior environment unit of analysis to social groups and social benefits, theories of social interaction and culture emerged. These conceptual frameworks illuminated context as critical in shaping roles, typical behaviors and function, human interaction, and so forth. As we discuss in Chapter 6, social role theory has provided a bedrock for theories that explain and lead to refashioning atypical behavior. As one of the seminal social role theorists, Wolfensberger (1972) originally posited normalization theory, which explained atypical behavior of those with impairments as a function of inadequate teaching/learning. In a similar but more abstract manner, Talcott Parsons (1954), a well-known functionalist, invoked a type of social exchange theory, asserting that reportable and observable relinquishment of typical social roles on the part of those who were ill is sanctioned and motivated by exchanging dependency for care. As we examine in subsequent chapters, the exterior environment theories that broach the subjects of power and privilege are critical in explaining the relationships that emerge between persons with impairments and those who provide services and care for them (Tregaskis, 2004). These theories have been called upon not only as explanatory but also as conceptual alleyways for change.

Thus, while longitudinal and environmental theories began as playmates in establishing disability as an internal environment condition that explained disability as a deviation from standard maturational expectations, these theories contain conceptual villi in which direction for change live and can emerge, given the opportunity.

Categorical Explanations

The theories that belong within the *categorical classification* explain human description as a function of group belongingness, or diversity patina. Within the large genre of categorical theories, types of groups range from those that are created by one's individual characteristics such as race, sexual orientation, diagnostic category, genetic makeup, and sex to those conferred by membership in various sizes of observable or constructed groups such as families, social groups, professional groups, gendered groups, cultural groups, religious groups, and so forth. To a greater or lesser extent, depending on the theory, group membership and responses to it are therefore seen as the primary factors that elicit human behavior and appearance and shape one's life experience.

This class of theory is central to early multicultural theories and civil rights movements, in which group members were seen and in large part shaped by, oppressed, or afforded privilege on the basis of racial, ethnic, social, and cultural group belonging. The expansion of multicultural theories beyond observable race and ethnicity saw the inclusion of other groups including, to some extent, disability. The perimeter that diversity patina draws around a group brings forth a host of advantages and disadvantages.

Historically, disabled groups fashioned their civil rights movements after others, and thus categorical membership created solidarity and political presence. However, while categorical theories define and have the potential to predict membership and imbue identity, they also simplify, essentialize, constrain, brand, and logofy (DePoy & Gilson, 2008). Branding and logofying involve the ascription of identifying symbols to groups that label them as publicly and privately recognizable and valued (or devalued). So while we support disability as a critical element of human diversity, we do not support its detention in the quagmire of diversity patina. We dissect these points in Chapter 8, as they are central to our social change agenda.

Systems Theories

In this category, human description (primarily behavior and experience) is seen as the interaction of subelements. Von Bertalanffy (1969), in response to reductionist theories that viewed organisms as no more than the sum of their parts, was the first seminal systems theorist. He posited that the elements of any entity were interactive and their relationships were not only interdependent but they defined the whole.

Systems theories have been applied to multiple human phenomena from individual corpuses in part or in total to large organizations and even more amorphous groups. What characterizes them all is the interaction between the subsystems, or elements that comprise the larger system.

Among the traditional systems theories, systems have been divided into two primary categories: open and closed. A *closed system* is delimited by impermeable boundaries inside which the system elements interact and influence one another. Because of its finite limitations, studying the behavior of one or more elements should logically allow the prediction of behavior of the other elements.

Open systems are those with variations in the degree of permeability of their boundaries. All open systems can be influenced by systems outside of their primary elements and all have the potential to influence other systems. In this class of systems, behavior is not as predictable as that of closed systems since it is subject to influences beyond the system turf.

We have included chaos theory in this class because it addresses systemic behavior. In this worldview, seemingly unrelated and nondeterministic behavior is a function of dynamic patterns that may not be directly ascertainable but can be posited. Thus, chaos in theoretical parlance does not mean random. Rather, it refers to a dynamic, nonlinear set of systemic processes.

As we discuss in Chapter 9, each of these approaches to understanding systems is relevant to legitimate disability definition and response. As example, embodied systems theories are nuggets to be mined in concert with interior environment theories as they serve as staging for scrutinizing the influence of atypical corporeal processes on other parts of the body and its function. On an organizational scale, within the disability service arena, systems explanations are used ostensibly to align disability services with articulated need (Kendrick, Jones, Bezanson, & Petty, 2006). The term *systems change* has been used to denote this aim. We follow up on systems change in subsequent chapters on policy and service responses to disability.

Contemporary and Emerging Explanations

In this class of theory, we include emergent theories such postmodernism, poststructuralism, postcolonialism, deconstruction, post-postmodernism, and related approaches. Moreover, although many of the theoretical frames of reference that we have included in this group have been in existence for centuries, they have only recently been revised and applied to explaining human phenomena and even more nascent, disability. As we discuss in Chapter 10, new political theory, although part and parcel of political science, is a potent framework through which to explain group identity and interaction that is so critical to understanding disability rights efforts in the late 20th century.

This class of theory adheres to and values pluralism, interdisciplinarity, and multiple interpretations to explain human description. Seminal to many of these musings is the significant role of language and image as symbol. For that reason, we locate Explanatory Legitimacy under this rubric. Finally, in this category, we include theories that note the importance of virtual contexts and technology. Technology has pushed the boundaries of the physical and social world to the point where traditional theory no longer may be able to provide potent explanations for human phenomena, particularly as the corpus becomes more tangential to identity, health, and function.

Intersectionality

Before leaving this theoretical overview, we bring your conceptual attention to the intersection of the five genres discussed above with the two explanatory categories of disability that ended our contemporary history chapter: medical-diagnostic and constructed. Remember that the medical-diagnostic explanation emerged and strengthened in the 20th century and became hegemonous and almost synonymous with the term disability. In opposition to this conceptualization of disability as medical deficit, disability scholars and activists in the late 20th and 21st centuries proposed an opposing approach, explaining disability as a construction of the social environment. Building on the social model approach, multiple explanatory theories of disability emerged, all of which we have referred to as constructed. As we present later in the text, a third approach, interactive explanations that take both bodies and diverse environments into account, is most cogent in approaching the complexity of disability.

Informed by theories, which derive their empirical credibility and power from experimental-type nomothetic inquiry, the medical-diagnostic explanation for atypical activity, appearance, and experience has successfully located the cause within the individual's corpus as a permanent impediment with diminished capability (Gilson & DePoy, 2003). These medical explanations, forms of biological and chronological determinism dancing with expected and chronologically prescribed, nomothetically derived, and verified norms of appearance, behavior, and experience, define *able-embodied* and its opposite, *disabled-embodied*. As their foundation, interior environment, and longitudinal understandings interact to create norms and deviations there from. To some extent, linear systems theories inform the medical diagnostic perspective as well, considering that the corpus and its organic contents are parsed into interactive systems. Thus, to support medical diagnostic explanations of disability, longitudinal and interior environment theories peppered with systems theoretical approaches act in concert. And as we discuss later in the book, the helping systems put in place take on the structures and processes of experimental-type inquiry, with the professional at the helm of understanding and response.

Camouflaged within the view of the disabled human as medical deviance is the historical perspective of the individual as object of charity or help (Machan, 1998). That is to say, any individual or group whose diagnosis fits the legitimate criteria for disability is expected to be compliant and thankful for the intervention offered by knowledgeable professionals in exchange for assistance.

Similar to the theory genres that comprise them, medical explanations of the atypical have been the subject of much criticism. Several of the major objections lie in the domain of devaluation leading to limited power, control, and access in the lives of individuals with permanent diagnostic conditions (Linton, 1998).

By definition, the notion of "within normal limits," regardless of its direct use or implication through euphemism, places individuals with permanent diagnoses that result in the atypical as pathological, not normal, labeled by others on the basis of a circumscribed body of private knowledge, and subject to control and judgment. While medicine has provided significant benefit to disabled people, there are some who suggest that the mere acceptance of theories inherent in medical intervention with regard to prevention, remediation, or maintenance of one's disabled condition in and of itself devalues the circumstance and experience of disability and, by default, the disabled person.

As we noted in Chapter 2, further antipathy toward the medical-diagnostic school of thought emerges from the gate-keeping function served by systems built on the medical-diagnostic model and its explanatory theories.

Of particular and final note in this section, is the issue of human diversity (Scotch & Schriner, 1997). According to disability scholars, the arbitrary attribution of disability status and the concomitant devaluation to specific diagnosed medical conditions is antithetical to human rights theories. We provide depth of analysis of this agenda later on in the book. But here, we remind you that the medical-diagnostic explanation and its concomitant theoretical foundations were operative and central in summoning a counter explanatory theme.

Constructed Explanations

Rather than prescribing standards and norms on the basis of what is most frequently and empirically observed, the explanations that fall under the constructed rubric explain *disabling forces* as relative and interactive (Gilson & DePoy, 2003). Moreover, dissimilar to medical-diagnostic explanations, constructed explanations of disability have their common foundation in exterior environment and contemporary and emerging theories. The notion that individuals and their activities are diverse rather than fitting within binary categories of "normal" and "not normal" is central to this approach. Why some areas of diversity are constructed as disabilities (e.g., atypical mobility in which individuals walk with assistance) and others are not (e.g., atypical vision), despite being correctable with adaptive equipment, is a fundamental question raised by these frameworks and informed by pluralism.

Among the numerous approaches that can be placed under the constructed umbrella are social, political, and cultural explanations of disability. We examine these in detail in Chapters 7–10. As we noted in Chapter 2, the social model of disability was one of the first explanatory frameworks developed in opposition to the medical-diagnostic view. As indicated by its name, scholars who proposed this model invoked exterior environment theories, synthesizing political, economic, and social theories to support the oppression and devaluation of atypical bodies and performances. Categorical and contemporary and emerging theories of performance, language, and embodiment joined the explanatory throngs, bringing perspectives beyond longitude and interior environment to bear on understanding the arbitrary nature of disability and related simulacra. Thus, disability was reframed from the failure to meet longitudinal normative expectations observed internally or externally to an experience of categorical inequality, devaluation, oppression, and exclusion. Empirical support for these explanatory claims included the exterior environment presences of negative attitudes, limited physical access, limited access to communication and resources, as well as exclusion from the rights and privileges of citizen groups. The constructed approach heavily drew on diversity-patina discourse, summoned to posit disability as a disenfranchised culture. Thus, whereas the medical-diagnostic explanations maintain disability as a private, internal condition, the constructed explanations have moved causes of, and thus responses to, disability into the public. These stances range from explaining atypical description as an interaction between person and environment to the large scope of disability as a civil rights issue.

Open systems theory informs those proponents of the constructed explanations of disability who claim that discrimination can have medically and behaviorally devastating effects that provide the continuing rationale for professional domination and control over the lives of disabled individuals. Consistent with longitudinal and environmental deviance theories, explicit or implicit expectations for the atypical serve to perpetuate it. The social causes of atypical description may be misinterpreted as the individual's intrinsic shortcoming, supporting the continued and even amplified need for professionally designed and directed systems to remediate deficits. Within constructed explanations, systems theory therefore reveals a twofold result: (a) benefit for the provider at the expense of the individual who is disabled by the provider's expectations and (b) continued devaluation of the disabled person.

Until now, we have discussed the constructed explanation as a negative and discriminatory experience for disabled people. However, it is interesting to note that some with reportable but not observable atypical experience are concerned with prohibitions that prevent their classification as disabled.

Consider, for example, people who under the medical-diagnostic model have multiple chemical sensitivity (MCS). This group is fighting for disability status in the presence of disbelief and negative attitudes toward the efficacy of the diagnostic explanation for atypical experience. Constructed explanations of disability in this case illuminate how questionable diagnosis intersects with negative attitudes to exclude a group from the resources that are afforded to those with legitimately sanctioned disabilities. Additionally, this explanation also holds the key for improving the lives of individuals in this group in that environmental changes to eliminate those substances that elicit extreme sensitivity (rather than individual remedies such as nonparticipation in public environments or even psychiatric diagnosis and treatment) would follow from a constructed explanation of MCS.

Before leaving this chapter, we attend to how the intellectual movement named post-postmodernism has influenced disability explanations. In the longitudinal scheme of theory development, constructed models were developed in opposition to linear medical-diagnostic thinking. Similarly, post-postmodern theorists rebel against the carnivalesque theories of postmodernism in which they see no conceptual work getting done. Thus, the post-postmodern theorists, surrounded in a context of virtual technology, blogs, tweets, and cognitive prostheses, have once again moved theory by opposition. Post-postmodernism seeks to reconnoiter methods and thinking to fill the conceptual and substantive emptiness posited by the postmodernists. Interdisciplinarity has emerged in universities as a post-postmodern structure and has catapulted the reemergence of corporeal systems ostensibly within interactive contexts as explanatory of disability. The term *neurodiversity* is reflective of contemporary post-postmodernism as it mixes two theoretical metaphors that previously have not fit together in conversation. In our opinion, caution must be observed when restricting diversity to organic, interior environment elements. While interdisciplinarity has the potential to advance progressive thinking and response, it also may be trapped in anachronistic medicalization and continued fragmentation of the diverse body. We discuss this point throughout the book.

6

Longitudinal Explanations

Introduction

Of particular importance to understanding contemporary disability legitimacy from a medical-diagnostic perspective are longitudinal theories. By themselves or with other genres of theory such as interior environment frameworks, these conceptual approaches to describing and explaining human activity, appearance, and experience have been operative in parsing populations into binaries of normal and not-normal, that can then be translated into disabled and nondisabled. Most frequently referred to as developmental, stage, phase, and life-course theories, we prefer to refer to this genre as longitudinal to reflect the common characteristic, the role of chronological time and maturation as descriptive and explanatory of humans. Some longitudinal theories posit specific stages through which individuals pass and must negotiate, while others see chronological maturation as a fluid process without discrete qualitatively different stages. Selected longitudinal theories focus on processes internal to humans, while others look at the interaction of multiple factors to describe and explain maturation. Some look at the full life span and others focus on specific age cohorts. From a cohort perspective, the age at which one acquires a legitimate explanation of disability determines one's label. As example, the legal term *developmental disability* refers to the acquisition before the age of 22 of an interior environment anomaly as explanatory of atypical description (Developmental Disabilities Assistance and Bill of Rights Act, 2000). After the longitudinal marker of age 22, disability is referred to as *acquired*. Regardless of the domain or age locus, all longitudinal theories have common elements presented in Table 6.1.

Table 6.1   Heuristics of Longitudinal Theories

Heuristic #1 – Longitudinal approaches are based on how individuals pass through chronological time. Thus, longitudinal theories are explicitly or implicitly concerned with the process of human aging even if they do not identify that focus. Movement through time counts the number of units (minutes, days, months, years, and so forth) and attributes differences to humans as they accrue increasing units.

Heuristic #2 – Longitudinal descriptions and explanations to a greater or lesser degree posit typical and desirable appearance, milestones, experiences, and logical explanations that inhere in a particular time frame in a human life. Conversely, they imply the opposite.

Heuristic #3 – Longitudinal approaches are descriptive, explanatory, and prescriptive. These theories not only describe what is typical for a particular age and why but also assert or imply what should be. Thus, the typical not only is the most commonly observed but also becomes the standard for comparison and desirability as well as the metric for the undesirable.

Heuristic #4 – Longitudinal approaches propose a unidirectional trajectory of life. That is to say, as one ages, one grows and changes both quantitatively and qualitatively. A person cannot "ungrow" or grow backwards. However, a person can be "delayed" or experience loss of development in disability parlance.

Heuristic #5 – As individuals develop through the life span, experiences are additive in that past events impact the present and contemporary events influence future development.

Heuristic #6 – Over time, humans become increasingly mature and complex until a certain point of decline.

Heuristic #7 – Growth and development are not uniform in a single life. That is to say, individual uniqueness emerges from the differential growth and development of some areas over others.

Heuristic #8 – Longitudinal approaches provide the platform for comparing and contrasting individuals and groups along specified standards. That is to say, longitudinal approaches identify the typical and desirable aspects of age ranges and their opposites.

Heuristic #9 – Specific longitudinal theories should not be used in place of grand longitudinal theories to describe and explain holistic phenomena. Doing so presents the unfortunate tendency to draw inaccurate general conclusions about humans on the basis of specifics and provides the foundation for essentialism, stereotyping, and discrimination.

As revealed in the heuristics, to a large extent, longitudinal theories advance the ideas that underpin many areas of life. They tell us what to expect as we reach certain ages, what not to expect, what distinguishes one age group from another, and the nature of maturity and aging. Of particular importance to understanding disability through a legitimacy lens, these theories provide the value-laden explanatory basis for typical and atypical unfolding of a life from birth through death. As such, these scaffolds build, establish, and evaluate individual lives and groups according to age expectations throughout the life span, compare individuals to expectations, and determine the extent to which they fit or do not fit.

As the epistemic basis for longitudinal theory, nomothetic inquiry seeks to quantify within-group commonality and between-group difference with the label of *normal* often ascribed to phenomena that are most frequently occurring at each age. Conversely, *not-normal* is attributed to the phenomena that are not as frequently observed. To us, this logic is curious in that it prescribes what *should be* from observation of what *is* most typical. Further, the leap from description to axiology is then translated into standards, further reifying *frequent* as most desirable. Quetelet extracted *moral man* from his creation and application of the bell-shaped curve to human reasoning and behavior (DePoy & Gilson, 2007). And thus, while longitudinal theory, based on Quetelet's normal curve, has been useful in creating expected chronological guidelines, we suggest its use as "fact" is ill-advised given the logical sequence that we have just described. The creation of prescriptive standards exclusively from counting functions to jettison those who do not "measure in" so to speak. So we may look not only to attitudinal and environmental barriers but also to the roots of these barriers in methods of knowledge creation and verification as potentially disabling.

Consider some exemplary theories to illustrate. Erik Erikson was perhaps one of the most influential theorists in locating behavior and age-appropriate tasks in specific age categories. The application of his work to assessment and diagnosis has been criticized for using metaphoric content as a literal translation of what *should be* by psychologists and other professionals concerned with the proper unfolding of a responsible life (Shane & Venkataraman, 2001). The roots of Erikson's grand theory can be found in Freud's psychosexual stages of development, which proposed qualitatively different and discrete stages of the human as he or she passed through childhood. According to Freud, chronological maturation was predetermined, and for people who are considered to be normal, it follows the sequence of increasingly harnessing the id and its sexual energy, under the watchful eyes of the ego and superego. Deviation from what Freud proposed as predetermined maturation had negative results, producing psychopathology that he referred to as neurosis or psychosis. These two classes of psychopathology were used as the basis for diagnostic categories through 1968 (American Psychiatric Association, 1968), and still inhere in the current diagnostic taxonomy of psychopathology, and thus disability, explained by aberrant psychological maturation (American Psychiatric Association, 2000).

Erikson not only extended development from birth through death but also "clothed" the series of challenges or conflicts that Freud sexualized. According to Erikson, failure to negotiate the central conflict of each age-related stage of life in the desired manner resulted in failure. Moreover, because Erikson proposed a grand theory, that which pervades the whole body and its behavior, poor outcome resulted in generalized psychosocial malfunction or in more contemporary terms, disablement. Erikson held three forces responsible for development: biological, inner psychological, and external social influences. This elemental triumvirate still dominates theory that cleaves populations into function/dysfunctional, healthy/ill, and able/disabled. Moreover, the epigenetic nature of stages, the notion that they build on one another, leaves the adult at risk from childhood if that person did not properly and sequentially resolve each psychic conflict. As an example, if a child were not able to emerge from the metaphoric conflict of autonomy versus shame and doubt into independence, the remainder of his or her life would be marred, even if the child were physically incapable of achieving the desirable outcome.

Similarly, predeterministic theories of specific areas of human description and explanation doom atypical longitudinal maturation to the status of abnormal. Consider cognition, for example.

One of the most prominent classical theorists who described cognitive development as a series of longitudinal steps is Piaget (1955, 1959, 1962). His work remains seminal as the foundation for much of the age-related educational and social policy and practice in developed countries, despite criticisms of his methods of inquiry and the application of his framework to diverse learning and thinking styles. Given that he developed his theory based on observations of his own three children and supported his hunches through open-ended observation of children playing (Campbell, 2006), it is therefore perplexing that he considered himself a genetic epistemologist and that his work has been so broadly espoused by the educational establishment. A close examination of Piaget's work reveals the strong genetic influence on his explanatory, biological perspective for human thinking, despite professed disdain for such explicit ideas in contemporary, politically correct parlance.

Integral to Piaget's thinking is the genetically predetermined, sequential acquisition of abstract reasoning, with some influences from the exterior environment (Huitt & Hummel, 2003; Perry, 2005). Considering that "heredity, physical experience, social transmission, and equilibrium" (Thomas, 2001, p.17) were posited by Piaget as the four factors that explained *normative* cognitive development, the potential for children with atypical phenomena in any of these variables, such as motor skills or even nonstimulating home environments, sets the definitional stage for abnormality and life-long embodied cognitive disability. Because Piaget generalized *thinking* to moral reasons as well and influenced seminal theorists of moral reasoning such as Kohlberg (Thomas, 2001), those who did not fit the prescriptive standards for normative development were potentially less morally developed than those who did.

Before leaving Piaget and his successors, we direct more focused attention to the critical importance of these frameworks in perpetuating disability in educational systems. As we noted, in the United States and many other developed countries, grades and curricula are organized according to age cohorts with expected typical competencies within each cohort. Those who deviate from expectations are considered of substandard or superstandard intelligence, disabled, or gifted respectively. However, given the theoretical presence of exterior environment resources as one necessary element in advancing thinking competence, shunting students who do not meet standards from the environments that provide "thinking opportunities" to excluded settings is contradictory to the very theories that are used to justify such practices (Kail & Cavanaugh, 2004).

We now move to another area of embodied disability that has been significantly shaped by longitudinal theories: physical description. Given the current hegemonic view of disability as embodied deficit, the longitudinal descriptive and explanatory literature on physical activity and appearance has been a major influence on disability legitimacy and response. Longitudinal theories of the body's maturation and change over time comprise a huge and diverse area of study and concern. To some theorists, including Piaget (1970, 1985) and his successors who we discussed immediately above, a clear understanding of descriptive and explanatory theories of the physical body is more important than any other arena of human experience (Thelen & Smith, 2006).

The point at which physical description and explanation begin and thus what defines a body are areas of immense controversy and particularly relevant to disability legitimacy. We deal with these in greater detail in Chapter 12. However, in this chapter, we bring your attention to the observable areas of the body that lend themselves to longitudinal examination: appearance, physical growth, and physical activity.

Similar to other areas of longitudinal theory, physical growth and activity were initially approached primarily from birth through attainment of early adulthood. However, several years ago, we went to see a portrait exhibit by the artist Dennis Ashbaugh (Wingate, n.d.), who used genetic codes rather than external bodily features as portraits. This exhibit was an epiphany for us in that we realized that portraiture and thus description of human embodiment and legitimacy of disability has expanded beyond the 20th century observables of organs, motor activity, and appearance to the interior world of DNA. We address this issue later in this chapter and in detail in Chapter 7 and continue with our discussion here of the legitimacy of physical development from birth through death as explanatory for disability.

Of particular importance to describing bodily development over time is the concept of developmental milestones in which typical appearance and activity are both described and prescribed as necessary, normative, and thus able-bodied. The Apgar (1953) scale is a well-known assessment of the viability of the newborn physical body. It provides norms for respiration, muscle tone, skin color, and reflex activity, beginning *description* with expected norms outside of which a child is considered to be atypical and potentially a legitimate member of the disability club. Moreover, there are numerous prescriptive and diagnostic assessments of infant growth and development including descriptors of size, weight, motor skill (Deitz, Kartin, & Kopp, 2007), and even sleep patterns just to name a few areas, in which an atypical score begets immediate and legitimate medical-diagnostic explanatory attention. In these scales, Quetelet (1969) remains alive as his construct of the normal curve underpins and thus describes how a typical, young child should look and act.

Expanding further forward in chronological, intellectual time, Arnold Gesell (1880–1961) was one of the first theorists to describe child motor development in detail, focusing on crawling. Building on this longitudinal description, Myrtle Byram McGraw (1899–1988) examined and characterized walking activity. Table 6.2 presents examples of important milestones for years One and Two (WETA, 2008; University of Pittsburgh Office of Child Development, 2005).

Not unexpectedly, milestone theories have formed the basis for many descriptive measures of normal motor maturation including the Denver II (formerly the Denver Developmental Screening Test; Frankenburg, Dodds, Archer, Shapiro, & Bresnick, 1992), the Child Development Inventory (replaces the Minnesota Child Development Inventory; Doig, Macias, Saylor, Craver, & Ingram, 1999), and the Bruininks-Bruininks (2009) Test of Motor Proficiency.

Through these longitudinal lenses, as a child matures, age cohort expectations and value-based preferences prescribe what is descriptively normative in height, weight, gross and fine motor activity, physical health, and so forth, with the normal curve allowing for some deviation, but not much. As children proceed toward adulthood, descriptive embodied expectations grow more complex both quantitatively and qualitatively expanding the repertoire and the efficacy of bodily growth, specialization, and competence. Thus the descriptive theoretical focus on the typical unfolding of height,

Table 6.2 Child Development: Typical Ages for Milestone Development

Age	Gross Motor	Fine Motor
Year 1	Lifts head and holds head steady Sits unsupported Rolls from back to stomach Crawls on all fours Pulls to stand Stands unsupported Walks aided, then independently (1–15 months)	Grasps objects and puts them in mouth Uses pincer (thumb and finger) grasp Transfers object from hand to hand Drops and retrieves objects
Year 2	Walks independently Walks backward Climbs stairs with assistance Removes clothing Improves balance and motor control Runs Kicks a large ball	Builds towers of three blocks Scribbles Turns knobs and pushes levers and buttons Throws ball
Years 2–3	Runs forward well Jumps with two feet Walks on tiptoe Stands on one foot with aid	Strings beads Turns book pages Writes using thumb and finger position Creates basic shapes in writing
Years 3–4	Walks on a line Balances on one foot (5–10 seconds) Rides and steers pedaled toys Throws ball overhand Catches ball	Builds tower of nine blocks Copies basic shapes Manipulates and shapes clay
Ages 4–5	Walks backward toe-heel Jumps forward ten times without falling Climbs stairs independently Turns somersault	Uses scissors to cut line Copies cross Copies square Prints some letters

(Continued)

| Table 6.2 | (Continued) |

Age	Gross Motor	Fine Motor
Ages 5–6	Runs lightly on toes Walks on balance beam Skips on alternate feet Jumps rope Skates	Cuts out simple shapes Copies triangle Traces diamond Copies first name Prints numerals (1–5) Colors within lines Masters adult grasp of pencil Establishes handedness Pastes and glues appropriately

weight, and gross motor activity of early childhood is enlarged with theory that characterizes typical performance in which embodied descriptors are synthesized, specialized, and applied to roles and functions such as work, play, and ultimately reproduction (Backett-Milburn & McKie, 2001). Each of these descriptive role areas of human experience forms a legitimate context for disability determination and system response, such as vocational/ career development and counseling, play therapy, rehabilitation, and even bioethical intervention.

Because of the ubiquitous assertion in classical longitudinal theory genres that embodied maturation peaks in young adulthood, subsequent chronological changes in description imply decline into embodied disability. The pinnacle for excellence is therefore embedded in early adulthood longitude, with description leading up to this age as preparatory and leading away as descent from desirable (Seifert, Hoffnung, & Hoffnung, 2000). During this chronological period, embodiment turns its short-lived gaze of excellence towards beauty, reproduction, and physical competence. Longitudinal description of the middle and elder years is retrospective and compared to what *was*. As we noted earlier in this chapter, this embodied longitudinal view does not bode well for the recent positive growth and development in middle and later years posited in grand theories as evidenced by the numerous efforts in Western culture, including plastic surgery, to retain a youthful physical appearance. However, we do not mean to imply that aging and wrinkles are accepted as beauty in any culture. Rather, as eloquently stated by a blogger on the Toddle Dredge website (2009), and consistent with Explanatory Legitimacy Theory, "the problem is not that we consider youth beautiful. The problem is that we equate beauty with worth." Thus, value and devaluation on the basis of longitudinal explanation frames legitimate responses such as attitudes that locate aging individuals in the disability camp and thus exclude them from full participation in work, communities, and so forth.

As the population in developed countries ages, theorists have attempted to align new thinking to reframe the devaluation of increasingly large segments of intellectual and fiscal consumers. Theoretical and market efforts have been initiated to attempt to characterize aging as positive development (Minkler & Fadem, 2002) and to detangle disability from chronological passage through time. Nevertheless, bodies at any age that are not consistent with early adulthood standards of beauty and function reside in the shadow of youthful beauty and saunter perilously close to the boundaries of unacceptable.

Longitudinal theories are not a mutually exclusive theory genre. They overlap with several others, and thus we now divide them into three subcategories: longitudinal-interior environment explanations, longitudinal-exterior environment explanations, and longitudinal interaction between the interior body and the exterior environment.

Longitudinal-interior explanations such as those that attribute physical development to normative neuromuscular and physiological statuses resulting from physical maturation support the basic notion that individuals develop (with some variation) in a similar fashion. Some variables that explain degrees of difference include gender and genetic codes. More recently brain maturation, perception, learning, and adaptive nature of movement have been summoned as important interior explanations for longitudinally appropriate motor development (Adolph, Weise, & Marin, 2003). Through these conceptual portals, atypical description is explained by unfolding pathology in one or more of these interior sets of conditions. Bioethical issues have moved into this longitudinal-interior territory, with much debate and disagreement about the morality of producing time-sensitive homogeneity through medical manipulation.

Theories that posit longitudinal-exterior environment explanations for physical development identify the exterior and opportunity presented within it as the primary loci that shape growth, competence, and their opposites over time. For example, Schmidt and Wrisberg (2004) link motor activity, performance, and learning in their framework of motor development, and they urge professionals to facilitate motor maturation through providing structured external environment opportunity. Dissimilar from the longitudinal-interior explanatory theories that support nature as causative of physical development or delay over time, longitudinal-exterior theories support nurture as growth-producing and thus indict it as causative of the atypical as well (Berger & Adolph, 2003).

Longitudinal-interactional theories explain chronological embodied description as the complex interplay of interior and exterior factors (Adolph,

Eppler, Marin, Weise, & Clearfield, 2000; Berger & Adolph, 2003). These interactive approaches are gaining popularity as post-postmodern explanations for human phenomena and are increasingly appearing in the literature and research that seek to unearth complex causes of atypical conditions such as those labeled as Autism Spectrum Disorders, among others. Within this post-postmodern perimeter, literature on embodiment and impairment has been instrumental in expanding interactional explanations for chronological development. As example, Schneider (2004) highlights the way in which one's physical appearance interacts with stereotypes to explain human activity.

Before we end the chapter, we turn our attention to a critical point that has had a significant impact on legitimate response to disability explained through longitudinal thought. Historically, longitudinal approaches to description and explanation have spanned the chronological domain from birth to death. However, currently, with the expansive technological, spiritual, and biological gazes, prenatal and even preconception description and explanations have nudged their way into *womb to tomb* theories, which posit prebirth description and influences on postpartum chronology. The expansion of theoretical geography prior to the point of birth opens the door for genetic maneuvering or termination of life before parturition for the purpose of avoiding the atypical, most often labeled as developmental disability.

Similarly, an event at any point throughout the life span that creates a deviated path between the expected and the observed in one's chronological cohort is considered atypical and undesirable through longitudinal thinking. The fissure between the chronological typical and atypical provokes dissonance, discomfort, and offers up the age-cohort deviant individual to the disability membership door.

Complexity of legitimate normalcy is further complicated as one moves past the chronological marker of skill and attribute procurement. At a certain age, while expected and typical, embodied difference described as loss and decline positions one as legitimately disabled and thus disability is linked to and almost synonymous with longevity. Therefore, unlike any other age cohort, in elder years disability loses its initial origin as atypical description in comparison to one's chronological peers. Rather, the comparative embodied description between youth and aging creates the operative platform on which all members of the "aged club" are considered legitimately disabled and assigned to the disability club without further explanatory ado.

Paired with interior environment explanations, longitudinal theories have been powerful explanatory determinants of legitimate disability club membership. Moreover, they have crafted responses that are developed along age lines, with the eldest members of the population all falling into the disabled abyss despite their comparative congruence with their own age cohort.

7

Environmental Explanations

In this chapter, we delve into disability explained through environmental theories, or those that describe the environmental element of behavior, appearance, and experience, and explain these human phenomena as a function of environmental influences. Before discussion, application to, and analysis of disability, we first clarify the meaning of environment.

A majority of definitions of the term *environment* depict it as a surrounding space or context in which a being exists or activity occurs. In these traditional definitions reflecting Enlightenment era thinking, environments are separate from the beings that inhabit or perform within them. More recently, however, postmodern fields such as technology, new media, and embodiment have redefined environments as "the entire set of conditions under which one operates," broadening the definition from a location outside of the body to a set of conditions in which the boundaries between corpus and not corpus are not clear. Moving from a binary that dissociates bodies from external environments creates an integrative and contemporary backdrop for analysis of environmental explanations of disability. In essence, post-postmodern theory suggests that one's body defines the environment since, without the body, environments and their meanings, elements, structures, and interactions cannot be perceived (Johnson, 2008).

For the purposes of clarity, and because much environment theory is still anchored on the distinction between space inside the body from that without, we divide our initial discussion of environment theories into two categories, interior and exterior. However, in Chapter 10, we address contemporary theories, which weave bodies and contexts into a complex textile in which weft and warp must coexist.

From a more classical view, interior environment theories are concerned with the description and explanation of embodied organic phenomena, such as internal organ systems, genetics, interior psychological structures, processes, and so forth. This intellectual domain has been of critical importance in proposing the meaning of legitimate disability as a medical-diagnostic phenomenon (DePoy & Gilson, 2004, 2007).

Exterior environment theories focus their gaze primarily on human description and explanations ranging from the view that behavior, appearance, and experience result directly from environment stimuli external to the organic body to the perspective of behavior, appearance, and experience resulting from exterior environmental factors mediated by interior environmental elements, such as intelligence, personality, power differentials, individual values, individual beliefs, and so forth. This subcategory of theories informs disability legitimacy from diverse sets of conditions, including ways in which built, social, abstract, cultural, and virtual contexts explain and then respond to atypical description. In previous work, we used the term *constructed* to differentiate this subcategory (and others) from classical interior notions of disability as explained by pathology. Rather, constructed explanations, including exterior environment frameworks, are those that characterize disability as *built* or created by elements that do not directly emerge from embodied deviance.

While interior and exterior divisions have distinct commonalities, Table 7.1 presents the heuristics that unite classical environmental theories.

Table 7.1   Classical Environmental Theory Heuristics

1. Classical internal and external environment descriptions and explanatory factors are conceptually separate and can be distinguished from one another providing that definitional elements have been clarified.

2. Environments are diverse, including immediate human, physical, natural, sensory, technological contexts, and more abstract social indirect and virtual contexts.

3. Environments are composed of multiple conditions.

4. Environments create context.

The heuristics reflect the notion of environment as context, or perimeters, created by sets of conditions in which an event or phenomenon is located and grounded.

Interior Environment Explanations

We now examine theories that explain humankind, and thus disability, as a function of interior conditions, or those that are delimited to the organic body. That is not to say that all of these theories eschew conditions external to the body as explanatory. Rather, they range from fully interior to interactive, but still retain the distinction between interior corpus and exterior sets of conditions. Table 7.2 displays the heuristics of interior environment theories that unite them and distinguish their difference from classical exterior theories.

Table 7.2 Heuristics of Interior Environment Theories

1. Interior environment theories are concerned with human phenomena delimited by the organic structures or "mind" functions of the body.

2. Interior environment theories describe humans in terms of interior conditions, structures, and processes.

3. Interior environment theories explain human description primarily as a function of corporeal phenomena.

4. No two humans are identical despite significant similarities in interior structures.

5. Individuals can be distinguished from one another by their interior environments.

6. Diverse groups can be distinguished by common interior characteristics.

7. Human description can be manipulated by changing the interior environment.

Theories that we have classified under interior environment are mostly concerned with the body; its conditions, structures, and functions; and how the body is causal of human description. Moreover, because no two individuals are seen as indistinguishable, even identical twins, a look under the skin so to speak can be important in differentiating one individual from another. However, organic similarities among diverse subgroups of humans are also seen as important not only as identifiers and explainers but also between group differentiators. As we will see, this last point is the vortex of much debate in Disability Studies, particularly in the context of contemporary scientific advancements that can manipulate the interior environment as the basis for remediating interior disabling conditions or bolstering anomalous interior processes that sustain life which otherwise could not continue.

Now let us begin our discussion with what we mean by the *body* and the interior environment.

What Is a Body?

Traditional views of the *body* define it as the organic systems that comprise its anatomy and physiology. The extent to which mind functions are part of the body or separate from it has been a well-worn and debated issue for centuries. Descartes has been credited with the distinction of the material body from the spirit (referred to as *dualism*) in which soul, thinking, and emoting occur despite the recognition that the Ancient Greeks documented the ideas (Robinson, 2007). From the corporeal standpoint, spirit functions are controlled by organic systems but in themselves have been parsed out of the materiality of the body. Thus, the observable container and its contents comprise the material element of typical interior environment theories, while cognition, emotion, and spirituality are embodied by ethereal processes. As we will examine in more detail, contemporary embodiment theories to some extent have reunited body and spirit as well as body and exterior (Merleau-Ponti, 2008). However, here we discuss the material corpus as it forms the basis of medical diagnostic explanations of disability and remains hegemonous despite the efforts that are emerging to infiltrate the legitimacy of this conceptual stronghold.

The Body as Measured

Of particular importance to disability explanation is the development of mathematical statistics and concepts of central tendency that we discussed earlier. Quetelet, his normal curve, and the ascendance of measurement resulted in the application of numbers to define and characterize bodies, among a range of other human phenomena (Altman & Gulley, 2007). Once numeric observations of bodies were divided into binary categories, the description of bodies was bifurcated into normal and abnormal. With the mathematical foundation of the normal curve translated into "scientifically supported prescriptive normalcy," the body became a major object to which standardized acceptable and healthy attributes, and thus undesirable conditions were ascribed. The viable and acceptable body was described through nomothetic methods of inquiry as most frequently occurring age-appropriate in its vital organ, functioning of correct size and weight, fitting into and functioning in public work spaces, and being able to use mass-produced, standardized objects made for consumption (DePoy & Gilson, 2004). Standards of bodily health and beauty were based on norms, and bodies that deviated from those norms were measured as anomalous. Moreover, atypical bodies became the object of medical and professional scrutiny, study, and correction, or what is referred to in contemporary theory and literature as *medicalization* (Conrad, 2007; Rosenfeld & Faircloth, 2006).

We briefly bring your attention to beauty here because this construct unveils the complexity not only of the desirable dimensions of the material corpus but also of the axiology embedded within framing scientific norms and desirables. Plastic and corrective surgery is evidence of the medicalization of beauty and its colonization by industries driven by interior environment measures.

Although asserted to be bias free, measurement is axiologically based (Martin & Lynch, 2009). Consider one of the major efforts to surveil and characterize disability across the globe: the International Classification of Functioning, Disability and Health (World Health Organization, 2010). This instrument is the most recent of multiple efforts by the WHO to develop and implement a measure of both health and disability that is standardized and therefore globally comparative. Methods of scientific measurement ostensibly follow a temporal and logical sequence, which begins with theory, reduces theory to its component parts, lexically defines the parts, and then translates them into measurement. Thus in this sequence, axiology determines theory choice, as there is a full array from which to select. However, when looking at the ICF taxonomy, it is curious to note its creation, which emerged not from existing theory but rather from a complex series of primarily inductive group processes (Changeaux, 2004), legitimating the proposed definition from the measurement itself. As described in the quote below, the body remains the locus of disability explanation, albeit with the addition of some contextual factors. Interestingly, dissimilar to the binary of disabled/not disabled posited in definitions that hold the body exclusively responsible for explaining its atypical condition, this definition aims to "typicalize" the atypical.

> The ICF puts the notions of health and disability in a new light. It acknowledges that every human being can experience a decrement in health and thereby experience some degree of disability. Disability is not something that only happens to a minority of humanity. The ICF thus 'mainstreams' the experience of disability and recognizes it as a universal human experience. By shifting the focus from cause to impact it places all health conditions on an equal footing allowing them to be compared using a common metric—the ruler of health and disability. (WHO, 2010)

This measure is only one of many contemporary exemplars of the application of measurement to bodies and their functions. As noted by Kertzer and Arel (2002), and more recently Martin and Lynch (2009), counting itself reifies categories through enumerating the magnitude of membership.

With the advancement and entrepreneurship of the medical community throughout the 20th and early 21st centuries, the medical espousal of embodied theories of disability and their concomitant measures have been powerful in defining and quantifying the body, and then colonizing the atypical as the purview of medical explanation, judgment, and when possible, revision.

Of course, in the technology-rich 21st century, the role of technology in measurement cannot be ignored as it is becoming increasingly critical in numeric assessment. Advancing in its functional capacity as well as surveillance capacity, technological enumeration has further enshrined interior environment explanations of the body and thus of disability. Cognition, for example, as we noted in Chapter 6, is a construct that could, until recently, only be assessed through behavior. Before technology peered inside the human skull, inferences about observable behavior such as language acquisition and use, abstract conceptual formation and manipulation, and problem-solving served as proxies for intelligence measurement. However, with contemporary technological methods such as quantifying the electrical activity, glucose use, and heat of various regions of the brain, cognition has acquired spiffy, observed explanations, tests and measures, elegantly visualized as interior neurophysiological functions (Tooby & Cosmides, 2000). Terms such as memory connectivity, neural network, information flow, and so forth depict the metaphoric usage of computer parlance to explain and assess human thinking as an interior process in which information is imported from the exterior environment and acted upon by biology and physiology.

Now, consider the human genome. Genetic cartographers hailed the completion of the genetic map in 2003. Genetic explanations and counting have been central to disability legitimacy for decades, positing genetically explained syndromes that justify immediate attention. For example, visit the work of Rothschild (2005) on contemporary prenatal practices. Remember back to our point about infant deformity in Ancient Greece in which, in some areas of Greece, infants were not considered human if, at birth, they deviated significantly from typical body structure? Rothschild notes that prenatal testing standardizes the acceptable interior environment through quantification. Interior environment characteristics that deviate too far from the standard become both explanatory of birth defects as well as the basis for lawful abortion. The application of this type of interior environment counting not only serves to idealize the acceptable interior environment but in doing so also functions to eliminate abnormal bodies. Does this practice sound familiar? In the United States and other developed countries, interior environment homogeneity reifies normalcy and measured deviance. Measurement then becomes the foundation for policies that allow not only lawful but also expected abortion of embodied difference. While we do not take a position on the efficacy and morality of selective abortion, we ask you to think of this practice in the context of history and disability and to see it as a window into the variable and contextual descriptions and explanations of the body over time.

Similarly, end of life issues emerge. As noted by Davis (2006), physician-assisted suicide policies, where legal, may only be invoked on the immediacy and magnitude count of interior environment decomposition. In the United States, legislation in Oregon (Death with Dignity Act, 2009) further stipulates that one's interior mental capacities need to remain measurably intact in order for individuals to make sound decisions about their right to die with medical assistance.

Theoretical Triumvirate

Human biology, physiology, and psychology are the three linchpin supports for interior environment theories relevant to legitimate disability explanation. These three conceptual cousins rely primarily on nomothetic measurement of the material body and its processes as their evidentiary sources.

Through the synthetic lens comprised of the three fields, the material body and its activity are parsed into subsystems which span description and explanation from minute structures only visible through technology to highly observable conditions. This scaffold segments bodies disabled by interior environment anomaly into disability types such as physical, cognitive, learning, psychiatric, and so forth. The mechanisms that activate this theoretical taxonomy as explanatory of disability are the list and enumeration of typical structures and functions, each of which has a quantitative range of acceptability beyond which disability is legitimated. Through this explanatory perspective, each subsystem must acquire and contain specific structures and components that perform according to empirically derived metrics over the longitude of a life. If these metrics are not met in a timely fashion, disability may be the result. Note that longitudinal theory takes its seat at the triumvirate table, drawing a linear continuum on which biological, physiological, and psychological phenomena unfold.

Toggling back and forth between theory and technology, the 21st century is rife with debates regarding legitimate embodied disability explanations. For example, consider how the increasing assertion of the neurological basis of mental illness, only ascertainable through contemporary technological observation methods, has become central as explanatory of the inferable of mental behavior, including but not limited to personality, emotions, motivation, and even vice. Drawing on this trend, Medina (2000) recast Dante's seven deadly sins as interior environment dysfunction. He asserted that envy, lust, gluttony, avarice, sloth, wrath, and pride, rather than being human, moral failings can be explained by biology and even more specifically by genetics.

Interior environment explanations give rise to critical legitimacy issues related to disability. We address these in subsequent chapters but here just identify that serious and controversial bioethical dilemmas emerge from explaining disability primarily through interior environment approaches. For example, when is a life no longer viable on the basis of deviance from typical interior environment system function? How does technology influence the interior environment, its characterization, its standardization, and even its functionality? How does measured intellect influence autonomy and rights to self-determination?

Interior environment explanations have been the subject of much criticism from disability scholars and activists. Several of the major objections lie in the domain of devaluation leading to limited power, control, and access in the lives of individuals with permanent diagnostic conditions (Linton, 1998).

By definition, the notion of *within normal limits*, regardless of its direct use or implication through euphemism, places individuals with permanent diagnoses as pathological, not normal, labeled by others on the basis of a circumscribed body of private knowledge and subject to control and judgment. While medicine has provided significant benefit to those with embodied diagnostic explanations for disability, there are some who suggest that the mere acceptance of medical intervention with regard to prevention, remediation, or maintenance of one's disabled condition in and of itself devalues the circumstance and experience of disability and, by default, the disabled person.

Further antipathy toward the interior environment theories, which drive the medical-diagnostic school of thought, emerges from the gatekeeping function served by medical, social, and health professionals in determining access to resources and participation in activities. Some of these activities are related to the providers' domains of professional concern, and some are not.

Another area of criticism is the assumed need for and unwanted imposition of formal services and professionals in the lives of individuals who are legitimated as disabled on the basis of interior environment conditions. Finally, and most important, is the issue of human diversity (DePoy & Gilson, 2009; Michaels, 2006; Nussbaum, 2001). According to disability scholars, the arbitrary attribution of disability status and the concomitant devaluation to specific diagnosed interior conditions is antithetical to progressive diversity ideologies and efforts to equalize access to resources and opportunity. Contemporary and emerging theories speak to those criticisms as we discuss in Chapter 10. To some extent, progressive exterior environment theories are useful in advancing rights and access as well. We turn to these explanatory frameworks now.

Exterior Environment Explanations

Because of the multiple of theories that address exterior environments, we have delimited this chapter to the genre of frameworks that both share the heuristics presented previously for all environmental theories and also contain the heuristics for exterior conditions presented in Table 7.3.

Table 7.3   Exterior Environment Heuristics

1. Exterior conditions are separate from the material body.

2. Exterior environments are diverse, including immediate human, physical, built, geographic, and natural sensory conditions, and more abstract social, indirect, and virtual contexts.

3. Desirable behavior, appearance, and experience are context-specific and change according to who or what is in control of the environment.

4. Because human and non-human exterior environments influence humans, individual and group behavior, appearance, and experience can be manipulated by changing external conditions.

Central to the explanations that we address in this part of the chapter is the disabling control on humans with a range of embodied atypical conditions exerted by known or tacit, exterior conditions. Let us turn to discussion, analysis, and illustration of three representative, theoretical frameworks now: behavioral and learning theory, social models, and usable/non-usable environmental theories.

Behavioral and Learning Theory

As we discussed previously, behavioral theory grew out of an intellectual opposition to explanations which could not be verified by observables.

Rather than inferring the explanation for description as a function of interior, psychosexual processes, for example, behaviorists concerned themselves with explaining measurable observables as a direct or mediated response to environmental conditions (Baum, 2004). Early behavioral theorists such as Watson (Watson, 1997; Watson & Schwartz, 2004) built on the work of Pavlov (1928–1941, 1957) and applied it to humans. Watson asserted that psychology should be concerned with the observation and empirical analysis of human behavior rather than with abstracts and inferred constructs such as the mind and the unconscious (Baum, 2004).

This work is particularly important to disability legitimacy in several ways.

First, choreographed with interior environment theories, behavioral theories align limited expectations for atypical and inadequate performance with medical diagnostic conditions.

Second, these theories map a multitude of empirically verified and well-used pathways for social role assessment, revision, and manipulation of these undesirables by systematically designed exterior environment philandering (Wolfensberger, 1972, 1980).

Third, learning and behavioral disabilities in themselves are considered as a subcategory of legitimate embodied disability despite their descriptive tenor. As violations of prescriptive desirables, explanatory interior environment inferences are guestimated. These suppositions are then used to guide pharmacological treatment responses to provoke behavior change. If the desired behavior is produced, the descriptive embodied diagnosis is tautologically confirmed.

Finally, as a playmate of longitudinal theory, behavioral theories residing under the rubric of social role theories structure age-appropriate behavioral expectations and deviations therefrom. Social role theories explain human behavior largely on the basis of social learning. That is to say, a nondisabled individual ascertains and enacts typical, preferred, and acceptable behavior from membership experiences in different age categories, such as child or adult.

Social role theorists share the common notion that social roles are learned from exterior environmental variables and are further ingrained through perceived or actual consequences. Applying social role theory to human illness, Parsons (as cited in Cockerham, 2003) proposed the "sick role" as one which embodied socially determined rights and obligations. According to Parsons, an individual who has been deemed a legitimate patient by a professional authority and who is being treated for illness by a professional is released from his or her normative role expectations in exchange for grateful compliance with the authority. The professional holds the knowledge and skill to restore an individual to health and function. The acceptance of the sick role concept has been operational in elevating health care and service professionals to perceived omnipotence and in locating them out of reach of skepticism or mistrust. While this model is still dominant in the disability industry, it is to some extent being eroded by contemporary and emerging approaches which challenge notions of homogeneity and need for standardizing human description.

Also concerned with the self and then deviant social roles, Goffman (1961, 1963) proposed a model of identity and interaction that he explained metaphorically through dramaturgy. That is to say, he described human identity as a function of interaction, suggesting that individuals invent and reinvent the *self*, their identities, through enacting and then revising their social role behavior in response to scripted messages from their social stages. Without the social stage, Goffman explained that a stable identity cannot emerge. Of particular importance to disability legitimacy was Goffman's analysis of the influence of the institutional exterior environment on individual residents and their identities. Goffman suggested that in the name of cure or community justice, deviant individuals are incarcerated, removed from civil social stages so to speak, and are subjected to exterior conditions that degrade and reshape their identities. The dubious outcome of institutionalization according to Goffman can be explained by individual response to social input in a direction not wholly anticipated by the professionals and others who control institutions and those held within them.

Similar to other social and behavioral theorists, Wolfensberger (1983, 1984, 1985) applied behavioral and social learning theory initially to rehabilitation and then more broadly to explaining and promoting social norms in legitimately disabled populations considered to be deviant, devalued, or at risk for either. Social Role Valorization (SRV) theory, building on the earlier politically disfavored moniker, normalization theory, suggests that there are socially valued descriptors that beget positive social and resource consequences. If an individual fulfills expected social descriptive norms, he or she will be rewarded. Conversely, those who deviate from the norm will be devalued and excluded from opportunity. SRV theory contains both explanatory and prescriptive orientations that guide professional manipulation of unfavorable description. That is to say, devalued roles can be changed or valorized through teaching role normative behavior (altering observable description) or revising social norms (changing the exterior environment).

As you can see, behavioral and social learning theories and their derivatives are important and diverse in their scope and focus. These theories underpin many contemporary educational, health, and therapeutic practices including behavior modification, health behavior intervention, applied behavioral analysis, and social marketing. Behavior modification is directed at purposive, systematically organized behavior change, using strategies such as positive and negative reinforcement.

In the practice of applied behavioral analysis, desired behaviors are broken down into individual tasks. Individuals who are the target of behavior change are then given opportunities to practice tasks which are reinforced. Singular tasks are added cumulatively and directed at approximating the desired response until the preferred behavioral patterns are achieved. This practice is known as *shaping*.

Social marketing (Kotler, Roberto, & Lee, 2002) synthesizes marketing strategies with behavioral and motivational theory. Desired behaviors are explicated in popular media such as television, magazines, the Internet, and so forth, and potent reinforcements are advanced through vicarious approaches. Siblings of social marketing and emergent from behavioral theories are branding and design. We discuss these theories in detail in Chapter 10 but here bring your attention to the power of marketed exterior environment influences on expectations, description, and praxis (Gilson & DePoy, 2009b).

Before we leave behavior and learning theories, we want to highlight the importance of technology in both expanding and contracting our notions of environments and their explanatory influence on human description. When behavioral and social learning theories were developed, technology as we know it today did not exist. There was no Internet, video surveillance, and so forth. Thus, theories were anchored on the premise that physical environmental conditions had a profound influence on behavior since individual action could be observed and could garner consequences. In the 21st century, interaction in virtual spaces may be shaped by the rules of behavior in that space, but the nature of consequences and their meaning beyond those spaces is unknown. Conversely, technology such as video Internet surveillance brings observation and consequences into unexpected and often surreptitious contexts. The technological environment creates a segue to our discussion of what are referred to as usable/nonusable environments. We use this term to reflect the elements of exterior environments that can be occupied, built, or manipulated for human activity. Note that we include nonusable in this descriptive term to indicate that these exterior environment conditions may not be usable by all and thus are disabling.

Usable/Nonusable Environment

Built, natural, virtual, and object elements of exterior environments have been the locus of much discussion and recently have been increasingly explanatory of disability. From this perspective, the environment, not the individual body is legitimately causative of disability.

A look into architectural design history illuminates the axiological and cartoonesque rather than functional origin of standards. *Institutionalized* by Le Corbusier, the elongated measurements and proportionality of da Vinci's *Vitruvian Man* form the foundation for architectural dimensions. We refer to da Vinci's ideal as cartoonesque because Vitruvian man is eight heads tall while the average adult human figure is approximately seven to seven and a half heads tall (Cross, 2001; Dimitriu, n.d.; Margolin, 2002). Le Corbusier's efforts to *scientize* design, or provide a rational, numeric, empirical foundation in place of economic, political, moral, or functional anchor as the basis for architectural thinking and action, were espoused even up through the 1960s by influential architects such as Buckminster Fuller (Cross, 2001). And while well-muscled, tall, male bodies may approximate a fit, bodies that stray too far from these mythic standards are met with discomfort, ill fit, and thus disability. It is curious to note that even with principles of universal design intellectually and morally developed, ostensibly to respond to the full range of human diversity from the outset of built environment planning, methods and policies guiding new and retrofitted construction provide guidance for partitioned and clearly labeled spaces for atypical bodies. Rather than fostering usable space for all, these policies and praxis result in disabling those for whom these segments of public spaces and locations are designated (Lefebvre, 1991). From this viewpoint, the disabling agent is therefore the built exterior environment, not the interior body. The use of these exaggerated, male standards as the basis for fashioning environments and products literally disable by design. That is to say, they distinguish "who is in" and "who is out," who can function and who cannot, who is desirable for a space and who is not. Moreover, these visible geographies serve to contain atypical bodies and brand them, further explaining them as legitimately disabled by their devaluation and removal from usability of space for typical bodies (Butler & Parr, 1999).

Standardized virtual and material product design adheres to similar disabling principles. Adaptive and assistive products are both abling as well as explanatory of disability. As we discuss in detail in Chapter 15, products for the disability industry may be rehabilitative and functionally assistive, but through branding and stereotyping bodies and their performance as atypical, they extract users from typical product markets and land them in disabling social geographies.

The social devaluation of disabling spaces and objects was one important provocateur for scholars in the latter part of the 20th century to birth the social model of disability.

Exterior Environment Social Explanations

Whereas the interior environment explanations maintain disability as a private, internal condition, initial social explanations advanced by scholars such as Oliver (2009) moved causes of, and thus responses to, atypical description into the public arena. Among the numerous exterior environment explanations, the social model was one of the first to be developed in opposition to medicalized interior environment causal schemes. As indicated by its name, the social model defined interior environment anomaly as impairment and distinguished it from the disabling influences of negative attitudes toward and devaluation of those whose bodies were impaired. Building on early theory, those who moved to the extreme conceptual end of the social model spectrum acknowledged that impairment might be present but was not necessary for social forces to be disabling to anyone who experienced oppression, negative stereotyping, inequality, or exclusion from environments and resources (DePoy & Gilson, 2004). More recently, the social model has matured and become increasingly sophisticated as well as diversified. Social institutions and negative attitudes have been indicted for truncating access to environments, human rights, and the capability to engage in citizenship (Nussbaum, 2001; Sen, 2009; Steinberg, 2001).

8

Categorical Explanations

In this chapter, we establish the foundation for examining theories that explain humans as members of categories currently and most commonly referred to under the umbrella of *human diversity*. This theoretical genre is of particular importance to disability given the effort on the part of Disability Studies scholars and activists to align disability with civil and human rights efforts that seek to eliminate categorical oppression and inequality. In previous scholarship, we divided our discussion on categorical explanations into two parts, category membership on the basis of interior characteristics and category membership on the basis of exterior context (DePoy & Gilson, 2007). This distinction illuminates the worth hierarchy of categories because it is typically assumed that one can move more freely in and out of groups that are not interior. Thus, category by force rather than choice begets more empathy and tolerance.

In this chapter, we look at disability as both exterior and interior category. As we will see, the prevailing view of disability as interior shapes conversations about disability as pathology, individual identity, and object of intervention, while the exterior categorical explanation repositions disability as a grouping that can be imposed and thus reversed by changeable public conditions.

Categories, most typically classified as interior, that are determined on the basis of appearance may impose membership on those who do not necessarily want to belong or exclude those who do.

Table 8.1 presents heuristics common to both interior and exterior categorical theory.

Table 8.1   Heuristics of Categorical Theories

Heuristic #1 – Categorical explanations are based on nomothetic principles and methods of inquiry. Nomothetic refers to methods that seek to identify, associate, and reveal common causes of group phenomena.

Heuristic #2 – Categorical explanations assume a common identity and set of experiences among members.

Heuristic #3 – Categorical explanations can provide positive guidance in identifying between group differences and within group similarities but also can be misused as essentialist, over-generalizing, stereotyping, and discriminatory. This heuristic is not about theory, but about the use of theory.

Heuristic #4 – Categorical explanations assume homogeneity in areas beyond the membership criterion, to a greater or lesser degree. That is to say, on the basis of category membership, assumptions are made about experiences, traits, and expectations unrelated to the membership criterion itself.

Heuristic #5 – Categories and membership criteria are dynamic and influenced by many contextual factors.

Heuristic #6 – Categorical studies to a greater or lesser degree examine inequality among groups. This heuristic has become increasingly entrenched over the past several decades, since categorical studies often form the basis for civil rights and affirmative action movements.

Heuristic #7 – Categorical studies have been referred to over the past several decades as Diversity Studies, with new groups desiring to join in order to advance rights, opportunity, and privilege.

As we have presented in other chapters throughout the book, and apply to categorical theories in Heuristic #5, this genre of theory has changed in response to contextual trends. Particularly relevant to embodied material perspectives of disability is Armstrong's (2002) work. He traced the emergence of the concept of *normal body* over the past several centuries and suggested that large-scale nomothetic screening and surveillance of the body in efforts to measure and distinguish health from illness was a major contributor to the establishment of groups along ideological, desirable, and unacceptable corporeal characteristics. Building on these ideas, Rosenfeld and Faircloth (2006) suggested that medicalizing bodies further served to carve up humanity into two groups, one of normalcy and one of deviation.

Mixing classical longitudinal theories into the contextual positivist batter further served to legitimize normal and abnormal groupings as scientific rather than value-laden (Rosenfeld & Faircloth, 2006; Rothbart, 2007). However, as postpositivism and postmodernism emerged and provided the conceptual tools to frame thinking about human diversity differently, groups who in traditional positivist theories were considered marginal or outside of the monistic norm so to speak, had a new opportunity to be characterized as valued and worthy of theoretical attention rather than simply portrayed as different and unlike the desirables. The extent to which this opportunity had a positive outcome is equivocal, given the linguistic shallowness of diversity dialogue. Because diversity has become a term that is applied to those who are not typical, it is euphemistic for *not normal*. While diversity groups have gained explanatory attention, group membership under the diversity patina banner sustains "them and us" thinking. In agreement with other contemporary scholars (Goldberg, 1994; Kukathas, 2003; Michaels, 2006; Rodriguez, 2002), we assert that diversity efforts have remained primarily at the integrationist level of practice (DePoy & Gilson, 2004; Goldberg, 1994; McClintock, 1995; Shiao, 2004), and thus diversity theory and application in large part have reflected segregated approaches to the promotion of civil rights for predefined groups, such as the disability subpopulation, that have been identified as diverse on the basis of what we have referred to as diversity patina, or observable difference. While there are essential and warranted benefits to restricting diversity theory and related responses to selected diversity patina subgroups who have experienced discrimination, there are many limitations as well.

Explaining diversity as oppression and marginalization has been an important intellectual and policy impetus for promoting social action that is designed to advance equal opportunity. Although it is beyond the scope of this book to identify all of the advances anchored on theoretical views of diversity as minority, oppression, discrimination, and marginalization, some primary examples related to disability include the Rehabilitation Act of 1973, the Disability Discrimination Act (Canada), the Disability Discrimination Act (United Kingdom), the European Union Disability Discrimination Project, the Americans with Disabilities Act of 1990, Amnesty International Declaration of Human Rights, and the UN Convention on Human Rights.

However, restricting diversity theory to marginalized and oppressed categorical conceptualizations has limitations. First, viewing diversity as a characteristic of *otherness* sets the theoretical foundation for separation and scrutiny of marginalized groups by those who are in the position to marginalize (Heard, 1997; Ishay, 2008). This phenomenon is particularly potent in experimental-type research about disability, in which theory is taken as true until falsified.

As stated succinctly by Shiao (2004), diversity conceptualizations based on population category membership promote discrimination by institutionalizing power hierarchies (Shiao, 2004, p. 17). As example, disability industry professionals who define disability as a medical-diagnostic interior condition function not only to create the knowledge context that perpetuates this definition, but also to determine legitimate membership and response. Paradoxically, as we noted in Heuristic #3, population-specific conceptualizations of diversity have the potential to maintain stereotyping (Bonilla-Silva, 2003; Moller Okin, Al-Hibri, Gilman, & Raz, 1999; Rodriguez, 2002; Schneider, 2004) and ghettoizing (DePoy & Gilson, 2004) by positing homogeneity within the very groups that are defined as diverse. Assuming group homogeneity on the basis of a single diversity patina characteristic such as disability has the potential to promote essentialist thinking and identity politics and to restrict theory application and community responses to assumed, nomothetic need.

A final point to note about explaining diversity as difference is that doing so only ascribes diversity to those who lie at the extremes of the normal curve. We suggest "flattening the curve" as a contemporary, socially just response. What we mean by flattening the curve is to use research and response strategies that expand the range of normal so that the greatest number of groups and individuals fit within the typical range to which responses are targeted. Figure 8.1 graphically illustrates the difference in narrow and broad bell-shaped curves.

Expanding the theoretical paradigm of diversity to extend beyond marginal group membership to include the uniqueness of all people provides many opportunities not only to maintain the important theoretical and applied gains that have occurred from civil rights concepts and movements, affirmative action, and other disability specific responses, but also to advance

Figure 8.1 Typical Ranges Under Narrow and Flat Curves

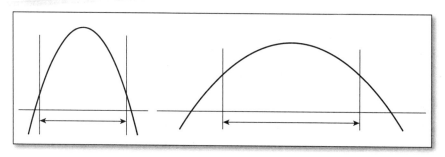

equal opportunity and justice through two important mechanisms, group symmetry and membership—two terms which are crucial to contemporary disability legitimacy issues.

Group symmetry does not naively posit that all groups have equal opportunity and access to resources (Nussbaum, 2001). Rather, it is progressive contemporary ideal that explains diversity of human description through the lens of equal value (Goldberg, 1994; Kukathas, 2003). Explaining groups as axiologically symmetrical has the potential of moving disability theory, research, and related social action beyond diversity patina conceptualizations to the second principle of diversity depth, membership.

We have chosen the word *membership* to denote belonging. In much of the disability literature, the word *inclusion* has been used to suggest membership and full participation in communities from which people were previously excluded. However, *inclusion*, to some extent, is disquieting for us because of its lexical definition and its application to multiple programmatic domains. We discuss these ideas in detail in Chapter 10 but here bring your attention to important explanatory points. Inclusion is defined as *addition*. Other synonyms are *enclosure* and *insertion*. Note the action orientation of the verb and the implicit gate-keeping hierarchy. Inclusion has to be crafted and enacted by those who have the power to facilitate entrance. The antonym of inclusion is *exclusion*, denoting the same action orientation but in an opposite direction, the exit door. In her discussion of inclusion, Titchkosky (2007) highlights how inclusion applied to special programs for disabled individuals is oxymoronic, and to some extent we concur. While intended to prompt equal participation (Allan, 2003), specialized inclusion programs designed for those whose experience disability, as explained by marginalization, continue to be grouped as help recipients, many times in the name of technical assistance or systems change. Specialized inclusive programs, therefore, continue to explain disabled groups as different and requiring help responses in order to participate. This inclusive status maintains a segregated and needy place, foregrounding disability in a dependent limelight.

In the model that we propose in Chapter 16, symmetry and membership explain the relocation of diversity patina and the right to full participation beyond category membership to the larger domain of diversity depth, or that of varied beliefs, ideas, and experiences that are part of human existence, thereby repositioning and legitimizing diversity as the property of all and the right to goodness of fit in all environments. This conceptual change has the potential to promote axiological value and tolerance for human difference and to eliminate grouped binaries (Kukathas, 2003).

Embedded within the larger dialogue of diversity, disability can now be unpacked and explained as both interior and exterior category, depending on one's theoretical stance. As we proceed through representative theories, we remind you of the axiological importance of the degree to which the embodied material membership criterion is observable. In the context of contemporary empiricism, observable often is translated to measurable, and measurable verifies existence. Conversely, reportables may factor lower on the disability membership and worth scale than those phenomena which can be counted.

Interior explanations of disability lie in two primary camps: medical-diagnostic and disability identity. Often referred to as impairment, the most prominent and well-accepted explanation of disability in contemporary, developed countries is a medical-diagnostic set of conditions that render the material body different in appearance, growth, and function. But this explanation is not so simple. It is ascribed and circumscribed to specific descriptive criteria unevenly. Thus, the location and extent of difference of description to which interior explanations are attributed and then legitimated as disability are not only a moving target but also are not predictable.

There are some clues, however, to what might be explained and thus addressed as a legitimate disability from an interior medical standpoint. The first clue is *longitudinal*. Once again, we see that descriptive deviance is not constant along the age continuum. Atypical is only present in comparison to typical within a specific age range. Consider walking, for example.

The second clue is *severity*. On the bell-shaped curve, deviance must be noticeably extreme in order to catch the attention of medical-diagnostic explanation.

The third clue is *verifiable description*. That is to say, observation directly or through measurement is most frequently required for the atypical to be credible enough to qualify for explanatory attention.

And fourth is *functional adequacy*. The extent to which an observable impairs function is crucial bait for catching disability explanations. Consider the example of walking again. Illustrating the longitudinal and severity backdrop necessary for description to garner explanation is the inability to walk. Walking only joins with deviance after a certain age and at an extreme point of difference. A 20-year-old man with a minimal limp might be the object of stares, or what Garland-Thomson refers to as a *staree* (Garland-Thomson, 2009), but it would not be likely that the limp by itself would be a magnet to attract medical explanation. If atypical gait were severe enough to suggest functional impairment, explanation would be warranted and sought from a diagnostician. The presence of an observable diagnosable interior environment explanation would be necessary but still insufficient for legitimate disability. Only in the presence of permanence or other acceptable explanations would an individual be legitimately disabled and responded to as such. Consider the youth who ingested excessive alcohol and could not walk. This temporary and devalued condition would not qualify as explanatory for disability legitimacy because of the extent to which the condition were by choice even if it were a regular occurrence. Furthermore, if an interior condition can improve, such as a fractured leg, it is not likely to be a legitimate disability. Once again, however, permanence and reversal are complicated in how each factors into legitimate disability explanation and determination. A man with a lower extremity amputation, regardless of his functional ability to ambulate with a prosthesis would be considered disabled, while that same man who moves from legal blindness to typical vision with the use of corrective lenses would not be legitimated as disabled. What is the difference between the last two exemplars? Logically, the situations are equivalent, but axiologically, contextually and politically they are not. Which interior categorical explanations qualify for disability and which do not are, therefore, dynamic and change not only over time but also according to context and value.

Micro-observables come into play as well in interior category explanations of disability (Betta, 2006). What we mean by micro-observables are the interior phenomena such as genetic materials and cell structures that can only be visualized by technology. As noted by Betta, the capacity to observe this layer of the interior material body has created a complex taxonomy in which quasi as well as full disability legitimacy can be theorized. Quasi-legitimacy would direct attention to the presence of genes that create risk for embodied deviance, while full legitimacy is conferred once the genetic configuration results in the presence of the impairment, not just the risk.

For the most part, interior categorical explanations at all levels of observation are the valued rationale for legitimate disability determination. Closely related to material embodied categorical explanation is disability identity. Building on the identity politics trends of other groups, identity explanations legitimate those with atypical phenomena as members in a disenfranchised social-cultural-political group who assert oppression or pride in their atypical interior conditions. Moreover, similar to other groups who have been successful in crafting awareness of their devalued and oppressed status, disability identity explanations are designed to beget the responses of awareness, right to equality of opportunity, resources, and privilege. (Linton, 1998; Siebers, 2008). Disability identity not only locates atypical bodies in a recognizable group, but also attributes meaning to the asserted collective appearances and experiences of that group.

While the cultural, social, and political elements of identity politics live in exterior categorical theories, we locate identity in part in the interior since it comprises the comprehension that one has about oneself as well as assertion of membership, camaraderie, and common experience in the disability group on the basis of one's atypical material body or what Takala (2009) refers to as bodily disadvantage. Of particular importance to identity are appearance and sense. That is to say, the relationship between appearance and sense of self is reciprocal (Negrin, 2008). Moreover, as we discuss in Chapter 10, identity is displayed in adornment, pointing to the importance of the aesthetics of "body objects" (e.g., clothes, public possessions, adaptive equipment) in framing identity, defining one's social role, and positioning self worth. Curiously, in the absence of observable atypical appearance, those who proclaim disability identity, declare a reportable diagnostic label to legitimate their membership, further pointing to atypical embodiment as the penultimate legitimate disability identifier. While disability identity may be a choice for some, aligning it more closely with exterior category status, legitimate ascription of disability for those with observable atypical characteristics is not always a choice.

In our 2007 book, *The Human Experience,* we located disability under the rubric of interior categorical theory because of the assertion that it is an embodied phenomenon. However, as we engaged in rethinking, we looked to our own work and the work of scholars, especially those early theorists who suggest that disability is exclusively a social phenomenon. While we still espouse disability as partly in the interior category, we must acknowledge the quagmire of this position, particularly when looking at disabling factors such as oppression, social exclusion, poverty, and axiological arbitrariness as disabling factors. The questions of why some embodied conditions that are correctable with adaptive equipment, such as eyesight and amputation, are differentially assigned or not as legitimate disabilities further confuses theoretical clarity. How is learning disability legitimated differently from low literacy, and why is the first a disability and the second not a member? We reconcile the confusion in Chapter 10 by positing disability as both relational and axiological.

In previous work, we referred to exterior categorical theories as part of the universe of constructed explanations. These retain the heuristics of categorical theories and encompass the set of explanations that locate the category of disability outside of the material body (Gilson & DePoy, 2004). Thus, while a medical condition or impairment may be present, it is not necessary for disability membership from the stance of exterior categorical explanatory theory. Several exterior category concepts have been seminal in the disability literature. One of the most prominent and contentious is the proclamation of disability culture.

To understand disability culture explanations first requires some discussion of the complex construct of culture itself.

- Looking at etymology, the word *culture* derives from the Latin root *colere*, which means "to inhabit, to cultivate, or to honor" (Wikipedia, 2010a). Traditional anthropologists such as Stocking and Tylor (1998), Mead (2001), Geertz (1973), and Boas (1940) described culture as the set of beliefs, symbols, moral imperatives, artistic practices and tastes, rituals, language, and customs that are both exhibited by and shape the lives of members of a group. Unlike contemporary scholars who imbue culture seemingly everywhere, classical scholars gazed outward from their own lives and geographies to discover patterns of behavior in isolated and circumscribed non-Western civilizations (Memodata Corporation, 2009).

- Epistemologically, the practice of systematically theorizing about situated geographies through ethnography has been brought to bear on contemporary locally positioned communities and subgroups within communities such as those with atypical characteristics. The use of ethnography or similar empirical methods that rely on inductive logic provides the opportunity for creating new theory and meaning and thus serves the creation of new definitions of cultures such as those now ascribed to disability culture (Ingstad & Whyte, 1995; McRuer, 2006).

Early discussion of disability culture suggested that disability is a culture of oppression. Individuals who define themselves as disabled and the objects of discrimination belonged to a unique group and shared a common cultural disability identity of devaluation and stigma (Linton, 1998). Membership in the culture was not attributed to diagnostic condition, since diagnosis is irrelevant in this approach to determining who is disabled. Those individuals who perceived themselves to be treated unfairly and thus constructed as undesirable by dominant social institutions were members of the culture of disability in that they shared disadvantage and curtailment of civil rights (Linton, 1998).

Against the backdrop of the prideful language and claims of the disability counterculture so to speak, dominant culture influences such as negative attitudes, limited or nonexistent physical and communication access, and the denial of rights and privileges are examples of just some of the social practices that have been identified to explain disability as an oppressed cultural phenomenon (Albrecht, 2005; Barnes and Mercer as cited in Barnes, Mercer, & Shakespeare, 1999; McRuer, 2006). This cultural model was potent in aligning disability with other minority cultures who sought to redress the abrogation of rights with affirmative strategies. However, more recently, disability culture, while not jettisoning its oppressed identity, has moved beyond by peering through humanities and cultural policy lenses to define its unique internal strengths. As such, disability art, literature, narrative, theater, dance, and other cultural productions have become central to defining disability as a group that shares *high-brow* cultural artifacts and characteristics. As example, the appearance of the film *Vital Signs: Crip Culture Talks Back*, produced by Mitchell and Snyder, was seminal in establishing disability humor and performance as public and worthy of attention. Other examples of disability high culture include the *Axis One Dance Troup*, disability poetry (Fries, 1997; Triano, 2003), organizations and websites such as the Institute on Disability Culture (Brown, 1998). For example, Brown (n.d.) notes current efforts to shift disability from an awfulized to a positive and unique human experience:

> The mission since 1994 [of disability cultural efforts] has been to promote pride in the history, activities, and cultural identity of individuals with disabilities throughout the world.

Consider the announcement below that we just received through e-mail:

> *Present Difference: The Cultural Production of Disability* (Manchester Metropolitan University in conjunction with BBC Northwest and the Cultural Disability Studies Research Network)

> This conference seeks to address the contemporary cultural production of disability within and across local and global contexts. Its focus is upon representation both in the sense of the production and circulation of particular narratives, ideas and images of disability and nondisability, and in the sense of the participation of disabled cultural practitioners in the production of culture.

As we noted, disability culture as explanation is contentious. Critiques challenge its existence on the basis of the essentialist assumption of homogeneity shared by those with diverse and dissimilar experiences and bodies. Opponents of cultural explanations decry the absence of interior environment explanations in constructed explanations (Shakespeare, 2006). Moreover, a recent study that sought to characterize disability identity and culture but did not find it outside of the academy provides further criticism for this lens (Gilson & DePoy, 2004). The inquiry illuminated the participation in high-brow cultural productions and assertion of disability cultural identity as limited to those with economic and educational privilege.

Other constructed exterior explanations have been posited as well, with similar criticisms. For example, the political construction of disability suggests that disability is an artifact of power imbalance and policy inequity (Nussbaum, 2006; Stein, 2006). Disability is explained as a subordinate group with truncated rights and negative valuation. Synthesized with systems theory, disability can be explained as the work that drives the disability industry. By virtue of receiving specialized services, disability is exploited and reified, providing ongoing economic benefit to those who perpetuate the category.

Building on economic exterior explanations are the explanatory lenses of design, marketing, and branding (Holt, 2004; Klein, 2003; Riley, 2006). Design, branding, and marketing are three dynamic, advanced capitalist legs that manipulate, locate, and seat consumption. The social model was one of the first conceptual frameworks to indict the built environment as a disabling factor. As examples, scholars and activists suggested the presence of stairs as an exclusive way to ascend and descend spaces, and limited methods of communicating information and so forth trumped embodied explanations for incapacity. More recently, geographers, architects, and urban planners have analyzed disability as a function of disabling spaces (Imrie & Hall, 2001), supporting environmental manipulation as the preferred response to decrease and eliminate disability. Given da Vinci's Vitruvian Man as the basis of standardized-built spatial dimensions and product design, it is not surprising that environments categorize and exclude those who deviate significantly from this proportional ideal (DePoy & Gilson, 2007). We revisit this point in depth in Chapter 10 when we discuss the role of embodied image and symbol as explanatory of disability. For example, the mere labeling of products as assistive locates those who use these category-specific items in the disability group.

Integrated categorical theories neither ignore the importance of the interior in differentiating groups nor neglect the importance of exterior social, political, economic, and cultural factors in explaining category membership. These theories span a continuum from examining disability as individual identity to analyzing and responding to it as a global category.

9

Systems Explanations

In this chapter, we examine systems theories, or those conceptual frameworks that explain disability as a set of interrelated parts. There are many variations and applications of systems approaches ranging from those that look at embodied or interior systems to those that examine human systems comprised of both humans and their exterior environments and even extending to systems that do not contain embodied elements such as institutional and policy systems, virtual systems, and so forth. Think, for example, of these systems: nervous system, family system, school or workplace, government, health care, and Facebook. All of these examples have the heuristics in Table 9.1 in common.

Table 9.1 System Heuristics

1. Systems theories posit that all systems are comprised of component parts that, to a greater or lesser degree, interact with one another.

2. Systems are dynamic. That is to say all systems change, albeit in different ways. Some change in a predictable manner, and some do not.

3. Some theories posit that systems can be influenced by exterior factors (open systems), while others examine system immunity from exterior environments (closed system).

4. Systems theory addresses relationships regardless of the parts and what influences them.

5. All systems are dynamic, though the nature and causes of change and movement differ according to the perspective.

6. Systems theories span a full scope of explanation from miniscule to universal.

As you can see by the heuristics, systems explanations all address an entity, no matter how large or small, as comprised and driven by one or more of its subparts. Change is a central tenet in systems theory in that systems are described as dynamic and relational. In concert with this tenet, the term *systems change* has proliferated in literature about disability policy and services, explicating the view of these abstract and concrete phenomena as comprised of parts that adhere to processes that are essential elements of systemic action. Consider this statement from Rowland and Mariger (2005):

> As Web accessibility garners increased importance and attention, there is greater emphasis on making systemwide rather than individual changes in our efforts to create a more accessible world.

This quote reveals the somewhat euphemistic use of the term *systems change* to refer to broad-sweeping changes in practice, in this case web-authoring praxis. However, as reflected in the heuristics, systems theory posits that change in any element of a system, even within an individual, is provocative of change throughout a system. The question of what parts are being included in this web access system are unclear and imply that the disabled web user could be peripheral and outside of the changing system. We raise this point to denote that those who are the objects of systems may not be part of the system that is being addressed and changed. This phenomenon is particularly prevalent in disability service systems for reasons which we explore later in the book.

You might also notice as you read that many of the theoretical explanations that we locate in this chapter could easily be categorized under other rubrics. For example, some mesosystems, which we examine below, could fit well within exterior environment theories. Conversely, you have already read about biological and cultural systems in Chapter 7. While those discussions also fit under systems approaches, we located them in the chapters on interior and exterior environment theories because of their primary substantive focus.

In this chapter, we delimit our discussion to explanations that extend beyond embodiment and thus do not address biological systems exclusively. To organize this vast literature within its chronological context, we begin a brief discussion of the history of systems theory and then move from exemplars of disability related systems organized from most proximal (close) to humans to most distal (distant).

History

What is most interesting to us about the history of the application of systems theory to disability is the way in which diverse methods and equipment have influenced the nature of systems ideas. In particular, the development of systems theory over the years has moved from simple description of the linear interaction of two or more related parts of a whole to nonlinear conceptualizations of systems as complex in structure and interaction. Most recently, systems explored through and exemplified by computers have been able to identify and illustrate systems concepts, which had previously been seen as disparate and chaotic, as organizing elements of phenomena. The capacity of computers to move human thinking beyond chronological time and geographically situated space has been critical in advancing systems explanations of disability and responses to it. Consider Olsen's (2008) contemporary work as an exemplar. On her blog, she notes, "All life, but maybe especially disability, is chaos theory in action. Any outcome might be true." By this assertion, she is both explaining disability and contributing to its interrogation and interpretation through computer technology. How her text will be interpreted and then applied by others is equally as unpredictable as she claims disability is. The blog responses move in diverse nonlinear directions, taking concepts of disability into conceptual and geographic fields afar. Such concepts and their communication have developed only with the advent of ubiquitous computer use.

Looking back to the first documented articulations of systems thinking, we return to Ancient Greece and Aristotle who coined the phrase "the whole is more than the sum of its parts." Numerous inventions and ideas over chronological time demonstrated elements of systems theory such as a feedback loop, the mechanism through which one part of the system receives information from another and then responds. Yet it was not until the mid-20th century that systems theory was developed and formalized by several theorists, of whom the most renown were Parsons, Luhmann, and then von Bertalanffy. These theorists have been seminal in explaining social interaction as a systems phenomenon, and thus their theories and those who built on their ideas have been foundational in explaining disability as a complex interaction of people and environments (Michailakis, 2003) that therefore must be addressed in a nonsimplistic manner.

Further building on this important school of thought, Parsons (1937) sought to characterize social action through a systems approach, in which environments and processes were seen as subelements of social action. Briefly, he suggested that social action could be explained by humans (behavioral organisms) interacting with environments of ideas and expectations (culture) within physical environments (space, objects, locations). This thinking is inherent in the early social model of disability (Linton, 1998).

Luhmann (in Paul, 2001) characterized systems as communication entities that had distinct identities. He described systems as separate from their environments and explained their function as the extraction and use of limited information from the exterior to communicate meaning.

Building on multiple disciplines including but not limited to philosophy, biology, and physics and the work of his contemporaries, von Bertalanffy (1976) advanced general systems theory. Simultaneously, *cybernetics*, the application of mathematical concepts to describe and explain communication and feedback mechanisms within systems, was also developed. According to von Bertalanffy and his contemporaries, a system is described as a set of interacting parts or activities that form a whole. Thus, while components of a system can be identified, they cannot be reduced to individual and discrete elements. Moreover, von Bertalanffy theorized social systems as open systems. That is to say, different from closed systems, which are contained by impermeable boundaries, *open systems* are influenced by forces outside of themselves. In other words, open system boundaries are penetrable. The category of disability itself is an open system, meaning that anyone can join.

Classical systems theories have been applied to explaining a range of units of analysis relevant to disability from family systems to organizational, social, cultural, and virtual systems. The open-closed distinction is particularly relevant to explaining disability. Closed system approaches are typically invoked in embodied explanations while open systems are applied to explaining disability as interactive. With the omnipotence of the computer and the hegemony of postmodern and even post-postmodern thinking, systems theory has undergone important conceptual changes. Contemporary systems theories explain disability as a complex system in which body and environment are not separate entities. Different from embodiment theories, which suggest that body and environment are indistinguishable, others (Hickman, 2007; Shilling, 2008) foreground the purposive systemic interaction among bodies and their contexts as the backdrop against which disability can be explained. As we noted above, Olsen (2008) equates disability with chaos, one of the most important contemporary systems frameworks. Chaos explains change in complex systems or those that are not reducible and predictable.

As you can see by the brief history, systems explanations have moved from deterministic, linear, and predictable to complex and unpredictable unless subjected to advanced modeling and computer analysis. Disability theorists drawing on this theoretical genre therefore have access to a rich and long theoretical tradition that is most useful in providing complex and dynamic explanations in which disability is not reduced to a single element. While potentially powerful in explaining disability and crafting responses, we will see in the chapters on legitimacy that systems theories leave the door open for vagueness and too many opaque layers of response.

Contemporary Systems Disability Explanations

Now let us turn to systems theories that have been useful in explaining disability. Albrecht, Seelman, and Bury (2001) have referred to Bronfenbrenner's (2005) thinking as valuable to understanding disability from diverse system levels and sizes. We concur to some extent and here briefly discuss Bronfenbrenner's bioecological theory before applying his work to disability explanations.

According to Bronfenbrenner, humans develop within the context of four exterior systems, from proximal to distal: micro, meso, exo, and macro. Thus, development itself is explained as a systems phenomenon. See Table 9.2 for descriptions of each level (Bronfenbrenner, 2005).

Table 9.2   System Levels and Exemplars

Proximal———————————————————————————————Distal				
	Micro	**Meso**	**Exo**	**Macro**
Definition	System that considers immediate surroundings	System consisting of sets of microsystems	System that indirectly influences an individual	Abstract system that guides and shapes systems
Exemplar	Family, home, school, work	Community, neighborhood	Mother's workplace, sister's school	

Over the past several decades, Bronfenbrenner and Morris (2006) expanded their description of the microsystem to include the individual and language and symbols to which an individual attributes meaning, thus creating the concept of the *biopsychosocial* human. These nested systems and their contents are particularly relevant to viewing disability as a set of interactive factors. While not seeking to elucidate the direct cause of disability, this microsystem lens explains disability from a logical ecological perspective or one which indicts the reciprocal influence of body and its surrounding as disabling (Albrecht et al., 2001).

Microsystem Theories

Microsystem theories locate disability explanations in the interstices between the body and the immediate environments in which individuals behave and act. Even before social models of disability were claimed by disability scholars, systems theory applied to disability recognized systemic causes of disability, many of which had little to do with embodied pathology.

Traditionally, the systems that have been interrogated at this level of concern are family and work. For example, a family systems approach (Appleby, Colon, & Hamilton, 2007) might explain an atypical child's disability as his or her family's stereotypical and overprotective treatment or the beliefs and values that guide how a family will respond to the birth of an atypical infant (Seligman & Darling, 2007).

Within family systems, caregiving is often discussed as a systemwide issue. Curiously, caregiving is a term that has been applied to diverse ways in which individuals give to and receive help from their families and more recently from a host of providers. Within the systems lexicon, caregiving often is depicted as a network of interrelated formal and informal human resources that in some sense has moved from the privacy of one's home into the public medical/professional domain. Those caregivers with the least access to public caregiving resources are often characterized as burdened, setting the stage for a professional literature and a specialized field with its own payment systems, rhetoric, and practices. The large literature on caregiver burden highlights disruption from typical family systems and prescriptive social and work interactions. Thus, from this vantage point, the care recipient as well as the caregiver are disabled and in need of public attention.

Similarly, negative attitudes and discrimination in the workplace experienced by those with atypical description might be characterized as a disabling microsystem. Note that in both examples the body in environment is considered, not just the body or the environment.

More recent microsystem causes of disability are tied to inadequate environments and what we refer to as body embellishments (equipment, or technology). Inadequate or stimulation-vacant environments had been charged as explanatory of disability as early as the 1960s (Kagan, 2002). Programs such as Head Start and early intervention were founded on theories in which children who were chronologically behind their peers were disabled with the root cause as the perceived absence of learning stimuli in impoverished home environmental systems. And while these youth were not classified as medically disabled, the assumption that they would be disadvantaged compared to their wealthier counterparts in the school system placed them in the needy category as subjects for public intervention. These children thus attend school in the name of Head Start before kindergarten (Kagan, 2002).

More recently recognized, and the object of civil rights legislation in several countries, are disabling attributes of physical microenvironments. Built barriers such as stairs, single models of communication that do not consider people who do not see and hear typically, and other concrete obstacles have been blamed for disability and exclusion. As we noted in the history section, the foundation for current architectural standards institutionalized by Le Corbusier harkens back to the elongated measurements and proportionality of Vitruvian Man (Gilson & DePoy, 2007). Bodies that stray too far from mythic standards of human size, locomotion, sensorium, and behavior experience ill fit and thus are disabled in geographies that are built according to Vitruvian bodies.

Moreover, and perhaps even more compelling, are the meanings of spaces themselves. As noted by Lefebvre (2001), physical space is not neutral but carries values in its design and purpose that affect its inhabitants. We discuss this point in the chapter on contemporary and emerging theories but raise it here as a systemic consideration. Spaces, whether built or natural environments are elements that play important roles throughout systems. Who can and should be in what microspaces, what activity takes place, economic value, social meaning, and so forth, not only link parts of microsystems but also are embedded in a complex, multidimensional web of diverse system levels as well. For example, environments in which services are delivered to clients with disabilities affect macrolevel cultures, economics, and policy as well as reflect them in the confines of local space. We refer to this large system as the *disability park* to note that while the locally situated space is a microsystem, its appearances, entrance and egress, practices, movement patterns, activities, economics, and governance are controlled elsewhere and are remarkably similar across geographies.

Before we leave physical spaces, we bring your attention to your computer. While we may not see computers as microsystems, to some extent they function as such when individuals use them for microsystem functions such as work and social life. The virtual environment at this level is therefore subject to the same scrutiny as the physical world, as evidenced by recent accessibility legislation. However, the *computer as object* may also be considered a body embellishment, in that it is a multipurpose object notwithstanding omnipotence and thus has macrosystemwide and diverse systemic relevance.

While the term *body embellishments* has been used to refer to adornment, in our work we use it to denote any objects that assist bodies to function, including but not limited to appearance and fashion. The dearth of needed body embellishment objects in a microsystem may be explanatory of disability no matter what one's body brings. For example, living in a rural area with no public transportation requires one to drive a car. If one does not have such a body embellishment in his or her system, disability occurs preventing one from engaging in work, family sustenance, activity, and so forth.

Or consider the teen who is ostracized because his fashions do not conform to the social system expectations at school. The operative principle with body embellishments highlights the role of objects and technologies in mediating disability. Some theorists suggest that disability can be eliminated with the presence of systemic body embellishments such as computers (Gleeson, 1999). In Bronfenbrenner's model, microsystems exist within mesosystems such as communities, neighborhoods, and so forth. This system level is comprised not only of individual microsystems but also of intricate relationships among them. Furthermore, mesosystems may unite microsystems under a conceptual meso-umbrella so to speak. That is to say, in addition to being concretely delimited, as is the case in communities or neighborhoods, mesosystems can be bounded within conceptual perimeters, such as people with disabilities. They are endless but all have in common that they organize, shape, and are shaped by both the systems levels in which they are nested and which they contain.

For example, Speaking Up for Us, drop in centers for disability category members, and organizations such as the Disability Section of the American Public Health Association, Society for Disability Studies, Association of University Centers on Disability, and so forth, are comprised of microsystem units but are wedged in between them and macrosystem abstracts. In some sense, mesosystems function as bidirectional conduits to exert control over microsystems and attempt to influence macrosystems from "down below," so to speak.

Exosystems are those that are related to and influence a micro-unit of analysis but are indirectly connected to it. We have referred to this system level as tangential-influential (DePoy & Gilson, 2007). In our recent work, we have identified the importance of tangential-influential policies that are relevant to but not directly related to disability and named them disability-implicit. Included are laws and rules at the community level that state seat belt regulations that reveal system values about disability but are not rhetorically specific to it. We might even look to engineering and architectural groups and most standards from this vantage point, as these both significantly influence disability but are only peripherally concerned with it, if at all. This system area is often overlooked in theory and praxis as its oblique angle to some extent obfuscates its view and thus its power in explaining disability.

According to Bronfenbrenner, macrosystems are described as abstract systems of ideas and practices that guide behavior and activity in exo, meso, and micro systems and are informed and shaped by changes in these systems. Further, Bronfenbrenner asserts the importance of understanding the macrosystem level, in particular social policy, in explaining behavior at other system levels. Applied to explaining disability, we suggest that policy is not simply a response, but contains significant explanatory power. For example, listen to Fries (2007):

> For the first time in close to eight years, Social Security has decided it needed a medical review to discern if according to their rules, I am still disabled. (p. 1)

Social Security policy explains disability by providing eligibility criteria for coverage. Explanations and their valuation both emerge from the social, political, economic context and shape disability as medical, long-term, profound and the object of specialized benefits.

Macrolevel systems are not limited to formal policies and rules however. Cultural systems, abstract social systems, communication and media systems, and now virtual systems beyond the individual computer level that we discussed above are part of the macrolevel explanation of disability. The macrosystem is particularly important in illuminating the interaction between laws, policies, cultures, and global trends and all systems embedded within this large system expanse.

The rational model of policy analysis (Fischer, Miller, & Sidney, 2006; Stone, 2001) fits well under this system level within classical linear systems explanations. Rational analytic models view disability policy formulation as democratic negotiation about the meaning of and response to disability among multiple system interests. System components are viewed as differential entities with varying degrees of competing interests and power bases. As these interest groups interact and provide feedback to one another, policies which best emerge from needs are developed, implemented, evaluated, and revised according to system feedback. For example, a rational view would characterize the 2009 Amendments to the Americans with Disabilities Act as an orderly and logical outcome of evidence-based negotiations among diverse interest groups. This policy would therefore explain disability as specified in its verbiage.

The beauty and use of Bronfenbrenner's systems theory lens is that it explains the behavior of multifaceted and complicated systems in logical and linear terms. However, explanatory legitimacy foregrounds value and purpose as central, and thus we suggest that logical deduction may not be most useful in understanding macrosystem explanations of disability. Rational disability policy analysis (Fischer et al., 2006) illustrates this point. Using this approach, the expected outcome of policy negotiation would be directly linked to disability definitions, and negotiation would proceed in a logical sequence. However, traditional systems theories, and thus rational analyses, have not provided the explanatory power to understand complex systems such as disability, which we suggest cannot be characterized through linear relationships because of their diverse and competing axiological and purposive foundations.

Complex Systems

Several contemporary approaches such as chaos (Wolfram, 2002), network (Barney, 2004), and conflict models have been posited and for us are most useful as applied to explaining disability. As noted by Berube (2009),

> disability is at once ubiquitous and elusive: once we consider its myriad forms, not only as medical syndromes but as variables that structure human social and environmental arrangements, we begin to understand just how difficult it is to understand the subject of disability itself.

Thus, these theories lend themselves to disability as checkered, striped, and multipatterned. Because these theories are mathematically complex and require computer-generated models to explain their behavior (Wolfram, 2002), a detailed discussion of their principles is beyond the scope of this book. However, let us look into some basic tenets of complex systems and how their explanation has informed disability.

Chaos theory, one contemporary explanatory theory, has been important in advancing analysis of complexity and unpredictability. Through this lens, system behaviors, which before computer-generated mathematical models seemed random, nonrepetitive, and unrelated, have been observed and explained as complex behavioral patterns. The behavior of chaotic systems contains the elements of predictable systems, such as feedback and change, but is explained by nonlinear mathematical concepts. For example, according to Parker, Schaller, and Hansmann (2003) and Livneh and Parker (2005), adjustment to acquired medicalized explanation for disability is not linear as suggested by other scholars, but rather is an unpredictable process, which is dependent on the coalescence of a multitude of variables within diverse contexts. Such labyrinthine phenomena can only be characterized through complex systems approaches.

Let us return to our example of policy analysis to further explore the potency of complex systems theories in explaining disability. In classical macrosystems theory, as we noted above, rational policy analysis and formulation are ostensibly an outgrowth of a careful examination and negotiation of social problems, needs, and resources, with the expectation that policies will ultimately produce desired outcome for the people who are targeted as the recipients of policy rulings and benefits. However, within the contemporary global economy, the relationship between disability policy and outcome is not simple or predictable, suggesting the need for nonrational models of analysis in which explanations and outcomes are seen as a function of complexity (Stone, 2001). We agree and thus have parsed disability policy into three subdivisions: disability-exclusive policy, disability-embedded policy, and disability-implicit policy. *Disability-exclusive policy* is the set of explicit statements that legitimate membership criteria in the disability category and guide responses to legitimate category members. *Disability-embedded policy* has a similar function to exclusive policy, but disability is one of two or more groups addressed in the policy. *Disability-implicit policy* does not name disability but tacitly defines and responds to it through its prevention, elimination, or manipulation. Note that through singly, directly, or obliquely addressing disability, it is explicitly or tacitly encased in axiological explanations. For example, prenatal screening policies in the United States and other developed countries explain fetal disability as genetic deficit by virtue of surveillance for the purpose of eliminating deviance arising from chromosomal diversity. Similarly, workplace regulations define disability as inability to work and thus structure exterior microenvironments in order to avoid injury that could truncate an employee's ability to fully participate in work. Note that we are not opposing these policies, but rather we are using them for illustrative purposes. Both of the exemplars explain disability differentially, one through genetic difference and one through harm resulting in loss of work.

Unlike the British social model, which explains disability primarily as socially constructed and would fit under linear systems, complex system approaches would acknowledge prejudice and discrimination as part of a tapestry of human rights violations. For example, theorists such as Nussbaum (2001) and Sen (2007) have advanced human capabilities as a framework through which to view human rights as a variegated picture of advantage and systemic values. Cross-fertilized with ethical models of distributive justice (Stein, 2006), explaining disability moves into the systemic realm of abstract complexity in which disability cannot simply be attributed to a social system. Rather, disability is explained through the interplay of diverse values, ethics, resources, and purposes that are dynamic and subject to contextual influences, many of which cannot be fully identified.

Before leaving this chapter, we bring your attention to another domain of complex systems, that of ideas and theories. Disability Studies has joined hands with other intellectual trends including but not limited to feminist thinking, queer theories, civil rights concepts, and so forth. Through this intellectual kaleidoscope, systems of theory are created by the turn of one's intellectual gaze. For example, heterosexuality and normality are both surreptitious and parallel partners in establishing systems of what should be and thus what should not be (McRuer, 2006), queerness and disability, respectively.

Systems theories are diverse, and each genre brings a different understanding to disability explanations. Unlike monistic models such as the medical model or social model, systems perspectives do not locate disability as either interior or exterior. Rather, even classical linear theories provide the richness of interaction to explanations of disability, with complex systems theories brandishing elegant and spectacular aptitude to inform disability and fertile response in the 21st century.

10

Contemporary and Emerging Explanations

We have discussed many contemporary explanations of disability in previous chapters, some from traditional disciplinary foundations (e.g., biology, longitudinal approaches, anthropology) and some from interdisciplinary fields (e.g., systems theory, network and complexity, categorical approaches). In this chapter, we delve into the world of disability explanations that can be framed within postmodern and post-postmodern lenses, or those that locate descriptions and explanations of humans within multidisciplinary domains. Contemporary disability scholars have welcomed and applied these theories to explaining disability from varied perspectives, which have significant potential to provoke intellectual and praxis change. Some explanations (particularly in the postmodern genre) highlight symbols, networks, cyber-phenomena, constructions, and human rights abrogations while others that we locate in post-postmodernist thought integrate what might seem like theoretical strangers, such as cognitive evolution and morality (Cognitive Evolution Laboratory, 2009).

Just for a moment, let's reflect on today's world to get a context for the work that we discuss in this chapter and that is profound for thinking about disability differently. We live in communities that are no longer defined by their geographic or even physical boundaries and thus can be in several places at one time (Bugeja, 2005). We can increasingly participate in global events when they happen through viewing them in action on screens that we can even carry in our pockets. Work no longer needs to take place in a physical workplace. We can create and revise our own virtual identities, functionality, and methods of interacting. We can shop internationally from our living rooms. We can communicate with great immediacy across the globe in languages that we may not even speak. We text message, e-mail, log on, and blog. We can access libraries and museums across the globe from our homes and can meet face to face even if we are physically situated in different continents. Time is no longer simply a linear chronological measurement. We live among people who originated from geographic locations throughout the globe. We challenge the intellectual status quo of separate disciplines and discuss concepts such as intersectionality, symbols, and constructed realities. And we can uncouple ourselves from our bodies as we interact, earn, play, and even engage in sex in virtual spaces.

Given these contemporary trends, it is no surprise that traditional theories explaining disability, such as those that are deterministic are no longer adequate. And so we come full circle theoretically to our last theoretical explanatory rubric, contemporary and emerging theories.

As you will see later in the chapter, we turn our analysis on the theoretical framework that organizes our discussion throughout the text, explanatory legitimacy. This chapter provides the theoretical and experience rationale for a legitimacy worldview, which does not eschew traditional disability theory but places it in a larger purposive and contextual framework from which to think about disability in our contemporary universe. We conclude the chapter with disjuncture theory, a contemporary explanation that reflects the principles of post-postmodern thinking and thus guides complex, relevant contemporary analysis, axiology, and responses to disability.

Heuristics

Table 10.1 presents the heuristics that bind the theories in this chapter under a single rubric.

As you can see by the heuristics, contemporary theories reflect the pluralism, complexity, flexibility, and sometimes even uncertainty brought about by technology, the "shrinking" of the globe, and the rubbing of material and virtual elbows (so to speak) of so many diverse ideas, experiences, and worldviews. As we have indicated earlier with regard to categorical theories, we refer to this phenomenon as diversity depth, a concept that has great relevance for eliminating the essentialism so frequently arising from seeing disability as a single corporeal reality. Contrary to diversity patina, which assumes and locates difference in the variable of embodied disability, diversity depth is seen as a universe of experiences, ideas, and worldviews

Table 10.1   Heuristics of Contemporary and Emerging Theories

1. The theories in this chapter share the characteristics of multidimensionality, pluralism, and complexity.

2. Theories range from explaining order to disorder.

3. Theories are supported by multiple ways of knowing.

4. Theories move beyond binary concepts of normal and abnormal to explain heterogeneity and progressive diversity.

5. Individual theories do not claim to be the single dominant worldview or truth.

6. The theories eschew traditional concepts of objectivity.

7. Theories are embedded in social, political, economic, expressive, spiritual, virtual, and cultural contexts.

(DePoy & Gilson, 2004). These theories provide us not only with the permission but also with the invitation to be uncertain and to engage in purposive and multiple ways of thinking about our worlds. They allow each of us to claim our own diversity regardless of the extent to which we sport bodies and background characteristics and to see other humans through our own values and views. They acknowledge and integrate context as an important element to consider rather than attempting to neutralize it as a biasing factor. And they do not prescribe human explanation.

Postmodernism

Theories that emerged in opposition to modernism have caught the intellectual gaze of many Disability Studies theorists. Looking in on itself, attempts to define and characterize postmodernism are vague and pluralistic and become victimized by the linguistic patterns and narratives that they critique. So we will try to discuss postmodernism and its application to explaining disability with the dilemma of language that we have addressed in previous chapters. In essence, postmodernism is not a theory, but a set of ideas that views the world and universe as a pastiche, or collage, of disparate beliefs, views, experiences, cultures, and practices. Thus, different from schools of thought such as the behaviorists, traditional systems theorists, and so forth, postmodernists deny that there is a grand narrative, or cultural-linguistic story, that unites humans under an explanatory umbrella. To the contrary, by design, postmodernism suggests that the myth of grand narrative masks the fundamental disparities of individuals and groups.

Of particular relevance to disability explanations is the postmodern eschewal of the grand narrative of science as truth, allowing for multiple explanations of disability beyond corporeal pathology (Davis, 2002). Challenging science has opened a portal through which Disability Studies has opposed the medicalized 20th-century notion of disability. Through looking at science as narrative rather than fact or truth generated by objectivity, the values and contextual bases which explain disability as an embodied phenomenon that is different from typical and normal can be unraveled and reconstituted within a pluralistic, purposive, critical frame. Furthermore, the preference of postmodernists to value local over global spawns the opportunity for tailoring explanations and thus solutions to uniqueness of context.

Remember that we discussed the pitfalls of applying theory developed on one population to another. Postmodernist methods of inquiry have the potential to eliminate this error. Of course, theory developed locally does not advance global explanations and thus for us, as we propose, is important to link with other more broadly conceptualized and useful methods of knowledge generation.

Unlike the modernists, who rebelled against and detested the order and form of Enlightenment theory, art, music, and drama, and mourned the fragmentation and disorder in the world (Cahoone, 2003), the postmodernists accept and celebrate the world as a carnival so to speak. What we mean is that the postmodernists describe the world as a set of juxtaposed, fragmented, diverse ways of being within an advancing context of technological and language symbols. Extreme postmodernists such as Baudrillard (1995) see nonsense rather than sense in our world and thus play with ideas, words, and images without assigning meaning or substance to them. Baudrillard used the term simulacra to describe symbols (signifiers in postmodern speak) that have no foundation or original source. We see this term as central to much of contemporary theory and potential social change and apply it later in this chapter.

Look at Powell's (1998) words to further clarify postmodern thinking:

> The mapmakers of the past centuries superimposed a fictitious grid upon the globe—the meridians—the lines of latitude and longitude. They charted narrow straits, far-flung exotic archipelagos, dark continents, prevailing winds, waves and currents. Similarly, postmodern intellectuals have attempted to map the contours of our rapidly changing world, its mix of identities, realities, cultures, races, gender roles, technologies, economies, cyberspaces, mediascapes. (p. 4)

As reflected in Powell's text, postmodernism does not discard the existence of knowledge but rather, concerns itself with the construction of knowledge as a pluralistic set of symbols within a purposive, political, and local framework. Viewing knowledge as diversity of ideas, or what we introduced as diversity depth, appeals to us, in that there is no prescribed worldview and there are many bodies of evidence, beyond traditional positivist designs but including them as well, that can support individual claims. Moreover, because postmodernists foreground purpose rather than fact as the foundation of knowledge generation, this school of thinking has significant application of knowledge for the intent of social change.

Of great significance to explaining disability is the emphasis of postmodern thinking on the role of technology (Warschauer, 2004). The omnipotence of computers and technological advances is central to much of postmodern thinking in that these innovations have changed the way in which we conceptualize, create, characterize, organize, store, and disseminate knowledge (Kim, 2001). Computers have created the paradox of digitized information, which can easily be changed with no discernable record of what came before but which ostensibly leaves a permanent and enduring electronic record. In essence, computers have ratcheted up the consumer element of knowledge. Knowledge is linked to advertising, can be purchased, and can be consumed. Just think about how many websites exist and then cease to exist without a publicly visible trace. And then who decides about what qualifies as knowledge and what does not? In postmodern societies, multiple forms of knowledge are acknowledged, beyond simply that which is supported with the scientific narrative. The Dalai Lama's (2005) most recent book is a prime example. In the prologue of his new work on the intersection of spirituality and science, the Dalai Lama says,

> I was never trained in science. My knowledge comes mainly from reading news coverage of important scientific stories in magazines like *Newsweek,* or hearing reports on the BBC World Service and later reading textbooks on astronomy. (p. i)

Yet, the Dalai Lama's writing is considered by many to be the pinnacle of scholarship and knowledge. Further, in concert with postmodern thinking, the Dalai Lama identifies the functional capacity of science as transformative, but then suggests that because of its limitations, science fails to produce a full understanding of humans. For this purpose, other knowledge sources are identified such as spirituality, moral discourse, and ethical analysis. Related to disability explanations, postmodernism has been a major champion of "nothing about *us* without *us*" (Charlton, 2000). This slogan refers to the right of disabled category members to be in the lead of creating knowledge about themselves in place of medical colonization of bodies. While pivotal in its time, this assertion is internally contradictory as the *us* is not defined as local, rendering the linguistic quicksand ready and waiting.

One major criticism of postmodernism has been that, because of its eschewal of predictive validity and global truths, it fails to answer fundamental questions necessary to guide informed praxis and action. For us, the postmodernists have opened the discourse about pluralism in many domains including disability. For example, what is the acceptable knowledge base for explaining disability? How can competing explanations be positioned to work? What we mean is, work is the intellectual, analytical, and knowledge base to inform understanding and equality of human rights.

Post-postmodernist theorists, in response to the uncertainty of postmodernism, are attempting to advance theories and knowledge that mediate the conceptual confusion and uncertainty left by postmodern thinking. This contemporary genre for us integrates the "best of all explanatory worlds" by synthesizing the advantages of diverse fields. DePoy and Gitlin (2005) and DePoy and Gilson (2008) have proposed post-postmodern models in their methodological works. Building on the work of Tashakkori and Teddlie (2002) and Shilling (2008), pragmatism, an early 20th century philosophy, makes its way back to the 21st century, joining disparate views and ways of knowing into goal-oriented interdisciplines that comprise post-postmodern thinking (DePoy & Gilson, 2008). We return to post-postmodernism after discussion of some of the central postmodern-type ideas that have framed disability explanations and continue to do so.

Social Constructivism

Social constructivism is a school of thought that views humans as the creators of reality. We place quotation marks around reality because according to the social constructivists, reality does not exist. Rather, reality is invented by humans and thus does not exist outside of human thought and action. By engaging in interaction and discourse, humans create knowledge through sharing and attributing meaning to symbols. Thus, different from disciplines that propose truth as the outcome of their research, within social constructivist thinking and inquiry, humans exist within contexts of meaning (Kim, 2001).

The social model has its origin in social construction, as it explains disability as the sets of attitudes, barriers, and exclusions faced by people regardless of their embodied characteristics (DePoy & Gilson, 2004).

Social constructivists give significant explanatory power to culture, meaning, and context. And as claimed in Explanatory Legitimacy, contextual and purposive bias, value, and diverse worldviews explain and delimit disability. There can, therefore, be numerous explanations, some which do not even include embodied factors, that can explain disability from a constructivist perspective.

Consider this example. A few years back, we received a grant to study the meaning of independence and quality of life for youth with special health care needs and disabilities. The study was intended (in concert with postmodern notions) to inform services and community supports to assist youth to become productive in their communities. So we set out to study the views of youth, their parents, their teachers, service providers such as health and social service professionals, and policymakers who develop funding and legislative guidelines for services and community supports. The findings posed quite a social constructivist dilemma. Parents saw the meaning of independence and quality of life for their children as living independently away from parents in a home of their own. The teachers explained independence and quality of life for the youth as their acceptance and actualization of responsible self-care, providers did not agree on the meanings, and policymakers delimited the concepts of independence and quality of life within fiscal constraints of public support. Most unexpected was the view of the youth themselves who seemed to achieve *intersubjectivity*, or consensus about the meaning of independence and quality of life, without negotiation. The meaning that they ascribed to both was equal opportunity. That is to say, they wanted equivalent opportunities among themselves and their peers for their futures and felt disabled by what they perceived as limited opportunity. As you can see, the two terms, *independence* and *quality of life*, not only have differing explanations depending on the context and people who were asked, but also have diverse definitions, context-embedded, and necessary to be negotiated if the knowledge gained from the study was to be useful in guiding social action (DePoy, Gilmer, & Martzial, 2000).

The example above raises another important point about social constructivism, the inductive inquiry methods used to support knowledge through this lens. The assertion that science and positivist inquiry methods are grand narratives is held by social constructivists. Because experimental methods are based on the philosophical foundation of monism and objectivity, research that seeks to find a single truth through implementing procedures which claim to eliminate human bias are not espoused or supported as a preferred methodology. Rather, narrative strategies which can yield multiple views, such as the inquiry that we described above, provide the evidence on which constructed claims are based. Narrative, storytelling, and other inductive methods, therefore, form the constructivist epistemology, or the way in which one can come to know anything (DePoy & Gitlin, 2010).

The methodological point above creates a good segue to the contemporary use of fields such as political theory, economics, literature, and visual culture as lenses through which to explain disability. Because of space limitations, we cannot discuss each of these important fields, so we have chosen visual culture to illustrate. You can extrapolate the concepts that we discuss to other fields as you read and think.

Visual Culture

Visual culture is a relatively new field that seeks to explain visual images in terms of cultural and social meanings (Rampley, 2005). Different from the study of art or art history, visual culture is concerned with a broad scope of visual images, including art and expanding to the host of digital, electronic, craft, film, mass media, advertising, photographic, scientific (Tufte, 1990, 2006), and other images that exist throughout exterior environments. Visual culture theorists cover the full expanse of human appearance, behavior, and experience, from microunit (individual) to the macrounit (culture; Bronfenbrenner & Morris, 2006), from genetic image to the meanings of abstracts in the media and in scientific narratives.

Perhaps the most obvious explanation for disability within the visual culture framework is the inability to participate in ocularcentric culture if one is not able to see. Yet, there are many implications for disability explanations beyond the physiology of sight within this field of thought. Of particular note is Kleege's (2005) urging that the image of hypothetical blindness, or what she refers to as *sightist* assertions applied to phenomena such as ignorance and lack of insight or understading, explains disability more than not seeing in a sighted world. However, visual culture is not simply concerned with sight as functional or euphemistic for other desirable attributes, nor is visual culture exclusive to images of the body. However, representations of bodies have been one central theme in visual culture that is of critical importance to Disability Studies, and so we now focus on reflections of the body in image and meaning.

Until recently, it was unusual to conceptualize the visual arts as theories so to speak, about biological explanation. Yet, consider how visual renderings of bodies have contributed to meaning over chronological time. In what she refers to as the art/science connection, Ione (2008) discusses early neurological illustration and imagery as a window into cultural beliefs about the role of intrinsic, embodied structures on human behavior and thinking.

Initially through dissection and more recently through technology that paints the body as an electrical, chemical, and structural phenomenon, visual imagery has shaped the sciences of anatomy and physiology (National Library of Medicine, 2009; Onians, 2008; Running Subway Productions, 2008). Consider the image of the human genome or a genetic portrait of an individual.

Genetic research and the technology to allow us to look at microanatomy, depict the human form by its bar code so to speak, a series of linear scratches that create visual genetic maps (Heiferman & Kismaric, 2005). Explaining *congenital genetic disability* as an atypical genetic composition can therefore be interpreted not only as medical deficit but also as meaning and display in visual image (Rothbart, 2007). Harkening back to Quetelet, the visual genetic picture that is most common is determined to be normal while deviation in genetic visualization is constructed as not normal and for some common deviations, explained as congenital disability (Anker & Talasek, 2009; Sandor, 2003).

Recent installations in several art museums and galleries have further highlighted the centrality of visual culture in defining valued and devalued bodies. For example, consider the exhibition that has appeared in multiple urban sites throughout the globe, *Bodies, The Exhibition* (Premier Exhibitions, n.d.). Through dissection, mortuary science, and artistry one can visualize the body as

> both captivating and edifying. BODIES . . . The Exhibition unveils the many complex systems of organs and tissues that drive every aspect of our daily lives and unite us all as humans.

However, the visual images are not messy, filled with fluids of fasciae. Rather, they are embellished with color and texture that is inviting and intriguing, catching one's gaze in webs of iridescently tinted neurons, vessels, and organs. Curiously thin, male bodies predominate with female bodies displayed in two exhibitions: the reproductive system and breast cancer. What are the meanings of visual images of the body in general and gendered bodies in particular? How do they explain disability by what is not present in the exhibition? While each viewer takes away an individual meaning, we were struck by the beauty of the artistry and the homogenization of the body contradicting the cultural rhetoric of diversity.

Similar to the juxtaposition of art and dissection that allows us to peer through the protection of the skin, neuro-imaging has created a videographic representation of structures and interpretive neural productions that form visual standards of desired neural embodied performance, outside of which lies pathology and disability (Sandahl, 2005; Siebers, 2000). To a large extent, visual body culture has replaced behavioral observables as the foundation on which pathological explanations are laid. Thus, the instrumentation as well as its capacity to render visual image is in itself often explanatory of disability. As suggested by Pauwels (2005), science itself speaks meaning through these visual images. In agreement, Carmen (2004) suggests that the human genome and its application to human behavior are and should be examined within the disciplines of political theory and axiology. Through his discussion of genomics, Carmen reminds us that science of human biology and physiology exist within an interpretative theoretical framework in dynamic and diverse contexts and thus is not a singular discipline. As evidence, look at the description of normal bodies offered by the United States National Library of Medicine (2009):

> The Visible Human Project® is an outgrowth of the NLM's 1986 Long-Range Plan. It is the creation of complete, anatomically detailed, three-dimensional representations of the normal male and female human bodies.

Not only is the meaning of *normal* posited but also culturally inscribed in visual museum display (National Library of Medicine, 2009). Conversely, the meaning of *not normal* is visualized by what is *not* on display.

There are some exemplars emerging that challenge the boundaries of the normal body as displayed in medicalized exhibitions. In large part, the difficulty of distinguishing the body from technology has provoked artists to move into bio art (Kac, 2006) in which bodies are represented as cyborg, transplantations, prostheses, and other renditions of biotechnology (Smith & Morra, 2007). Contemporary figures such as Aimee Mullins and Pistorious have been important visual culture images, calling into question where the boundary lies between the embellished and the disabled body. But visual culture does not simply meet disability through direct depiction of bodies. Rather, visual culture is ubiquitous in our universe and thus influences disability through multiple ocularcentric genres of images.

Post-Postmodernism

Design and branding are closely related to visual culture because of their frequent reliance on visual image. These frameworks have only recently been applied to explaining disability (DePoy & Gilson, 2009; Gilson & DePoy, 2009a; Pullin, 2009). The integration of these fields moves this discussion into the realm of post-postmodernism. In response to postmodernism, which cannot find reality and agreement among knowledge productions, post-postmodernism seeks to posit knowledge that can be useful but not monistic. In order to achieve this aim, fields that have been disparate are called into play, creating an active vortex of thinking which forges synthesized but flexible viewpoints to be harnessed for application and advancement. Sunami (2009) refers to reconstructivist art as exemplary of post-postmodernism:

> [This] work builds upon prior, deconstructionist artworks and techniques, but adapts them to classic themes and structures, with the goal of creating works of genuine emotion and significance. In this way, reconstructivism (when it works) combines the vitality and originality of deconstructionism with the comforts, pleasures and rewards of classicism. The overall purpose of reconstructivism is to reawaken a sense of the Real in a world where everything has been demonstrated to be an illusion.

In the emerging tradition of post-postmodernism, we have brought together disability and design and branding in our previous work. Because we see design and branding as more expansive than visual culture, we have located it within contemporary thinking that has the power to elicit informed change (Gilson & DePoy, 2007, 2008, 2009b). Clearly the visual dominates design and branding, as images are typically consumed through vision. However, as we discuss below, design and branding within the 21st century global market economy are critical in shaping identity, category, and place, whether visualized or ascertained in other sensory or abstract methods. We begin with definitions and then apply these contemporary frameworks to disability explanation.

Design

Design is a complex construct that has been increasingly used to describe abstract and concrete human intention and activity and to name a property of virtual, physical, and even abstract phenomena.

Figure 10.1 presents representative lexical definitions of design.

As reflected in the definitions and consistent with post-postmodern thought, design is purposive and may refer to decoration, plan, fashion, functionality, and influence. What is evident in the diverse definitions is the broad scope of phenomena to which design applies, including but not limited to the activities of conceptualizing, planning, creating, and claiming credit for one's ideas, products, and entities as well as the inherent intentional or patterned characteristics of bodies, spaces, and ideas (Margolin, 2002;

Figure 10.1   Definitions of Design

1. To create, fashion, execute, or construct according to plan: DEVISE, CONTRIVE (Merriam-Webster, 2010a).

2. Means any design, logo, drawing, specification, printed matter, instructions or information (as appropriate) provided by the Purchaser in relation to the Goods (Tomohawk Products, n.d.).

3. A set of fields for problem-solving that uses user-centric approaches to understand user needs (as well as business, economic, environmental, social, and other requirements) to create successful solutions that solve real problems. Design is often used as a process to create real change within a system or market. Too often, design is defined only as visual problem-solving or communication because of the predominance of graphic designers (Nathan.com, n.d.a).

4. The plan or arrangement of elements in a work of art. The ideal is one where the assembled elements result in a unity or harmony (Worldimages.com, n.d.).

5. Both the process and the result of structuring the elements of visual form; composition (Ackland Art Museum, n.d.).

6. A clear specification for the structure, organization, appearance, etc. of a deliverable (Ten Step, 2003–2005).

7. Intend or have as a purpose; "She designed to go far in the world of business" (POETS, 2009).

8. A plan for arranging elements in a certain way as to best accomplish a particular purpose (Eames, 1969, in Munari, Eames, Eames, Guixe, & Bey, 2003).

Munari et al., 2003). Despite the ubiquitous and diverse use of the term, of particular note is the post-postmodern commonality in all definitions of design as purposive and intentional. That is to say, design is not frivolous but rather is cultural iconography, which is powerful, political, and is both shaped by and explanatory of notions of standards, acceptability, membership, and desirability (Foster, 2003; Munari et al., 2003).

Branding

In contemporary Western economies, design is closely related to branding. Given the emergence of branding from the fields of marketing and advertising, brands within this constrained conceptual framework are defined as the purposive design and ascription of logos to a product for the intent of public recognition, addition of value, and consumption. Of particular importance to disability explanations within the scaffold of branding is the construct of value-added. Interpreted broadly, the addition of value does not necessarily imply an increase or elevation but denotes the cultural inscription of value that can span the continuum from extremely pejorative to most desirable.

More recently, scholars have enlarged the definitional scope of branding as a critical, culturally embedded, symbolic set that commodifies and reciprocally represents and shapes value, ideas, and identities. Brands are design stories that unfurl and take on meaning as they are articulated and shared by multiple authors so to speak. Because symbolism and dynamism both inhere in branding, Holt (2004) has suggested the term *cultural branding*, which elevates brands to the status of icon and marker of identity and idea. While Holt's term is relatively new, the notion of branding as explanatory of one's cultural, social, and individual identity and comparative social worth was originated in the early and mid 20th century by thinkers such as Horkheimer, Adorono, Noerr, and Jepgcott (2002) and McLuhan and Fiore (2005). Although divergent in ontology and domain of concern, these scholars were seminal in introducing branding as an identity-assemblage and projecting entity. That is to say, through the process of choosing and adopting cultural iconography in the form of products, fashions, food, music, and so forth one ostensibly defines the self and displays value to others (Holt, 2004).

Contemporary literature reveals a more complex analysis and debate about the directionality of the choice-adoption-display sequence of branding. Some scholars adhere to the classical view that choice of style and design brand is a self-determined effort to align one's identities with preferred cultural-media images (McLuhan & Fiore, 2005) while others suggest that branding is surreptitiously ascribed to groups and individuals by market forces. We suggest, however, that the post-postmodern purposive nature of design and branding manipulates individuals and groups into believing that they can and do autonomously choose their identities but, in effect, do not, regardless of what icons they may select from a provided menu of options.

Building on design and branding theory, the conceptual portal of design and branding is potent for unpacking and analyzing the purposive, political, and profit-driven nature of embodied labeling, identity formation and recognition, stereotyping, and responses that explain disability and give meaning to it as a category. The explanatory importance of this conceptual framework lies in the processes and purposes of design and branding as deliberate, complex, and potentially able to manipulate meaning of self, others, and categories (Licht & O'Rourke, 2007).

As we noted, while product branding is part and parcel of popular visual culture, it looms larger and more powerful in explaining disability populations and affixing their value. Visual logos do not have to be present in order for disability to be recognized and valuated or branded. As noted by Lefebvre (1991), for example, physical space is not neutral. Referred to as *brandscape*, location carries value or devalue-added meanings within its perimeter, design, purpose, and use. Understanding disability through the powerful contemporary post-postmodern lens is particularly timely and thought-provocative within advanced global market environments (DePoy & Gilson, 2009; Pasquinelli, 2005).

In a recent presentation entitled "Designer Disability" that we gave at the Society for Disability Studies, Guzman, (personal communication), remarked that marketing theory did not do explanatory justice to understanding disability as a cultural group that experiences social discrimination and exclusion. In concert with Riley (2006), we disagreed, suggesting that in the 21st century and consistent with post-postmodern thinking, disability is no longer exempt from the market economy, business, and its design and branding processes (Adair, 2002; Pullin, 2009; Riley, 2006). Rather, this synthetic lens is seminal to explaining disability as marked, circumscribed, and commodified by designated products, spaces, and abstracts that not only brand its members but also position them as a target market segment ripe for commodification and economic exploitation (Seldon, Bartholomew, & Myddelton, 2007). However, this complex analysis reveals new actionable pathways to social change.

Before moving to more abstract design domains such as policy and services, we return to visual culture as concrete exemplars of this complex but compelling explanation.

Product Design and Branding

Similar to Fussell (1992), whose classic work asserted that owned, displayed, and used objects are explanatory and demonstrative of social class, specific disability products are designed as functional, recognizable, identity assigning, and manipulative of those who use them and those who view them. In essence, these products by their aesthetic design and distribution outlets brand and thus explain the user as disabled. For example, consider these two photos of shower seats. Despite identical functionality, Seat A in Figure 10.2 is designed as prescribed durable medical equipment while Seat B in Figure 10.3 is designed for commercial sales and voluntary selection and universal use. The family sporting the medical equipment is often branded as the object of pity, with lexical symbols such as caregiver, assistive technology, and health insurance further reifying and providing explanation of disability as pathology.

Figure 10.2 Seat A

Figure 10.3 Seat B

Conversely, a perusal of websites and catalogues of commercial companies reveals that they sell "high brow" (Foster, 2003) designed and marketed household and lifestyle products that were originally branded and in some outlets (rehabilitation, assistive technology, and medical products) still are disability-branded. In comparing the products, difference in the functional use is not discernable, but the design distinctions are often obvious (see Figures 10.2 and 10.3) and thus ascribe *sub rosa,* an explanatory brand label to those who have and use designer disability products. Consistent with visual culture theorizing, the brand in turn manipulates meaning, behavior, and value and serves to institutionalize and maintain segregated status quo between disabled category members and their nondisabled counterparts. Consider two more examples: headphones and attire.

Bodies diagnosed with conditions that contain the symptom of distractibility are often met with medication and medical products to filter out irrelevant stimulation and aid in concentration. However, those same distractible people, without diagnostic labels, were the subject of a recent article in the *New York Times* reporting use of mainstream, high-tech, noise-canceling headphones to eliminate ambient noise, help people focus, and reduce noise-related stress in urban environments (Walker, 2008). Different from the devaluated signifier of assistive technology, this genre of technology is referred to as *fashionable technology* by Seymour (2008).

As part of a current exhibition at the Royal Ontario Museum entitled, *Out From Under: Disability, History and Things to Remember,* Phillips (2008) draws our attention to attire, not haute couture but another type of fashion. She displays a photo of adults clothed in identical, drab gray sweat suits (called track suits) next to the actual suits themselves. What becomes clear in the visuals and further elucidated in the textual explanation is that this attire not only homogenizes those who wear it but also strips them of individual identity and brands and devalues them as disabled institutional litter regardless of where they live or what they do.

The exemplars above depict what we refer to as devalue-added explanatory status or the negative valuation inherent in a brand. However, disability product design does not always carry a pejorative connotation. As shown in Figures 10.4

and 10.5a and b, items such as racing wheelchairs and futuristic prostheses often brand and thus explain disability as superhuman, inspirational, and remarkable, but never fashionable.

Anderson (in Rampley, 2005) discusses fashion as an academic discipline and calls our attention to its increasing presence in theory about humans. Its relevance to disability explanation is visualized in examples 10.2 through 10.5.

Fashion, defined at the microunit as bodily dress and adornment, is particularly relevant in explaining disability. What Rampley (2005) means by this point is that individual selection of fashion displays a descriptive image of the fashion consumer to others and provides important explanatory meanings such as one's cultural context, gender identity, wealth, status, and sexuality. Moreover, within the complex contexts of the information age in the Western world, fashion has been explained as a critical factor in selecting a social group and establishing and illustrating one's group membership.

The foundation for current architectural standards institutionalized by Le Corbusier harkens back to the elongated measurements and proportionality of Vitruvian Man (Gilson & DePoy, 2007). Bodies that stray too far from mythic standards of human size, locomotion, sensorium, and behavior experience ill fit in geographies that are built according to Vitruvian bodies. It is curious to note that rather than being designed for a larger range of human diversity, contemporary methods and policies guiding new construction and retrofitting of existing built environments provide guidance for partitioned and clearly labeled spaces for disabled bodies. The result is that segments of public spaces and locations not only are designed for disabled bodies but also serve to contain them as well (Butler & Parr, 1999; Sherry, 2000),

Figure 10.4   Racing Wheelchair

Figure 10.5a Racing Prostheses

Source: Photo Courtesy of Ossur Americas, www.ossur.com.

Figure 10.5b Racing Prostheses

Source: Permission granted by Aimee Mullins. Photograph by Howard Schatz © Schatz Ornstein 2000 (from the book *Athlete*, HarperCollins 2000).

Figure 10.6 Parking

Source: © Can Stock Photo Inc.

branding them as atypical and explaining them as different by their occupation of the very space that ostensibly was designed for greater access and participation. Consider the examples in Figures 10.6 and 10.7. Figure 10.6 demonstrates the cleavage of space into distinct and separate locations for standard and atypical bodies with accompanying simulacra in Figure 10.7, the cultural icon that denotes spaces exclusively for disabled bodies whether or not those bodies use wheeled mobility. We refer to the wheelchair symbol as simulacra because of its diffuse meaning coupled with its recognition and devalue-added component.

While the media have been typically thought about with regard to shaping attitudes towards characters,

Figure 10.7 Disability Icon

Source: © Can Stock Photo Inc.

its power in explaining disability, particularly in the media-rich context of the 21st century, cannot be understated (Riley, 2006). Numerous media venues have been analyzed including but not limited to film, television, virtual and social networking, and print. For example, in film analysis, Scott (2008) asserts that science fiction is potent in creating design imagination and actualization, as exemplified by films such as *AlphaVille* and *Blade Runner*. These two films, along with others, depict "fables of the future" that provide templates and conceptual blueprints for urban designers (Scott, 2008).

Connor (2007) suggests that disability-positive films such as *Shrek* and *Finding Nemo* can counter more typically dismal media portrayal of disability. Different from films such as *Scent of a Woman* and *Million Dollar Baby* in which blindness creates rancor and permanent injury creates intolerable life, *Shrek* and *Finding Nemo* depict difference as heroic and atypical embodied characteristic as incidental, respectively. Post-postmodern analysis would bring multiple analytic models to bear on media representations, identifying a potential range of explanations in a single character. For example, *Forrest Gump* and *As Good As It Gets,* often vilified for actors playing disabled roles, represent the juxtaposition of pathology and deficit adjacent to accomplishment and potential.

Haller (2000) links diverse news media portrayals to policy formulation, suggesting that public opinion towards the Americans with Disabilities Act has been significantly influenced by media messages explaining disability through nine models: medical, social pathology, supercrip, business, minority, civil rights, legal, cultural pluralism, and consumer models. Each model elicits a differential response and is purposive and powerful in reifying disability within an explanatory frame.

Building on the policy/media work of Haller (2000), we now turn to the synthesis of design and disability explanations within the service and policy arenas. One typically sees disability services as altruistic, professional, and helping. We do not dismiss or vilify these important aspects of disability services that are so critical for increasing participation and access to some extent in our current world. However, the picture is not that simple. As early as 1992, Gill published work that revealed the economic advantage derived from disability by providers, professionals, product manufacturers, and so forth. DePoy and Gilson (2004) referred to this phenomenon as the disability industry and more recently the disability park (DePoy & Gilson, 2008) in which economic survival and profit too frequently trump the goals of facilitating meaningful, full participation in community, work, recreation, and civic life for people who are considered or identify themselves as disabled. Our more recent thinking asserts that in the current global context, economic advantage, and value-added services not only can coexist but also must do so in order to be viable (Gilson & DePoy, 2009). We discuss this point more fully in Chapters 11–15 on legitimacy of response.

For analytic and guidance purposes, we call your attention to the term *environmental simulacra*, originally coined to describe theme parks that are not easily distinguished from the reality they represent (Galician, 2004). Rather, these spaces and what occurs within them are designed for the purpose of shaping and encouraging consumerism. Given the current economic and sociopolitical context of the service environment, we suggest that this term and its principles are relevant to disability environments and the disability signifiers that are explanatory within them. The service environment or what we now refer to as the *disability park* is comprised of all physical and abstract spaces and activity as well as explicit and implicit sign, product, and signifier. Besides service delivery as the articulated purpose, implicit branding both influences and reflects the value or devalue-added partitioning of these spaces and the relative groupings who interact within them (e.g., consumer or provider; Tregaskis, 2004).

Aligned with disability products, spaces, and services, which serve to brand those who use and inhabit disability geographies and parks, the very notion of disability policy as a separate entity is an exemplar of abstract (nonvisual) branding through segmentation. Typically, disability policy has been categorized into two areas: policies that guide the provisions of disability services and resources, such as the Social Security Disability Insurance Act (SSDI) established by the Social Security Amendments of 1956 in the United States, and more recently those such as the Americans with Disabilities Act (ADA) and the UN Convention on the Rights of Persons with Disabilities that purport to protect and advance the civil rights of populations that are considered or identified as legitimately disabled.

Building on this binary taxonomy, we suggest that that policy is much more complex than its explicit verbiage and articulated outcomes. As noted by Kymlicka (2009), in his recent analysis of multiculturalism, global human rights policy is plagued by two overarching problems.

The first is the failure of current categorical frameworks to do viable work in carving up humanity into useful categories. Kymlicka's assertion provides one of the foundational pillars of our view, as we question the legitimacy of so many diverse and vague explanations for disability and thus the usefulness of the category for achieving the asserted purposes of full participation.

The second problem identified by Kymlicka is the time sequence of designing and implementing targeted and generic policy. Applied to disability, we suggest that targeted distributive and protective legislation in itself is explanatory of disability. Those who qualify for benefits and protections of disability policy are defined as disabled if they meet the explanatory criteria. Separate policies institutionalize disability explanations and the disability park by partitioning abstract principles and language and applying them differentially to disabled and nondisabled individuals (Tregaskis, 2004). For example, above we noted that people who are considered disabled use assistive technology while nondisabled people who use identical products use technology or, as Seymour (2008) asserts, use fashionable technology. Consider the need for help that is implied in the word *assistive* and the institutionalization of this concept in the Assistive Technology Act passed in the United States in the late 20th century.

Another consideration regarding the sequencing of targeted and generic policy was illuminated by Badinter (2006) in her discussion of gender equality. She suggested that the maintenance of specialized rights and policies negates their articulated aims of equality. This insidious process occurs by surreptitious design in which recipients of resources and rights only granted by specialized policies are defined by their eligibility for protection and thus continue to be required to remain segregated as victims. Those who are covered under disability policy are explained as vulnerable, in need of specialized assistance, and in the disability park that provides employment and economic opportunity and advantage to providers and disability designers. Analysis of disability policy reveals it as a grand narrative, a brand of designed disability policy that on the surface speaks of resources and equity, but in essence serves up populations identified or identifying as disabled to the disability park and thus explains disability by location of service consumer within the park.

Similarly, the UN Convention on the Rights of Persons with Disabilities, while theoretically enacted to raise awareness and reduce discrimination and disadvantage experienced by populations identified or identifying as disabled, is often persuasive in the abstract but lacks substantive content. Thus it is explanatory as well. The presence of specialized and protected policy worldwide and the location of disability adjacent to other groups explain all of these groups as needy of legal protection rather than as citizens with the rights and responsibilities afforded to typical citizens.

Both nationally and internationally, we recognize the value of these policies for redressing discrimination and exclusion, particularly in a context in which population-specific policies and resources are the predominant distributive model. However, through a post-postmodern lens, the explicit intent of policy is open for interrogation and analysis as the basis to advance social change and equality of opportunity and to move from the oxymoron of population-specific equality to population-wide equality and justice. We discuss these responses more fully in the chapters on legitimacy.

Post-postmodernism has gifted disability explorations and explanations with both intellectual and utilitarian richness. Consider, for example, the metaphoric propinquity of the designer disability items, orthopedic shoes, queerness, and evolutionary theory (Fries, 2007). Fries elucidates stunning relationships among his travels and phylogenic theories of natural selection, legitimately reintegrating science into discussions of disability. Similarly, the neuro-diversity literature allows for the reintroduction of biology into explanations of disability while advancing progressive views in so doing. For example, using this post-postmodern view, diagnoses of brain disorder such as bipolar disorder, schizophrenia, autism, and so forth are reframed as diverse rather than as pathological (Antonetta, 2007; Seidel, 2004–2009).

Given the recency of post-postmodernism and its theoretical vagueness, how this thinking will respond to post-modernism and influence explanations of disability are evolving processes. As we promised, however, we now discuss Explanatory Legitimacy as a post-postmodern theory. Although we originally conceptualized it as post-modern because of its acceptance of multiple explanatory frameworks within an axiolgical context, we suggest that legitimacy thinking about disability provides the opportunity for reconciling and rejoining theories that have been previously divorced, bringing theoretical synthesis to inform contemporary and progressive local through global legitimate response. Theoretical wealth and informed, productive, and negotiated social action can result when both monism and skepticism are transcended. We therefore conclude this discussion with a post-postmodern explanatory theory of disability, disjuncture theory (DePoy & Gilson, 2008; Gilson & DePoy, 2009b).

Disjuncture theory, a synthetic explanatory scheme, provides a powerful framework for examining disability as a complex host of interactions. Understanding disability from this vantage point provides a rich and multifaceted rationale that transcends disability legitimacy determination as a binary. Disjunctured explanations lay the bedrock for progressive responses, which meet Davis's and Kymlicka's challenge of jettisoning useless categories and replacing them with progressive and compelling social change.

Disability as Disjuncture

At the end of the history section we identified two major theoretical and praxis challenges for the 21st century, reconstituting the body and reconciling the medical-constructed binary. In this final section of the chapter, we posit disjuncture theory as an important integrative explanation for healing the intellectual chasm in Disability Studies and the study of disability for reunifying the body and for creating legitimate collaboration in theorizing about and responding to disability.

Intellectual Foundation

Our initial thinking about disjuncture emerged from a conversation in a Disability Studies class in which we asked students to reflect on the current rationale for typical and accommodative standards for built and virtual environments. The students indicated that they just took these environmental features for granted and had not thought about why doorways, chair heights, computer access, and so forth could not be reconceptualized differently. After this conversation, we set out to learn more about environmental design history and the rationale for accessibility standards that comply with the Americans with Disabilities Act. Our research revealed that built and virtual environmental and product design standards for industrial and postindustrial contexts are constructed around Enlightenment ideals of the human body, its balance, proportion, emphasis, rhythm, and unity (American Institute of Architects, 2010; Margolin, 2002). Literally translated from Greek as "measurement of man," *anthropometrics* has created an important foundation for design in that it is devoted to the measurement and numeric characterization of human bodies. Variables including but not limited to body configuration, weight, sensation, and typical movement provide the averages that shape environments and products, from skyscrapers to seating to computer and cell phone keypads. Although anthropometrics is ostensibly concerned with human variation, given its retention of *man* in its Greek translation, it is not surprising that da Vinci's logico-deductive canons of proportionality, based on his representation of the male figure, have been apprehended to serve as contemporary mechanisms to guide the design and control of environments, products, and those who act within them and use them respectively (Margolin, 2002). Considered one of the most influential modern architects, Le Corbusier used the golden ratio developed by Vitruvius and operationalized in da Vinci's Vitruvian Man as the human standard around which to design and build urban environments. (Cross, 2001; Dimitriu, n.d.). His efforts to *scientize design*, or provide a rational, numeric, empirical foundation in place of economic and political trends as the basis for architectural thinking and action, were espoused through the 1960s by influential architects such as Buckminster Fuller (Cross, 2001).

Also seeking to scientize design, the recent creation of the field of human factors has contributed diversity and flexibility to theory and design of human-environment interaction (Salvendy, 2006). Emerging from *ergonomics*, classically defined as the study of work, human factors theory and application is informed by multiple disciplines including "science, engineering, design, technology, and management of human-compatible systems" (p. 4). Of particular emphasis in human factors literature is its philosophical grounding in progressive views of environmental diversity and the response of environmental, product, and technological design to meet the broad range of human skills. Specific to disability, Salvendy eschews the disabled/not disabled binary, cautioning readers that skill-specific design responses may position a single individual in diverse locations on the bell curve with regard to competence. For example, an individual with limited vision might excel in auditory skill and vice versa. So designing to individuals as disabled or not disabled cannot create environments in which individuals can function optimally. Within the human factors rubric, disability is explained as "the inability to accommodate to the world as it is currently designed" (Salvendy, 2006, p. 1388). However, even with its praxis focus on environment and artifact design, the material body remains the locus for disability. Nevertheless, we see human factors as foundational to healing disjuncture as we discuss in Chapters 16 and 17.

Further advancing the understanding of disability as interactive, as early as 1999, the National Institute on Disability and Rehabilitation Research (United States Department of Education, 2007) published the following explanation: "disability is a product of the interaction between characteristics of the individual (e.g., conditions or impairments, functional status, or personal and social qualities) and the characteristics of the natural, built, cultural, and social environments." This synthetic explanation positions disability as mobile and context-embedded but fails to identify the point or range at which the interactive product moves from ability to disability. Similar to the human factors definition, within NIDRR's viewpoint, the atypical body remains the habitat of disability as depicted in the parenthetical clarifier in the definition above. Nevertheless, in response to the bifurcation of disability as embodied or exclusively a function of social discrimination, NIDRR's explanation is progressive in its effort to bring both bodies and contexts in contact once again.

As noted by Davis (1997, 2002), disability is an unstable category and thus has been in need of reconceptualization. Davis posited the revision of the category to include every *body* regardless of its current status. This important viewpoint foregrounded the limitations of outdated models of identity politics that crafted policy responses for subpopulations even with the recognition that everyone can join the membership roster of disability. Similar to NIDRR's definition, Davis retained the body as the entry point into the disability club, referring to Christopher Reeve as exemplary of how quickly one can change embodied status.

Building on this work and the work of other theorists who explain disability as interactive, we have posited disjuncture as one of many explanations that could form a solid axiological, as well as praxis, foundation for legitimate disability determination and response. Unlike NIDRR and Davis, however, we do not look to the body for the initial entrance into disability. Moreover, dissimilar from human factors theory, the material corpus may be, but is not necessarily the home of disability. Rather, we recognize body and environment as equal vestibules and suggest that a potent explanation of disability is not simply an interaction but rather an ill fit between body and environment. Figures 10.8 and 10.9 visually represent disjuncture. As depicted below, disjuncture is a continuum rather than a binary, with ascending degrees of separation between environment and body denoting more severe disjuncture and vice versa.

Consistent with all explanatory genres within Explanatory Legitimacy Theory, the explanatory disjunctures between atypical bodies and their contexts in and of themselves are not the locus of disability until a determination of legitimacy is made on the degree to which the ill fit is disabling. As discussed in previous chapters, bodies and environments are broadly defined and thus this explanation engenders a multitude of response options.

Diverse approaches to design, therefore, are not only central but also critical in framing responses that we see as promoting equality of opportunity, human rights, and social justice. In Chapters 16 and 17, we posit theory and directions for social change and illustrate how change has been and can be implemented to enhance the future of communities.

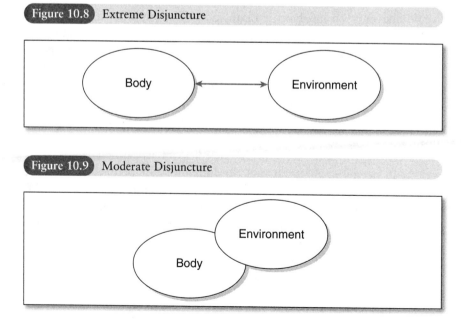

Figure 10.8 Extreme Disjuncture

Body ←——→ Environment

Figure 10.9 Moderate Disjuncture

Body / Environment

PART III

Legitimacy

11

Legitimacy—What Is It?

In this chapter, we devote our attention to the clarification, exploration, and illustration of the construct of legitimacy. We briefly introduced legitimacy in Chapter 1 as it emerged throughout history and then specifically applied it to disability determination and response.

Similar to other legitimacy theorists, we apply the construct of legitimacy to examine the explanatory criteria that are considered credible and acceptable to confer a status, in this case disability status, and then fashion responses to it. Because legitimacy theories aim to unclothe and display explicit and tacit values, pluralistic ideas, and power relations that determine authenticity, we find legitimacy to be a powerful disambiguating microscope to magnify and clarify why one becomes considered as disabled, the location of disability within social hierarchies, and the responses afforded to category members on the basis of worth. Thus, the third element of explanatory legitimacy focuses on judgments and beliefs about the viability and correctness of explanations that create the conceptual and empirical footing on which determination of group belongingness and response are made (Simmons, 2001).

Applied to disability, we suggest that the attribution of legitimate disability status to an individual or group is a dynamic, value-based categorization that has little to do with the atypical description, but rather with judgments and beliefs about the explanations attributed to descriptive elements. Because values are a major theme in many current theories of disability and are central to legitimacy approaches, we now attend to values and distinguish them from terms that are similar but not synonymous.

What Are Values?

Debates about the nature of values, what they are, and what they are not have contributed to multiple definitions and theories of value. Table 11.1 reveals the findings of our recent Google search on values.

Table 11.1 Value Definitions

- The quality (positive or negative) that renders something desirable or valuable; "the Shakespearean Shylock is of dubious value in the modern world"
- The amount (of money or goods or services) that is considered to be a fair equivalent for something else; "He tried to estimate the value of the produce at normal prices"
- Prize: hold dear; "I prize these old photographs"
- Respect: regard highly; think much of; "I respect his judgment"; "We prize his creativity"
- Measure: place a value on; judge the worth of something; "I will have the family jewels appraised by a professional"
- An ideal accepted by some individual or group; "He has old-fashioned values"
- *Value* is a term that expresses the concept of worth in general, and it is thought to be connected to reasons for certain practices, policies, or actions (Wikipedia, 2010b)
- Value is the respondent's estimate of how much the property (house and lot, mobile home and lot, or condominium unit) would sell for if it was for sale (For more information, see "Specified Owner-Occupied Housing Units"; US Census Bureau, 2005)
- The power of a thing to command other goods in exchange; the present worth of future rights to income and benefits arising from ownership (OfficeFinder, 1995–2010)
- The monetary worth of property, goods, or services (NCBuy, 2009)
- An expression of monetary worth of a particular piece of real estate (New York Real Estate, n.d.)
- Our sense of what something is *worth*; financial benefits (Nathan .com, n.d.b)
- Value is the respondent's estimate of how much the property would sell for on the current market. For vacant units, value is the sales

price asked for the property at the time of the interview and may differ from the price at which the property is sold. The "sales price asked" includes the price of a one-housing-unit structure and the land on which it is located. The sales price asked may also include additional structures such as garages, sheds, barns, etc. (US Census Bureau, 2005)

- Is not only what the Museum was or would be willing to pay for the object. It also reflects the return on that investment in the number of visitors that choose to see it, the number of students that wish to refer to it, or the number of images that are sold or licensed throughout the world. It is a measure of demand for that particular work. It also should contain an element of what economists call Net Present Value (Conservation Online, 2010)
- Monetary measure of the contribution to human welfare provided by project outcomes; numbers in an analysis; society's or an individual's view of a thing (EcoSurvey, n.d.)

Source: http://www.google.com/search?hl=en&lr=&client=safari&rls=en&oi=defmore&defl=en&q=define:value

And although diverse in their scope and nature, what all these definitions of value have in common is the core foundation of value as human belief of what is desirable. Moreover, while not synonyms of value, morals and ethics are inherent in them as suggested by Resnick (1997), who defines ethics as

standards of conduct that distinguish between right and wrong, good and bad, virtue and vice, justice and injustice. Some ethical standards, i.e., morals (or morality), are highly general and apply to all people. Other standards apply within the context of various institutional, organizational, professional, or familial roles, such as medical ethics, academic ethics, military ethics, etc. (University of Wyoming, 2009)

Synthesizing the common elements of values definitions and the scholarship that informs our framework, the following definition of value guides Explanatory Legitimacy:

- The set of beliefs about the desirability and worth of descriptions and explanations (DePoy & Gilson, 2004). In agreement with Lewis (2000), values are distinguished from other types of beliefs by their moral and action orientations.

Thus, applied to disability legitimacy (and more important in Explanatory Legitimacy), values designate which descriptions are of interest and fit, giving the theory its moniker: Values are selective and parse explanations of human description that qualify for membership and response from those that do not. Group assignment therefore occurs within a value perimeter from the acceptance of theories of human behavior as viable disability membership locators to the determination of which members will receive what type of response.

Because of the ethical and moral foundation of values and value determinations, the importance of analyzing the context and shared beliefs in what is right, sound, and good, is critical for understanding disability legitimacy decisions.

The recognition of the role of values in group assignment and identity is not new. In the social and minority models of disability of the late 20th century, for example, values are addressed primarily as they are applied to those who have already been perceived or identified themselves as disabled (Albrecht, Seelman, & Bury, 2001; Linton, 1998; Oliver, 1997; Silvers, Wasserman, & Mahowald, 1998). According to Pfeiffer (2002), values determine the boundaries of normal and abnormal and thus set the stage for acceptable and unacceptable human difference. However, our stance is a significant departure from recent models of disability in that in Explanatory Legitimacy Theory the value element of disability attaches itself to explanation, precedes categorization, and most important is itself the defining element of disability. That is to say, unlike conceptual models that define disability directly by description or explanation, Explanatory Legitimacy Theory asserts that disability is determined not by either, but rather by the set of beliefs, value judgments, and expectations attributed to the explanation. We are not suggesting that people or groups who are determined to be disabled do not act, look, or experience atypically or that medical, social, and economic factors do not influence life experience and community support. However, we see description and its explanations within the domain of human diversity. Value judgments and beliefs, on the other hand, create the acceptable limits of diversity beyond which individuals are determined to be disabled and thus categorized as such.

In concert with the tenets of Explanatory Legitimacy Theory, disability is a state rather than a trait not because, as asserted in current literature (Gilson & DePoy, 2003), medical or social conditions that disable individuals can change but rather because judgment and belief—the disabling designators—differ according to who is judging whom, when, and why judgments are applied and the context in which judgments are made. Because of differential values among individuals, theoretical perspectives and systems, and even changing values held by a single person, the definition of disability changes despite the equivalence of atypical description and the explanations for it (Jost & Major, 2002).

On the heels of disability membership, the second important part of legitimacy arrives, namely, legitimate response to disability category membership. Values regarding the explanations for location in the disability club play a significant role in crafting responses as well, ranging from conferral of privilege to oppression, exclusion, and even eugenics.

The late 20th century social and minority explanations of atypical activity, appearance, and experience identified and analyzed responses to disability status as purposively or unintentionally undesirable, while conceptualizations, such as that made by Stone (1986), highlighted the benefits of being labeled disabled. A careful and comprehensive analysis of value is therefore warranted to prevent a simplistic, static, or essentialist (Fuchs 2005; Jost & Major, 2002) view of legitimacy, of disability determination and response.

Legitimacy decree and responses occur and can be examined from numerous stances. Because legitimacy can be an interior or exterior environment process (DePoy & Gilson, 2008), we have separated the construct into two major stances: legitimacy from without and legitimacy from within. While both can occur simultaneously, we discuss them as separate for instructive purposes.

By legitimacy from without, we mean the stance of value sets particularly guided by longitudinal, exterior environment, and systems theories. While individuals with these explanations also may adopt legitimate disability identity of their own, these theoretical lenses by their very nature and content explain human development and behavior in comparison to specific established metrics as in the case of longitudinal theory, or in response to variables in the exterior environment or exterior interactive systems in which individuals are situated. These three genres posit explanations of *not normal* or not functional on the basis of what is typical and desirable within a cohort of systemic context. Thus, someone else confers disability status first before it is possibly adopted as accurate by the individual sporting the label. Value assertions and responses embedded within each of those theoretical genres might address conformity, morality regarding the degree of perceived control over one's circumstance, and locus of control (Yzerbyt & Rogier, 2001). However, over the past decade, legitimacy from without has become nudged into the global market economy and thus would be informed in part by contemporary and emerging theories as well (DePoy & Gilson, 2009; Riley, 2006). Logos, symbols, and marketing strategies have become forceful not only in directly designing disability but also in branding disability as well. Moreover, the brand assigns value to disability status depending on the explanation that landed an individual as a member.

Legitimacy from within encompasses the posture of individuals and groups in proclaiming their own legitimate membership in the disability club. Theoretical principles from interior environment perspectives as well as those from contemporary and emerging genres are operative in this slice of legitimacy. Included within this panorama are constructs such as disability identity, self-determination, and diversity depth.

From the discussion above, it is clear that within and without landscapes are not mutually exclusive. Consider how interior environment theories can be harnessed by professionals to confer and respond to disability membership while also being responsible for and accepted by individuals as a self-determined identity. However, the reference points and purposes of self-definition differ from those of being assigned membership by others. Moreover, the conceptual fabric of legitimacy illuminates the importance of how groups perceive the positions and cohesiveness of other groups and interact with them (Tregaskis, 2004) regardless of the actual positions held by individual group members as important determinants of category worth and response (Jost & Major, 2002; Valadez, 2001). We discuss these points in detail in subsequent chapters.

By identifying and analyzing contemporary value issues, we can approach the complexity of legitimacy as clearly as possible. Each of the theory genres discussed in Chapters 6–10 is relevant to stances of legitimacy from within and from without. However, as our discussion of legitimacy proceeds in the next chapters, we highlight why we made the interior/exterior stance distinction and placement of each issue.

Much of the current literature from disability studies, as well as that describing the experience of disability from those who have accepted or asserted legitimate disability status (which we label *legitimacy from within*), has been created in response to the judgments, attributions, categorization, and responses to explanations for atypical description on the part of nondisabled individuals and groups. To fully understand and analyze the stance of legitimacy from within, the vantage points and related actions of those who created the disability category and who have determined membership legitimacy therefore need to be explicated. Chapters 12–17 take on this important task.

12

Who Is a Legitimate Category Member?

In this chapter, we analyze how diverse theories discussed in Part II shape and thus legitimize membership criteria in the grand category of disability, and frame response. For each theory genre, we unpack values inherent within the theories themselves as the basis for understanding how categories of human diversity are allocated and located along axiological continua. We then situate theory in disciplinary fields as they relate to disability in preparation for subsequent chapters.

Following the sequence in which theory genres were discussed in Part II, we begin our discussion with longitudinal theories as they remain omnipotent in shaping and explaining expectations and thus responses to disability.

Longitudinal Legitimacy

Although longitudinal theories are diverse in their foci and values, all share the values that are listed in Table 12.1.

Looking closely at the narrative of longitudinal theories, the inherent value on averages emerges as central and relevant to disability determination. That is to say, longitudinal theories hold what is typical and most common for an age cohort as generally desirable and what is not typical as anomalous, exceeding, or underachieving desirability criteria. According to longitudinal theorists, as individuals age over time, they should exhibit similar trajectories that increasingly build on previous experience, skill, and

Table 12.1	Common Values in Longitudinal Explanations

Value 1 – Average is desirable.

Value 2 – Conformity to averages is desirable.

Value 3 – Average is prescriptive.

Value 4 – Orderly, prescribed progression through chronology is desirable.

Value 5 – Quantitative and qualitative growth are associated and both unfold over time.

Value 6 – Experience-rich environments produce learning and growth.

Value 7 – Environments and objects should be age appropriate.

Value 8 – Supportive, appropriate environments produce longitudinally typical learning and growth.

Value 9 – Maturation, learning, and growth up to the point of decline are desirable.

Value 10 – Nomothetic evidence (generated by examining groups) provides the foundation for verification of theory.

capability. Through this lens, as we analyzed in Chapter 6, disability is therefore explained as nonconformance, most typically underachievement, to preferred chronological metrics. Deviation from the average may, but does not necessarily, locate one in the disabled category. The value judgment that determines disability membership status is made both on the degree of difference and the reasons for it.

For example, body size that strays too far from the average is labeled by terms such as person of short stature and then diagnostically determined as disability if a medical-diagnostic explanation is paired with the atypical observable. If function is atypical for one's age cohort, disability status is even more likely to be ascribed.

Of critical importance to understanding disability through a longitudinal lens is the reciprocal relationships between the chronologically developing interior environment of the body and the exterior environment. Longitudinal theories prescribe the proper interior and exterior environments to foster typical growth over time.

Consider our previous discussion of the built environment and the basis for architectural design. Contemporary standards are based on anthropometrically determined averages for size, shape, mobility, and so forth. These averages become prescriptive and form the basis for what *should be* at specific ages. Similarly, public schooling in most developed countries is organized along chronological parameters of expected average interior cognitive, physical, sensory, social, and intellectual growth and achievement and thus seeks to shape these traits, homogenizing chronological development according to age cohort. Those who fail to achieve the average or the *norm* at an expected age are considered on an atypical continuum from immature to severely disabled.

To a large extent, as noted in Table 12.1, the values inherent in longitudinal theories have much to do with the preferred epistemology that creates and supports them. That is to say, coming to know about averages is a nomothetic inquiry process, or that which seeks to identify within-group commonalities and then to distinguish groups from others. Understanding the relationship between methods of knowledge generation and knowledge production clarifies how averages become valued as *truth* and thus drive response. Being aware of the methods of knowledge generation also provides insight into the direction of disability legitimacy. Since nomothetic inquiry methods are specialized techniques that are conducted by trained researchers and used by many health and human service professional groups to guide assessment and response, it logically follows that longitudinal legitimacy, at least initially, is conferred from *without* and mostly but not always is married to a medical-diagnostic, interior environment explanation. Consider the term *intellectual disability* to illustrate. Intellectual disability was previously referred to as mental retardation but because of the stigma of the label was changed to an ostensibly less pejorative name. While the language issue itself highlights the devaluation of the circumstance, further evidence of legitimacy based on values is revealed through closer examination.

First, consider the diagnostic legitimacy for intellectual disability. This label is determined by several criteria, the first and most legitimate being underperformance on an age-referenced test of intellectual function. As is characteristic of longitudinal thinking, theorizing the norm is derived from observations of the most frequently occurring phenomena, in this case scores on an IQ test. These frequencies are then translated not simply into norms but into desirables. Deviation from the average is considered atypical, with lower scores attracting the attention of disability diagnosticians. Within the past few decades, intellectual disability has moved from interior longitudinal explanation to interactive. As demonstrated in the definition below, function within specified contexts has joined IQ scores as legitimating criteria for intellectual disability. From the interactive longitudinal theoretical stance, classifications of severity based on age-appropriate scores on credible intelligence tests (developed nomothetically), indicate the degree to which and the nature of what a person with an intellectual disability can learn and do within diverse environments. Building on theory developed by nomothetic researchers, diagnosis is the legitimate domain of medical or psychological professionals who are educated in these methods, theories, assessments, and evidence-based treatments. Thus knowledge production, legitimate disability determination, and response are owned by a select group of professionals and researchers whose work displays the values listed in Table 12.1.

Curiously illuminating an awareness of a hierarchical value stance, which locates deviant bodies as subordinate, is the change in definition of intellectual disability (American Association on Intellectual and Developmental Disability [AAIDD], 2009). Reading this definition, the longitudinal interior condition is primary with rhetorical additives of context. Further professional hegemony in determining and responding to intellectual disability is built into the verbiage.

- Intellectual disability is a disability characterized by significant limitations both in intellectual functioning and in adaptive behavior, which covers many everyday social and practical skills. This disability originates before the age of 18.
- Intellectual functioning—also called intelligence—refers to general mental capacity such as learning, reasoning, problem solving, and so on.
- One criterion to measure intellectual functioning is an IQ test. Generally, an IQ test score of around 70 or as high as 75 indicates a limitation in intellectual functioning.
- Standardized tests can also determine limitations in adaptive behavior, which comprises three skill types:
  - Conceptual skills—language and literacy; money, time, and number concepts; and self-direction
  - Social skills—interpersonal skills, social responsibility, self-esteem, gullibility, naïveté (i.e., wariness), social problem solving, and the ability to follow rules/obey laws and to avoid being victimized
  - Practical skills—activities of daily living (personal care), occupational skills, health care, travel/transportation, schedules/routines, safety, use of money, use of the telephone
- On the basis of such many-sided evaluations, professionals can determine whether an individual has an intellectual disability and can tailor a support plan for each individual.
- But in defining and assessing intellectual disability, the AAIDD (2009) stresses that professionals must take additional factors into account, such as the community environment typical of the individual's peers and culture. Professionals should also consider linguistic diversity and cultural differences in the way people communicate, move, and behave.
- Finally, assessments must also assume that limitations in individuals often coexist with strengths, and that a person's level of life functioning will improve if appropriate personalized supports are provided over a sustained period.

It is interesting to note that according to the AAIDD (2009) description, intellectual disability is no longer considered a legitimate medical diagnosis but now has been shifted into a permanent and complex functional state. Unlike so may embodied conditions, this example illustrates longitudinal theories as primary and not necessarily linked to medical diagnosis for legitimate determination of disability. Still, the label, while not a medical diagnosis, requires professional designation and typically does involve medical scrutiny and surveillance to identify the organic cause, both major emphases of legitimating disability through longitudinal theorizing.

As we discuss in subsequent chapters, longitudinal responses to intellectual disability, while varied, most often take two primary forms: specialized efforts to promote typical functioning to the extent possible, or when that approach fails to homogenize behavior and produce desired results, compensation and ongoing support. Specialized efforts include strategies such as special and remedial education, socialization training, vocational habilitation, and so forth. These responses are designed to teach the competencies necessary for individuals who have been labeled as intellectually disabled with the skills necessary to function adequately in age-appropriate roles. For those who are not able to achieve the desired level of functioning, compensatory strategies such as supported employment, sheltered employment, life skills rather than academic education, and specialized, supervised living arrangements are often proffered to people who are considered intellectually disabled. Note here the euphemism *support*, a term that is used to describe formal and informal services for those individuals who do not match the desired age norms for their cohort.

Of course, intellectual disability is only one of many legitimate disabilities within the longitudinal genre of theories. Terms such as motor impairment, psychiatric disability, and developmental delay are diagnosed through comparing individuals to age-similar cohort metrics of average. Who is considered as a disability category member and who is not is a moving value target subject to context-based and dynamic norms, an acceptable degree of deviance from norms, and rationales beyond longitudinal deviance—most often medical diagnostic conditions.

Of particular importance to legitimacy determination is the extent to which the deviance is under one's control or perceived to be involuntary. Regardless of the distance from typical, those who are perceived to have a choice over their conditions are less valued and thus less legitimately disabled than those who do not. For example, the description of poor grade level school performance would not be considered a legitimate disability if it were caused by laziness, truancy, and so forth, but would be considered a disability if a diagnosed interior environment explanation were validated by a professional. Moreover, the legitimate explanation would be eligible for responses in the form of accommodations, special services, and other resources.

Longitudinal legitimacy therefore locates individuals in the disability category based on the valuation not only of their deviance from age appropriate norms but also for other rationales that are offered as complimentary.

Remember back to Chapter 6 in which we discussed the recent expansion of longitudinal theory beyond birth through death, in large part due to the ability of technology to visualize prenatal physiology, genetics, and structures. Because of the presence of contemporary instruments, professionals have penetrated prenatal skin and even interior organs of the body to scrutinize the typical maturation of micro-observables such as genes, neurophysiology, and so forth. Conferral of legitimate disability status begets professional attention and the sanction to halt further anomalous development in cases where legitimate and profound longitudinal deviation is predicted. Longitudinal explanations, despite the rhetoric acknowledging support for diversity and away from conformity, remains potent and powerful in determining legitimate disability.

Longitudinal theories form the foundation of many professional disciplines. And although they do not carpet social sciences from wall to wall, longitudinal theories are one theoretical species that either inhabits valued areas of social sciences or provokes other theories through opposition. Merged with interior environment theories, to be discussed next, longitudinal theories provide the *normal* backdrop against which deviance is contrasted and explained as disability.

Environmental Legitimacy

In Chapter 7, we defined *environment* broadly as a set of conditions that are both interior and exterior to the physical body. Woven together with longitudinal explanations, interior environment theories remain most central to understandings of disability as medical-diagnostic phenomena. Before analyzing legitimacy through this integrative stance, we discuss the values that bind all environmental theories.

Four values (in Table 12.2) are inherent in environmental theories to a greater or lesser degree. Environmental theories identify the set of conditions that are valued and the specific outcomes resulting from exposure to these conditions and frequently advance the processes through which these conditions can be created to produce preferred outcomes. For example, interior environment conditions such as *proper* weight and nutrition are prescriptive

Table 12.2   Values Common to Exterior and Interior Environment Theories

1. Separation of interior and exterior environments best enhances understanding of human phenomena.

2. *Healthy* environments produce desirable behavioral results.

3. Desirable environments comprise healthy structures and healthy processes.

4. Environments that harm humans and impede growth and development should be changed.

despite changes in research support for what is desirable to eat or, in dynamic and fickle cultural norms, that define bodily beauty. When linked to longitudinal explanations, desirable interior conditions become an important determinant of quality of life, another powerful value judgment about what elements comprise a good life at diverse ages over the life span. Similarly, desirable exterior environments such as "good families" are the object of scrutiny and give rise to responses to promote the actualization of these values.

Interior environmental conditions, the explanations that we have referred to as medical-diagnostic, and particularly those that are observable and involuntary, are currently the most valued legitimacy criteria for disability status. However, even the mere presence of a long-term or permanent interior condition may be inadequate for disability qualification. The hierarchy of legitimacy determination is organized along an axiological continuum with the highest pedigree belonging to conditions that are observable, measurable, and create atypical appearance. If interior conditions require specialized adaptive equipment such as wheelchairs for mobility, these conditions are even more legitimate than those in which one can pass (Riley, 2005) as unimpaired to the untrained eye.

While interior environment conditions remain dominant as legitimate explanations for disability determination, exterior environment conditions are gaining some explanatory legitimacy, particularly those that follow the minority or social model of disability that foreground discrimination and exclusion as disabling factors. We suggest, however, that regardless of the rhetoric, interior environment explanations continue to trump exterior legitimacy as the body remains the locus of attention and the rationale for exclusion and thus for exterior environment policy and praxis responses such as disability rights policies, which are guided by exterior environment explanations, but themselves use embodied conditions as legitimate eligibility criteria.

Exterior environment theories have been important in guiding responses to disability explained by interior environment and longitudinal frameworks as well. We discuss these approaches in more detail in Chapters 13–17 but here bring your attention to exterior environment services to address disability explained as interior medical diagnostic. For example, techniques such as applied behavior analysis are frequently used to change activity for individuals who are determined to be disabled due to interior *brain developmental disorder* causes of autism. We see these approaches in some sense as illogical leaps, in that responding to embodied explanations with exterior environment strategies seems to ignore the proposed causal factors. For example, suppose disability is determined on the basis of a neurological explanation. Shouldn't the response address the posited causal explanation or at least look at the extent to which these proposed explanations are improved even if alternative responses are chosen as intervention?

Environmental theories appear as explanatory intellectual tools related to disability in many disciplines. Interior environment theories are omnipresent in the health and human service professions, biological sciences, and social sciences, which seek to explain human behavior as a function of environmental stimulation and body-context interaction. Exterior environment theories inform, but are not dominant over, interior environment theories in health professions but play an important explanatory role in human services and social sciences. External environment theories drive professions such as architecture and engineering, among others, as these fields are concerned with the disabling elements of the built, virtual, and natural environment.

Categorical Legitimacy

As we have discussed in detail in Chapter 8, categorical theories both contain members and shape group-specific responses to disability. We were unable to extract values common to all since categorical theories, by their very nature, separate and distinguish groups and thus their value stances from one another. While several theoretical frameworks may initiate legitimate membership in the disability category, we see this theoretical genre as most critical in framing and guiding the nature and timing of legitimate responses to category members.

Previously, we have referred to categorical theories as bodies and backgrounds diversity or diversity patina. Category assignment and responses assume that category members, if legitimated as bona fide, have a host of similar characteristics and needs on the basis of category membership alone. It therefore follows that categorical responses treat members as homogenous and distinct from nonmembers. Historically and even currently, members of categories that are included among diversity patina grouping have been oppressed and excluded from full participation. However, only some groups gain admission to this metagroup. And not unexpectedly, diversity patina grouping as well as their membership criteria change with political, chronological, economic, and embodied context as well. For example, homosexuality was considered to be a mental disability until 1973 when political pressure and context removed it from the racks of psychiatric deviance. Look at the following description (Herek, 2009):

> In 1973, the weight of empirical data, coupled with changing social norms and the development of a politically active gay community in the United States, led the Board of Directors of the American Psychiatric Association to remove homosexuality from the *Diagnostic and Statistical Manual of Mental Disorders*. (*DSM*; Herek, 2009)

It is also possible for conditions to permeate the perimeter of disability membership. Consider shyness (Lane, 2007). Until 1980, shyness was considered a typical human trait. By 1995, it was not only included in the *DSM* but was explained as social anxiety, elevating it to a credible disability awaiting medical response. It is curious that some subgroups prefer to be jettisoned from disability membership while others seek entry. The nature of response is the key ingredient in this equation.

Responses span the continuum from exclusion to conferral of special rights and privilege. Those pursuing membership do so in order to obtain privilege. Yet, while group specific privilege has been one response to oppression and disadvantage, it also creates the long-term consequence of segregation and outsider status. As noted by Titchkosky (2007), inclusion programs paradoxically create excludable groups by maintaining and illuminating those who require inclusive programs as different and separate.

Within the grand category of disability, while all eligible members share legitimacy from without primarily on the basis of a medical-diagnostic explanation, there is a hierarchical taxonomy of subgroups as well, also explained by the type of medical diagnosis. Subgroups are distinct from one another on some criteria but not on fundamental valuation for disability group membership. However, assumptions of homogeneity within the subgroups, once again, are made on the basis of the medical-diagnostic type. For example, consider the terms cognitive disability, physical disability, and psychiatric disability: Each has as its core legitimacy criterion a set of diagnoses that are attributed to atypical function in each of these embodied areas. In concert with politically correct diversity patina rhetoric, disability subgroups are further cleaved into essentialist gendered, racial, and ethic divisions, each with its own commonalities within.

Thus, disability legitimacy is a collage which can be seen and responded to in total or in parts. Responses such as policy promulgation, to a greater or lesser extent throughout the world, respond to and thus further legitimize these groups and patchwork taxonomy. Cultural competence within disability services provides a clear exemplar of legitimate categorical responses and foregrounds group membership as the conductor of all subsequent responses through this lens. We critically discuss this point more fully in subsequent chapters, but bring it to your attention here to illustrate how categorical theories operate in explaining similarity and difference as group belonging.

Categorical theories are also potent in determining legitimacy from within and in shaping responses that are similar for other identity groups. Disability identity, or self definition and disability culture, can be a powerful political, social, and intrapsychic process. From an extreme position of the social and cultural models, disability can be legitimated simply by proclaiming that one is disabled and part of disability culture, regardless of embodied condition. The quotation with the instructive guidelines table below demonstrates the use of essentialist cultural competency strategies that are borrowed from ethnic and racial identity group responses:

> Many individuals with disabilities contend that they represent a distinctive cultural group based on the shared experience of disability. Just as strategies can be developed by health care providers to ensure competence in addressing ethnic and linguistic differences, so strategies can be developed to enhance cultural competence in relation to disability. (Institute on Community Integration, 2005)

Strategy	Ethnic/Linguistic	Disability
Hire interpreters	Hire bilingual interpreters knowledgeable about health care terminology	Hire staff trained in American Sign Language, familiar with technology-based communication, knowledgeable about health care terminology
Create a culturally-friendly atmosphere	Have signs in multiple languages, hire culturally-diverse staff, have cross-cultural and multi-lingual reading material in waiting areas	Configure service counters for wheel-chair approach at eye level; hire staff with disabilities; have disability publications, and large format and Braille reading material, in waiting areas

Source: Institute on Community Integration, University of Minnesota, 2005.

Categorical theories are ubiquitous and not specific to any discipline. Parsing humans into groups, ascertaining commonalities within them, and distinguishing among groups is an important aim of social and hard sciences, humanities, and professions.

Systems Legitimacy

Systems explanations focus on interrelationships, communication, and feedback as determinants of and responses to disability. As we discussed in Chapter 9, systems can be characterized in many ways, from closed linear entities to complex macrocosms whose chaotic behavior can only be understood through computer modeling strategies. Regardless of their size, shape, and activity, the values in Table 12.3 are common to all.

Systems theories legitimate disability as an interaction between body and environment. What distinguishes this approach from environmental interactive theories are the values on change, maintenance, adaptation, and preservation. Thus, while systems theories to some extent provide a contemporary and progressive explanation for disability as interactive, this genre is most prominent in legitimate responses to embodied disability. Of particular importance to responses, specifically to the maintenance of the disability park, are Values 7 and 8. Maintenance, adaptation, and preservation of systems are desirable. For example, this axiological tenet is particularly visible within managed care, which provides yet another layer to organize, preserve, promote survival, and render teams of providers efficient and cost-effective.

Table 12.3   Systems Values

Value 1 – Systems are purposive.

Value 2 – Positive change is desirable.

Value 3 – Feedback should produce positive change in system components and in systems.

Value 4 – In order to provide positive feedback, sound and efficacious communication among system elements and influences is necessary.

Value 5 – Stable but dynamic systems are desirable.

Value 6 – Direct and indirect influences on systems should be identified as essential to understanding system operation and change.

Value 7 – Maintenance and preservation of systems are desirable.

Value 8 – Adaptation is a desirable system characteristic.

Furthermore, in order to ensure its survival, the park must maintain individuals as disabled, and thus responses explained through systems theory approaches reify disability through identifying it as a set of weaknesses and needs that can only be fulfilled by complex casts of providers. The maintenance of disability-specific legislation, policy, and services, as well as the guidance to promote disability identity, can be well explained by systems theories as the park and its inhabitants struggle for self-preservation and adapt themselves to reach this aim. Furthermore, given the value on change, systems can morph into different but constant entities in response to contextual and potentially threatening variables. For example, systems that opposed medical labeling of disability may have disappeared if their agenda of full participation were met. These adaptive and dynamic systems are now once again focusing on quasi but politically correct labeling, meeting the valued systems criterion of preservation. Consider the AAIDD. In response to politically correct language trends, this organization eschewed its former name, The American Association on Mental Retardation, as well as its fundamental definitions and assessment strategies for intellectual disability (no longer referred to as mental retardation due to its stigmatizing and pejorative meaning).

Systems theories, while used as explanatory in many fields, are particularly prominent in professional fields that address legitimacy of disability determination and response and seek to continue to do so.

Contemporary and Emerging Legitimacy

Because contemporary and emerging theories are concerned with symbols, meanings, complexity, pluralism, and context, they are particularly relevant to explaining and responding to disability in contemporary global and local panoramas. What is common in the values, or what we refer to as value texts, of contemporary and emerging theories is the view that values are not universal, but rather are texts and narratives that are encased in situated boundaries that shape not only the articulation of the values but also the multiple and different meanings that are attributed to this symbolic and expressive text called *values*. (See Table 12.4.)

Contemporary and emerging explanations have brought disability legitimacy into the 21st century. Rather than opposing the explanatory categories and values that we have already discussed, contemporary and emerging legitimacy introduces and finally marries theories which were seen as explanatory enemies. Because frameworks are viewed as situated in context and meaning, they can be combined and synthesized purposively, opening a rich

Table 12.4 Value Texts

Value 1 – Purpose should shape knowledge and action.

Value 2 – To understand symbols we need to look at how meanings are constructed within political, economic, expressive, intellectual, and social contexts.

Value 3 – Pluralism is good.

Value 4 – Monism is a myth.

Value 5 – Diversity should be celebrated.

Value 6 – Monism stifles diversity.

Value 7 – Grand narratives are myths designed to derail equality.

Value 8 – Local is valued.

Value 9 – Interdisciplinary is good.

legitimate definitional and response dialogue. Of particular centrality to disability legitimacy within contemporary and emerging theories is the potential to legitimate disability beyond deviance of the material body and to respond to it through contemporary strategies which are legitimate beyond the category of disability itself. Contemporary and emerging explanations have the potential to harness the assets of the 21st century as the basis for destroying the perimeter that encases and segregates disability into an essentialist category in which its members are denied full civil rights in order to maintain special services within oppressive and exclusionary contexts. Legitimately determining disability as a complex ill fit between body and environment opens vast possibilities for legitimate responses. Medicine can be reintroduced into Disability Studies parlance. Exterior and interior environmental explanations and responses can live together and create new options and diversity depth can be achieved with disability being a legitimate part of it.

Because of the post-postmodern aim toward interdisciplines (DePoy & Gilson, 2009), no single field owns contemporary and emerging legitimacy.

13

Legitimate Humanities Responses

In previous chapters, we have discussed the role of the natural sciences in legitimately determining and responding to disability, particularly given the hegemony of these disciplines as the theoretical foundation of medicine and thus medical-diagnostic explanations of disability. This chapter explores the current and future potential of humanities to illuminate disability legitimacy and responses. First, we start with a definition of the humanities.

The Free Dictionary (Farlex, 2010c) defines humanities as:

a. The study of classical languages and classical literature

b. The Latin and Greek classics as a field of study

c. Literature, philosophy, art, and so forth, as distinguished from the natural sciences

d. The study of literature, philosophy, art, and so forth

These definitional elements refer to humanities in its classical sense, the disciplines that hold themselves apart from natural and applied sciences and specialized professional fields. However, within the past several decades, the boundaries between humanities, sciences, and even professions is blurring as disciplines such as new media, digital humanities, and design emerge as interdisciplinary and able to extract and synthesize knowledge from fields previously considered to be strange bedfellows. Consider the work of Tufte (2006) and Pauwels (2005), who both address empirical data as beautiful visual imagery. Given its broad scope, we therefore define the humanities from both traditional and contemporary stances. Historically, the humanities are comprised of art, music, literature, philosophy, religion, and language. Throughout the book and in particular in the chapters on history, we have touched on the manner in which these fields have shaped and reflected disability, contributing to its value or devalue. To a large extent, humanities in their classical sense continue to critically analyze images of bodies and experiences and thus frame disability legitimacy through cultural visuals, performance, and metaphor. As we have demonstrated, the field of history has been particularly important in illuminating how atypical bodies have been defined and responded to over the years, with the twists and turns of this crooked response path, determined by contextual factors, chronological imagery, and cultural beliefs (Albrecht, Seelman, & Bury, 2001).

More contemporary definitions of humanities not only enlarge its impact but also revise the fields that are contained within its boundaries. For example, in examining inclusive education, Ware (2003), suggests that a humanities-based Disability Studies moves the emphasis of disability definition and response away from the atypical, pathological body towards an understanding of disability as cultural artifact. Even the study of prostheses benefits from embodiment theory as demonstrated by Morra and Smith (2005) who have assembled a series of papers that exemplify the metaphoric and cultural meaning of prosthetic technology.

Numerous threads have been followed in this large humanities literature. For example, a major area of scholarship on disability in literature is the surveillance and analysis of body images and their meanings inscribed in text. This work focuses on the manner in which portrayals of bodies, behaviors, and even fashion (Negrin, 2008) imbue legitimate meaning in embodied deviance (Siebers, 2008). For example, science fiction films are potent in creating image. Works such as *AlphaVille, Star Wars, Matrix*, and *Blade Runner* depict "fables of the future" (Scott, 2008) that provide templates and conceptual blueprints for rethinking legitimacy of disability and response. Similarly, animated films such as *Shrek* and *Finding Nemo* have brought embodied difference into popular culture without attaching pejorative meaning to it.

Another major thread in humanities scholarship involves the challenge that disabled bodies launch at cultural standards of beauty, fashion, and conformity to embodied standards (Kuppers, 2003). Consider for example, the historical exclusion of disabled bodies from traditional dance, theater, and film. Segregated programs such as Very Special Arts (VSA) in the United States have been developed to engage disabled artists in parallel but separate arts worlds with embodied disability rather than artistic talent as the legitimate entrance criterion. Similarly, the Nalaga'at Theater in Jaffa, Israel, provides deaf and blind actors with the opportunity to engage in theater, again with the legitimate entrance criteria as the inability to see or hear.

In concert with our views of juncture and human rights, more recently, some progressive arts venues are integrating diverse bodies into the arts and performance. Cirque du Soleil, Axis Dance Company, and Merce Cunningham consider diversity of mobility styles as artistic with the eligibility criterion being talent.

Another rich humanities arena analyzes disability language, interrogating how terms such as blind, crippled, and deaf are apprehended as metaphor for undesirable human traits or behaviors. This usage then further shapes and inscribes legitimate disability definitions and response of devaluation (Rodas, 2009). A host of authors have sought to align Disability Studies with other identity fields such as queer studies (McRuer, 2006) in an effort to examine how difference through its questioning and contrast with conformity has the potential to unravel and thus recreate legitimacy in a standardized world. The work on disability and humanities is a growing literature in many areas including performance, media, architecture, art, and so forth.

At the end of the history section, we noted that one of the fundamental challenges for Disability Studies in the 21st century was to reconstitute the fragmented body. Post-postmodernism provides us with the powerful thinking tools to reunite schools of thought that have the intellectual power to see the body as a whole entity while still preserving the benefit of specialties. Moreover, because humanities seem to be more concerned with productions of bodies rather than the functioning of bodies themselves, these fields provide the foundation on which to design a world that responds to diverse bodies in ethical, moral, and just ways (Davidson, 2008). Perhaps, along with social sciences, which we discuss in the next chapter, one of the most important roles for the humanities in Disability Studies is its power to apply human thinking about right and wrong and to represent this thinking and potential alternatives to promote equality of human rights. McClennen (2007) suggests that human rights cannot be understood or fostered without the help of ethics and cultural theory. Affirming this position and adding literature and art to the mix was the recent world-class event, *Witness: Arts, Humanities, and Human Rights*. The speakers inscribed a human rights history and current principles in narrative, literature, art, and performance, showcasing the relevance of language arts, recitation, and image in critically and artistically promoting fairness through human thinking and productions.

Because the focus of this chapter is on disability legitimacy rather than on humanities itself, we devote the remainder of this chapter to the future and suggest how two major areas in the humanities, ethics and art, can be used to make profound changes in disability legitimacy and human rights.

Ethics

The Free Dictionary (Farlex, 2010b) provides the following definitions of ethics:

1. A system of moral principles: the ethics of a culture

2. The rules of conduct recognized in respect to a particular class of human actions or a particular group, culture, etc.: medical ethics; Christian ethics

3. Moral principles, as of an individual: His ethics forbade betrayal of a confidence

4. That branch of philosophy dealing with values relating to human conduct, with respect to the rightness and wrongness of certain actions and to the goodness and badness of the motives and ends of such actions (usually used with a singular verb)

In essence, although there are numerous definitions, ethics refers to judgments, rules, and behaviors denoting what is valued as good, what should be, or what should not be. Disability Studies, through the lens of Explanatory Legitimacy, is a conversation about values and ethics, what explanations for atypical bodies are desirable and thus *should be*, what explanations for atypical bodies should *not* be, what bodies should be assigned to disability status, if and how bodies should be manipulated and changed and what specialized range of responses should be afforded to those who are members of the disability category. The difficulty of determining what is ethical lies in the diverse decision criteria and logical processes that can be used to assert and support an ethical claim. Does one act on the principle of equal distribution despite the outcome? Does one act to try to maximize outcome despite the methods that are used to achieve it? Does one act on the principle of duty? Or are ethical and virtuous behaviors built into humans and thus guide their behavior? Of course, there is no single answer, and thus ethical debates emerge not only on disagreements of substance but also on the basis of how decisions themselves should be made, enacted, and evaluated. Consider the differences in thinking between Peter Singer and Harriet McBryde Johnson (Koch, 2006). Singer, a utilitarian philosopher, asserts that distributive justice should occur along egalitarian principles and, as a result of this distributive ethic, parents should be able to euthanize severely disabled children who require too many resources for a poor quality of life. Johnson, a humanist attorney, challenged Singer on his assertion that disability decreases quality of life. Rather, she defined a good life by one's richness of relationships. Moreover, she argued that resources should be readily given to preserve lives worth living. Each resource starts at a different content point, posits varied criteria for the value of a life, and uses different logic to arrive at his or her claim about the ethics of responding to devalued lives by eliminating them.

Disability legitimacy hurls significant challenges at ethics, cultivating a field in which ethical thinking can be sewn and applied to human life in general. As stated by Scully (2008), disability by its mere presence introduces ethical discussions and considerations into cultures. Scully suggests that Disability Studies moves away from a medical sociology of impairment toward a bioethical discussion of the limits of acceptable difference and what responses should be undertaken when that limit is exceeded. She urges bioethical considerations to move beyond life and death discussions of abortion and euthanasia to fundamental human considerations such as independence, autonomy, physical appearance, and so forth.

We agree with Scully (2008) and perhaps go further in suggesting that Disability Studies is a field of ethics that interrogates *goodness* of body types and functions and the viability of responses that are afforded to diverse bodies.

Ethical questions just to begin the debates could include:

1. To what extent and on what parameters should human worth be linked to body appearance, capacity, and difference?

2. What are the ethical dilemmas of segregated responses due to impairment?

3. What alternative, ethical responses, besides segregated responses, should be devised, and how will they be supported with resources?

4. What evaluative outcome criteria should be applied to determine the success of distributive solutions?

5. What is an acceptable ethic of care for bodies with limited life spans? With limited capacities for contributing to the economy?

Of course, the ethical issues and questions are numerous, complex, and important. Calling on the humanities to inform this critical thinking and action is just a beginning but clearly points to a remarkable and central role for humanities in clarifying disability legitimacy. We now move to art and design, fields within the humanities that not only can provoke thinking and debate but also have the power to make change in the legitimacy of definitions and responses to disability through image and icon.

Arts and Design

Given the post-postmodern trends towards interdisciplinarity, it is therefore curious that in the contemporary market economy, schools and universities are paying short shrift to humanities and performing arts. Perhaps this trend emerges from a failure of these fields to demonstrate their relevance to 21st century issues and needs or the complex language that we use in our work may limit its accessibility for some readers. Yet, looking back and ahead, it appears as if the enduring human productions are located in arts and music. Our museums are replete with artists' renderings, classical music seems timeless, and classical theater endures. Harnessing these fundamentally human phenomena to fashion a 21st century global environment that legitimizes and responds to diversity depth is a challenge for the humanities, not just for the purposes of criticism but rather for the purposes of significant change. Building on the excellent work of the humanities and Disability Studies, we propose that the humanities fields of art and design hold significant promise for healing disjuncture and providing legitimate responses to advance equality of human rights (Gilson & DePoy, 2009a).

In Chapter 10, we already introduced design as explanatory of disability. Remember that we discussed ways in which explicit and implicit design of bodies, natural and virtual spaces created a continuum of disjuncture to full juncture, with disability residing in disjunctured explanations. Just as design can be disabling, creating the disability park, it can also be enabling. Using contemporary arts and design practices that are aligned with larger powerful global trends typically not thought of as disability and human rights scholarship provides the opportunity for significant change.

We have already introduced universal design in previous chapters, and at this point it might appear as if this ideology is the panacea to be used by designers to bring disability into nondisabled culture. Unfortunately, however, while the ideology may be laudatory, its actualization is flawed, maintaining the disability park intact. While the conceptual foundation of universal design emerged from the humanities and can be traced to designers such as Marc Harrison (Hagley Museum and Library, n.d.), it soon became colonized by disability activists. This well-intended effort opened the door for universal design to become the property of rehabilitation as well as the basis for minimum legally mandated accessibility design for the built environment. The principles of universal design, advanced by North Carolina State University, therefore took on an unintended meaning of design for disability access despite its theoretical progressiveness and views towards equality of access. Moreover, as pointed out by Pullin (2009) and Gilson and DePoy (2009a), design is more than access and functionality. It is a culturally embedded human phenomenon that has a long history in producing identity, class distinctions and valuation. It responds not only to different abilities, but also to different preferences, tastes, sizes, and so forth. Thus, any design theory which suggests that products and spaces can be fully inclusive are either too complex or miss the point of design for diversity depth. For example, consider the chair. Although taken for granted as an essential piece of furniture, the history of the chair reveals its origin in distinguishing royalty from ordinary citizens. Contrary to the notion of the chair as ergonomically sound, healthy and optimal human sitting posture is not consistent with contemporary chair design (Cranz, 2000). Chairs were initially designed for preference and power.

Based on an understanding of design as reciprocally producing and responding to cultural trends, Gilson and DePoy (2007), Imrie (1996), and Pullin (2009) have identified art, spatial, and product design as a critical humanities field in promoting social change. According to Pullin,

> mediocrity must be avoided. In design for special needs mediocrity, thereby undermining the highest goals for social inclusion, can result in people being further stigmatized by the very products that are intended to remove barriers for them . . . If design for disability positions itself as quite distinct, somehow, in opposition to mainstream design, it inevitably will be less influential. (p. 64)

Consider the work of Strzelecki (2009) and Gilson and DePoy (2008), who all experienced exclusion from sports and fitness participation and who have met this inequity with innovative design responses. Strzelecki fabricated aesthetically pleasing crutches to support adaptive walking and hiking, and Gilson and DePoy (2008) have designed several commercially available, aesthetically contemporary sports innovations for skiing, running, and jogging. Of particular note, in concert with Pullin's ideas, is that these products are designed for a broad commercial market, eliminating the stigma of their segregated use. These products and their design are consistent with Holt's (2004) thinking as well, which we now call on to guide our recommendations. Holt identifies brands as cultural icons. He rethinks branding from simply a marketing tool to powerful cultural iconography in which image and its design have significant power to elicit attitude and behavior change. Capturing the art of image for branding and meaning-making, according to

Holt, holds cultural opportunity for profound change and thus Holt challenges cultural activists to take the artistic reins of design and branding for the purpose of global social development. According to Holt and relevant to disability legitimacy is the realization that iconic branding has activism inherent in it if it is conducted by those to whom he refers as cultural activists and to others who have been named media activists (Riley, 2005). Thus, both media and visual culture (Jianli, 2009) are two humanities fields that are being summoned by Holt to the human rights table.

The work of Pullin (2009) further illuminates the critical relationship between design and disability. Pullin notes that there is a tension between functional and aesthetic design which does not have to exist.

Building on this important work, we suggest that art and design are critical humanities fields to bear on Disability Studies. On social science responses, design is a powerful and essential tool for promoting human rights and equality of access to resources for all people.

14

Legitimate
Social Science Responses

This chapter examines how diverse social science disciplines legitimate and respond to disability. We begin with a definition of social sciences.

The Free Dictionary (Farlex, 2010e) defines social science as:

1. The study of human society and of individual relationships in and to society.

2. A scholarly or scientific discipline that deals with such study, generally regarded as including sociology, psychology, anthropology, economics, political science, and history.

Considering that history is listed as a humanities and psychology is included in the professions, the distinction between these two divisions is not always clear. However, a major difference lies in epistemology, as social science scholars use systematic, evidence-based inquiry rather than sole reliance on tools (such as language analysis and logic) to support knowledge claims (Bryman, 2008). Moreover, the focus of social sciences is on the *social*, from micro- to macrosocial relations, institutions, and abstracts.

Each of the fields in the social sciences has weighed in on disability explanations. In this chapter, we delimit our legitimacy discussion to sociology, political science, and economics, leaving psychology for the next chapter on professional legitimacy. And as we discussed in the history section of the text, while social science has not unseated biological medical legitimacy, social science fields have gained credibility and thus have guided legitimate response since the 1980s.

Sociological Legitimacy

We have already discussed the social model at length and here just remind you that this approach to legitimate determination of disability emerged from the field of sociology. In opposition to biological sciences, sociologists in the 1970s and 1980s posited social exclusion, discrimination, and oppression, not pathology, as the legitimate explanations for disability. You can refer back to Chapters 3 and 7 for an in-depth look at the social model and its importance in bringing social sciences into the legitimate scholarship on disability causes and responses.

As we have pointed out, the literature has been replete with sociological accounts of embodiment, of attitudes towards bodies, and of institutional influences on disability policy and response. It is curious that prior to the development of the social model from the United Kingdom, early nonmedicalized Disability Studies conferences and scholarship in the United States took place within economics and politics. For example, the Western Social Science Association was the original organization from which Society for Disability Studies (2009) emerged and then seceded. Although the social model was concerned with the outcomes of discrimination to some extent, the literature took a *disability from within* turn and primarily focused on the processes of oppression and exclusion, disability identity, pride, and culture. As advanced by Garland-Thomson and Longmore (2009), the following principles have guided social science legitimacy within the Society for Disability Studies:

> Everything related to disability and people with disabilities is in the process of being rethought and needs to be rethought. The academic study of disability has primarily been shaped by ideologies that define it as limitation in the performance of expected social roles due to underlying physiological pathology. That definition inevitably prescribes medical treatments and habilitation or rehabilitation as the appropriate solutions to the problems of people with disabilities. Yet those approaches have had only limited impact in ameliorating disabled people's socioeconomic marginalization. In contrast to these traditional modes of addressing and studying disability, Disability Studies takes as its domain the relationship of social values to societal organization and public policies, professional training and delivery of services, individual behavior and interpersonal encounters, cultural representation and technological and architectural design. Disability Studies utilizes a multidisciplinary approach to analyze the intricate

interactions among social, cultural, political, economic, and physiological variables. It seeks neither to jettison, nor to embrace medical paradigms of disability, but to transcend them. It explains personal experiences of disability, not simply in terms of the functioning of bodies that operate in nonstandard ways, but by locating those differences within the larger context of the cultural milieus that shape disability experiences.

While important in creating and promoting a new academic field and for advancing solidarity and political advantage, the focus on marginalization seemed to get stuck in personal narrative, thinning the substantive and sophisticated economic and political analysis that now is returning to Disability Studies.

Despite the assertions of bringing the body back into the Disability Studies debate, as we noted earlier in the book, the body remains fragmented and is thus a repository of social value or devalue. For example, Howson (2004) reminds us that the sociologist's attention to the body is devoted primarily to the human form as social being, one that interacts with others, performs social roles, and carries cultural image. Siebers (2008) goes further in stating that "embodiment and social location are one in the same" (p. 23) and affirms the body in fragments by stating, "embodiment is a bone of contention in Disability Studies as it seems caught between competing models of disability" (p. 28).

Thus sociology has been a major player in defining contemporary legitimate disability determination and response. While we acknowledge the significant intellectual contribution of sociology to disability legitimacy, we ultimately view political science and economics as most crucial in defining disability and crafting responses to it. So we now turn our focus primarily toward political and economic legitimacy of disability and the extent to which these fields have regulated legitimate responses that lie outside of the individual body and its social relations with diverse social units.

Political Theory and Human Rights Legitimacy

More recent social science work in Disability Studies has increased the complexity and thus the legitimacy of social sciences in intellectual determination and response to disability. Moving from disability as problem to disability as challenge to policy and human rights discourses, seminal thinkers such as Nussbaum (2006), Sen (2009), and Stein (2006) have taken on disability in their work. Nussbaum and Sen both use disability as a condition to analyze human rights policy and theories and support their human capabilities approach to disability legitimacy. Challenging social contract theories (Rawls, 1999), which in essence diminish disabled bodies from the exchange of power necessary for just governance to exist, human capabilities asserts that all humans should be able to exercise basic human freedoms. Thus, unlike social contract theory in which government power is legitimated by an exchange between government and subordinate citizens of equal status, the capabilities approach addresses the issue of human asymmetry caused by poverty and disability. Sen, and Nussbaum in particular, offer social justice theory in which all people, no matter what their embodied bargaining chips are, are legitimately worthy of living dignified lives. They assert that local, national, and global policy should reflect this approach and guarantee that all people have the opportunity to attain human capabilities.

New political theory has been busy as well in questioning more traditional conceptual and actualized power structures as legitimate. Kymlicka's (2007) skepticism in the legitimacy and utility of current human identity politic categories has been useful for stimulating thought about reframing policy that maintains and perpetuates specialized categorical responses. Similarly, Benn Michaels (2006) has challenged the scepter of identity categories, suggesting that language and attention to bodies and backgrounds as the current legitimate seat of diversity serve to shroud the reticence of individuals and groups who hold wealth to carry on conversation about redistribution. Derailing such conversation effectively serves to suppress and even halt negotiation and restructuring of legitimate power and distribution of economic resources.

Closely related to human rights and governance is the critical role of economics in disability legitimacy and response. We turn to this discussion now.

Economics of Disability Legitimacy

While the discourse about poverty and exclusion from remunerative, competitive employment is one important part of the economic picture of disability, it is only a small part of the canvas. We have referred to these issues in Chapter 3. Here we focus on the role of, as well as the potential for, the disability industry in crafting disability legitimacy for profitability. Concurrent with Gill's (1992) assertion that economics trumped helping processes or outcomes of rehabilitation, Albrecht (1992) uncloaked the disability-rehabilitation industry and the role of economics and politics in shaping the nature of legitimate disability responses. Albrecht (2005) denuded disability as the seat of multiple profit centers and a multibillion dollar industrial opportunity. Pharmaceuticals, professions, managed care, rehabilitation product manufactures, insurance companies, and so forth are all cashing in on disability. Moreover, because disability is ubiquitous, the disability marketplace is extensive. Corporations do not simply profit in developed countries. Rather, the disability industry has a global reach and impact. As stated by Albrecht (2005),

> there is little doubt that multinational corporations in the disability-rehabilitation business are selling their ideas and products to whomever will buy them. It is not at all apparent, however, that the needs of disabled people are being met. Potential profits, market share, return on investment, and shareholder value are forces that drive the system. (p. 597)

Moreover, one's personal wealth influences the nature of products and services received, illuminating the profit dominance of the disability-rehabilitation industry (Albrecht, Seelman, & Bury, 2001) and thus the role of one's economic status in defining disability legitimacy and worth for responses.

Building on Albrecht (1992; Albrecht, Seelman, & Bury, 2001) and Gill (1992) in our previous work, we examined the history of disability services and products and noted that disability has moved from charity and care to commodity and corporatization. We referred to this phenomenon as "bake sale to commodity," depicting the capture of disability by corporate health care.

Riley (2006) and others have posited a 21st century relevant view of the disability industry as we have noted in Chapter 10. Riley suggests that disability is a viable market that has yet to be fully exploited. However, according to Riley, rather than being seen as victimizing, he attributes great potential to the disability industry not only for profit but also for driving significant change. According to Riley, new business opportunities can centralize products and services into the commercial world, eschewing stigma and unseating this cash cow from health care corporations, which use gatekeeping and control to maximize profits without attention to population needs. We agree with Riley and other scholars in suggesting that disability products and services can become part of the mainstream of commerce and relegitimation of disability as human diversity and value. This trend is becoming visible as companies and catalogues such as Skymall (2009), the FeelGood Store (2009), and even gadget distributors such as Herrington (2000–2009) increasingly showcase products that just a few years ago were available only through medical providers and product distributors. We discuss what we see as the essential role of politics, business, and economics in legitimate disability determination and response in more detail in Chapter 16.

Many questions remain to be answered about disability legitimacy within social science (Simmons, 2001). These queries provide fertile ground for debate, rethinking, and renegotiation of disability legitimacy within the 21st century. Here we pose some to keep our intellects well-oiled.

Questions

1. What is legitimate citizenship and who is a citizen?

2. What are the diverse levels of citizenship and what is the role of atypical embodiment in defining a legitimate citizen?

3. How should economic contribution be factored into legitimate citizenship given a discriminatory employment market?

4. When and what type of social welfare should be legitimated as a response to embodied dependence?

5. How does personal wealth influence disability legitimacy and response?

6. What is the role of economics in legitimizing disability determination and response?

7. What is the role of policy in legitimating disability determination and response? How can these processes be used differently in the future to advance juncture?

15

Legitimate
Professional Responses

C hapter 15 examines how diverse professions currently define and respond to disability. We provide some direction in this chapter for rethinking professional research, knowledge, and praxis in the fields of public health, medicine, rehabilitation, education, social work, psychology, engineering, architecture, and business but wait until the next chapter to advance and illustrate a theoretical synthesis to guide action that disassembles the disability park while promoting full juncture.

We realize that each of the professions is multifaceted and complex and that there are variations in the manner in which practice is enacted. We therefore address general knowledge and tenets that unify each profession as the basis for thinking about current and future possibilities for refashioning disability legitimacy.

Public Health

According to Rimmer (2009) and Rowland, White, and Wyatt (2006), because of its traditional orientation as a preventive field, public health professionals have only recently accepted disability as part of their professional purview. Within the history of public health, disability, along with chronic illness, was seen as a condition to be prevented through the practice of public health strategies such as vaccination, injury and violence reduction, improvement of environmental quality, and so forth. Disability-adjusted life years (DALYs), a public health measure, refers to the quantification of burden of disability on a life in terms of shortened longevity as well as quality of life limitations (Lee, Buse, & Fustukia, 2002). Developed by Murray (1994), DALYs were intended to set cost-efficient priorities for public health interventions. "A good buy is one that is both cost-effective and addresses a large burden of disease" (Lee et al., p. 145). DALYs, therefore, allocate resources on a standard that values "big bang for the buck," turning away from low incidence conditions as well as devaluing embodied phenomena such as advanced age and atypical functionality. Implicit in DALYs is a standard quality of life that can be promoted by cost-conscious distribution of public health strategies.

As we discussed previously, quality of life itself is a construct that conceptually homogenizes *the good life* and thus diminishes embodied and functional diversity. Measures of quality of life further inscribe this construct as prescriptive and then use it tautologically to define and assess the worth of an individual's life. These measures and numerous other global measures of health operationally define health in part as the ability to engage in typical functional and quality-of-life activities such as walking, lifting, running, and so forth, activities which do not bode well for individuals with mobility impairments, for example. Including *function* within definitions of health automatically locates people with atypical function in the less healthy and less qualitative category of measurement, despite other theoretical and conceptual approaches that legitimate health, quality of life, and disability as different entities. Thus, public health measurements themselves often diminish the health and worth of people with disabilities, not on the basis of organic disease and pathology but because of how health and quality are lexically and operationally defined. These methodological practices, although still hegemenous in many medical and health professional fields and a staple of health disparities research, are in the process of being examined and revised.

Once disability and health are uncoupled, ambitious public-health agendas that clarify, measure, and address public health separate from typical functionality can be enacted. Attesting to this importance of reframing legitimate definitions of disability as well as public health was the recent establishment of the disability section as one of 25 primary sections within the American Public Health Association (APHA). Rimmer (Rimmer, Chen, McCubbin, Drum, & Peterson, 2010) discusses the importance of this structural shift in bringing disability issues into the public health domain. The action agenda of this section is to identify the special and unique public health needs of disabled groups. While we agree that this intermediate step is necessary, future efforts should be planned that expand the full range of diverse functionality under the rubric of the public. Continuing to fragment public health into strategies for most, and enacting special responses for those who do not fit, while a sound step in the right direction, needs to be expanded in order to put the *public* into public health.

Rimmer suggests that another major task of the disability section of the APHA is to educate providers and professionals in the special health needs of disabled people. After instituting this intermediate step, once again, we would propose that public health education move in the direction of educating all professionals in the full range of health care needs and relevant responses for an increasingly diverse public. This approach to public health has the potential to eliminate the disability park in the long run by creating professional-public juncture in which all people are included as part of the public.

Medicine

We have discussed medicine throughout the book, as it has been the seminal profession in defining disability legitimacy regardless of who or what professions are crafting response. Generally, the tenets that underpin medical practice are as follows:

1. Illness is specific—Each illness has a specific set of observables and reportables that are identifiable and that differentiate one illness from another or from nonillness.

2. Illness is universal—The manifestation of each illness will be the same across time, people, and cultures (Weitz, 2000).

3. The explanation for illness is considered to be based on a unique etiology—Specific pathology exists within the individual or is caused by unique environmental conditions such as microorganisms that cause pathology.

Guided by these principles, medical approaches to disability legitimacy are based on two criteria: (1) the presence of atypical activity, appearance, and/or experience explained by a diagnosis and (2) longevity of the diagnosis. Because the epistemic foundation of medicine lies in positivism (Depoy & Gitlin, 2010), it is assumed that the identification of the explanatory pathology and its legitimacy as disability is *true*, value neutral, and scientific (Weitz, 2000).

The medical model therefore legitimizes disability as an embodied pathological condition of long-term or permanent duration. Legitimate medical responses to disability are primarily diagnosis and, when indicated, treatment. Because the desired or preferred outcome from a medical interventive response is a return to an absence of illness or to maximum health, it is curious that legitimate response to disability may not always be within the scope of medicine since, by definition, disability is not curable. However, medicine is busy in the disability park. Medical legitimacy of disability determination underpins legitimate responses for most professions and specialized, segregated policies as well as lay definitions and understandings of disability. As the process of medicalization (Conrad, 2007) has expanded, medical approaches to disability legitimacy have further ensconced physicians as primary decision makers and active gatekeepers in areas that are both related to and distant from medical decision making, such as employment, educational response, and even preferred parking (Bassnett, 2001; Stone, 1986).

In concert with sociologists such as Conrad and Schneider (cited in Weitz, 2000) and as asserted by Pfeiffer (2002), we agree that medicine, despite its assertion of objectivity is not free of social values. Just the assumption that a medical diagnosis is a scientific fact rather than a descriptive text is in itself an epistemic and ontological bias. Think about alternative explanations that others have used for what is often described as illness and cure. For example, religious beliefs, social conditions, and so forth are often invoked as causes and cures of conditions.

The question that remains is, in the context of increasing medicalization, how to rethink legitimate medical determination of and response to disability in order to reduce and ultimately eliminate the disability park. Given that the category of disability is not likely to be dismantled anytime soon, what makes most sense to us is for physicians to engage in *good* medical practice, beginning with individual descriptive medical need rather than categorization. Doing so allows treatment responses tailored to individual diagnostic circumstances rather than assumed nomothetic response, which may not be accurate for the full range of category members. A simultaneous effort would delimit medical gatekeeping as the eligibility criterion for nonmedical responses. As example, medical model legitimation of medical diagnostic explanations of disability in educational settings is the primary qualifier for service under current specialized policy. However, mixing professional metaphors, so to speak, is not useful to describe educational need and thus diminishes the expertise of educators to identify atypical educational performance and verify explanations that then support cogent educational responses to learning needs. Finally, a careful and honest examination of the disability park as a medical profit center needs to be undertaken as the basis for revision and production of improved outcome for the individuals who receive services.

Rehabilitation Professions

The legitimate scope of disability practice in rehabilitation professions is to restore, foster, or maximize function in a specified domain of professional concern (Mackelprang & Salsgiver, 2009). We use the term *function* here to reveal the normative stance of rehabilitation. That is, based in large part on longitudinal and exterior environment explanations, rehabilitation professions assume a desirable set of typical activities within age and role norms and only recently have included diversity patina variables in assessment and practice.

In concert with longitudinal theory genres, each of the rehabilitation professions makes a determination of what is atypical by collecting observables and reportables and analyzing them in comparison to performance norms or expectations typical of an individual's age and circumstance relevant to the embodied slice of each professional domain. As example, occupational therapists contrast atypical activity to normative performance in daily tasks and life roles (Kielhofner, 2002) while physical therapists are primarily concerned with the functioning of the skeletal scaffold, its musculature and its neurological drivers. Of course, a more expansive and profitable mission, albeit vague, is promoted by the American Physical Therapy Association (2010) as the general enhancement of the longitudinally normative physical health and functional abilities of individuals.

For each of the rehabilitation professions, the explanation for atypical embodied circumstance or functional performance is primarily medical pathology. Some rehabilitation professions such as occupational therapy invoke exterior environment barriers as disabling but, for the most part, legitimacy for rehabilitation services is anchored on medical diagnostic explanations. In order to obtain services from rehabilitation professions, a medical referral, a self-referral, or a request for evaluation and assessment from another health or social service worker is initiated. A legitimate determination of disability, similar to medicine and nursing, is based on a medical explanation for an atypical circumstance within one's delimited wedge of the body. As we discussed above in the section on medicine, the medical profession is busy within rehabilitation. That is to say, explanations for atypical description are anchored in medical-diagnostic rationales, but rehabilitation responses do not seek to remediate diagnoses. Rather, rehabilitation responses address descriptive need and work with individuals primarily in that domain. The desired practice response outcome involves achieving the maximum assisted or unassisted typical activity, frequently not even referring to the medical explanation for legitimate response guidance.

Rehabilitation professions have much potential to craft relevant, complex, contemporary disability legitimacy, both definitionally and responsively. However, we suggest that rehabilitation is paradoxically both excessively slim and too rotund. By slim, we are referring to conceptual limitations in that legitimate disability within the rehabilitation professions not only lies in the material body but also is further subject to the same fragmentation that poses the challenge that we have launched at all professions to reconstitute the body. While parsing the body into slivers aids in specialization, this conceptual approach to disability limits legitimate response to segmented body parts and lends itself to the simplistic application of evidence-based practice at the expense of addressing individual need as person-pervasive. For example, when Stephen injured his rotator cuff, the well-meaning physical therapist suggested that he lie prone on a large ball, balancing with his arms as the ball moved. While this technique has shown excellent results for shoulder rehabilitation, Stephen, who has a fused hip, is unable to drape his torso over the ball, a simple matter that was overlooked by focusing on only one body part.

Rehabilitation, as we noted, is also too rotund. Here we refer to its similarity with other medicalized professionals who have unintentionally further institutionalized the disability park while simultaneously, conceptually narrowing legitimate and complex understandings of disability. The great value of rehabilitation is its capacity to teach new skills or help those who have lost skills to find new ways to achieve their goals. However, too many people with embodied conditions that qualify as legitimate disabilities become the ongoing work of rehabilitation and thus remain institutionalized as *lifers,* as patients, or as clients in the disability park.

The application of multiple explanatory theories of disability to rehabilitation would be warranted to expand narrow disability legitimacy and bring disability from without perspectives as well as the whole body into rehabilitation praxis. Explanatory perspectives including, but expanding beyond, the medical diagnostic would be warranted to recognize and dismantle the disability park while logically restructuring rehabilitation thinking to address descriptive need and reunite explanation and response. We would see this last suggestion as an important step for the survival and improved efficacy of rehabilitation, in that services would be available for many who do not currently legitimately qualify under medical-diagnostic explanations but who still could benefit from rehabilitation knowledge.

Education

Lexically, the primary scope of practice for educational professionals involves teaching and learning. This broad area of practice includes preschool through postsecondary education.

In the United States, public education programs, primary through high school, for children observed with atypical description consistent with the diagnosis of intellectual or learning deficit or exhibiting atypical, disruptive behavior were first mandated under federal legislation in 1975 with the

Education for All Handicapped Children Act and then extended to cover preschool-age children in 1968 with the passage of the Handicapped Children's Early Education Assistance Act. In general, under these policies, the qualifying or legitimacy criterion for the determination of disability once again has medical personnel busy in that they are the diagnosticians who qualify legislated medical-diagnostic conditional categories. Psychologists have hectic roles in this legitimacy activity as well in that they test and diagnose intrapsychic and cognitive deviance. To some degree, legitimacy criteria, such as those for which medically specific diagnoses based on observables can be made, are clear. However, in reportable areas with inferred explanations, such as atypical learning or behavior, there is much greater contention in terms of legitimacy.

The impact of this credibility chasm is twofold. First, the resulting variability of legitimate disability categorization and response may allow individuals to participate in and benefit from services that, under strict or firm delimiting legitimacy guidelines, would be denied. Second, variability can also be used to exclude individuals in one locale or region who might legitimately qualify for services and supports in another.

Based in large part on longitudinal explanations, regardless of the medical qualifier for disability services, the desirable outcome according to the education professional is a student's age-appropriate learning and performance on standardized and accepted assessments. As we mentioned above, we find it odd that despite educational responses being comprised of specialized teaching, legitimate eligibility for these services relies on medical-diagnostic explanations. This eligibility-response sequence seems illogical to us as it maintains medical explanations, and thus professions, as gatekeepers in a system in which they do not have primary expertise. The context of public education provides the forum for many noneducators to become involved in disability park ideology, planning, and educational practice indirectly related and thus only reportably relevant to educational process and student academic achievement. First, by virtue of public fiscal support, K–12 education leaves the educational professional group open to significant and variable public opinion, from local geographies with active lay school boards to federal debates in the US Congress defining how the civil right of public education will be actualized and accountable for all children and youth. In each of these contexts, the tension between and debate about inclusive versus separate education is played out with rhetorical ideology and diversity patina rather than depth, often driving educational practice for students with diverse explanations for disability. It is not uncommon to see children whose disabilities are explained by longitudinal delay placed in regular education classrooms structured according to age norms without specific attention to their learning needs, or sent outside their communities to school districts that are reportedly able to provide a full array of supports for students with medical-diagnostic explanations for atypical learning.

In higher education, note that US legislation governing educational inclusion and access changes from education-specific policy to the Americans with Disabilities Act. It is thus the responsibility of the student to assert disability legitimacy through seeking and providing a pedigree of acceptable, qualifying medical evidence. Because higher education is not seen as a civil right, the inclusion of students with disabilities on college campuses comes under the same jurisdiction as nondiscrimination in the workplace, community, and so forth.

For the most part, university and college disability student services maintain the disability park on campuses as they are typically segregated from general student services. Faculty response is variable in that disabled students have only recently become an identity group in higher education and, unlike gender, racial, and ethnic groups, one that is suspect for inclusion. Issues such as who is otherwise qualified to be admitted in higher-education in general and some majors specifically, how faculty are required to respond with accommodations, and the degree to which disability is aligned with campus diversity discourses vary significantly from campus to campus. Access to the physical and virtual environments remain fortuitous, although these issues are moving to the forefront of academic concern and discussion in some circles. Unfortunately, however, these efforts to address disability in higher education are further institutionalizing the disability park by focusing on the creation of specialized services and educational programs for potential students with embodied differences in function and learning. A more productive discussion for advancing the rights of all students to attend higher education might challenge the current assumptions and trends regarding one's right to be part of a campus community as judged by capacity to graduate rather than simply participate in a knowledge environment.

The need for students to medically qualify for special services maintains the disability park from the playground through the student union. Because financial issues rise to the top of educational policy and formulation of educational institutional structures, public education, particularly in the United States and now even higher education have fiscal muscle at the heart (Seldon, Bartholomew, & Myddelton, 2007). From the perspective that asserts and reifies the scarcity of fiscal resources for education and public services, how money is spent as well as received within specialized education of disabled students is often a contentious issue. Parents, educators, school administrators, policymakers, and community members often cannot reach consensus on how resources should be divided, especially when professional and lay groups compete over expenditures, income, and survival.

Given the current educational system, which is organized around longitudinal theoretical age-appropriate standards, we see the temporary relevance of disability services. However, in order to diminish and ultimately terminate the disability park, teacher education must be revised to educate teachers in multiple explanations for atypical human learning and in skill acquisition so that teachers and faculty can address a full range of student learning needs and styles rather than standard learners. An intermediate step preceding the disposal of the disability park in education would be wresting disability legitimacy away from noneducational gatekeeping professions and capturing it for debate and complex rethinking in the hands and intellects of educational experts, the teachers themselves.

Social Work

Because of its large scope of practice, social work can be diverse in its disability legitimacy determination and response. However, chronologically moving away from its early 20th century history of poverty and group work, current trends are institutionalizing social work professionals as the largest segment of clinical interventionists in the mental health and related systems, with only few practitioners entering into other practice domains. Thus, in large part, given that the praxis tail wags the theoretical dog, despite social work's professional mission to eliminate poverty, oppression, and discrimination, legitimate disability determination and response are driven primarily by its rootedness in mental health practice and thus on longitudinal and intrapsychic theoretical explanations of human deviance with limited attention to exterior environment theories such as economics, ethics, and political science (DePoy & Gilson, 2007, 2008).

However, considering that social workers, particularly at the undergraduate level of preparation, still work in human service and public protective agencies, the legitimacy criteria for the determination of disability by a social worker or as the result of an interaction or set of interactions with a social worker may vary and extend beyond the predominant longitudinal or intrapsychic explanations. Yet, in individual, clinical encounters supported by public or private health insurance, the ascription of disability legitimacy is most likely to occur in a manner common to many health practice arenas by applying a long-term, chronic diagnostic explanation to a set of atypical activities, appearances, and experiences. As the arena of practice moves beyond the individual to the family or groups of individuals with similar constellations of atypical activity, appearance, and experiences, legitimacy determination is commonly made on the basis of fit with preexisting eligibility criteria for safety net or public services. As we have noted, the essentialist assumption that disability automatically signifies poverty and the need for public support and charity is operative in this system of legitimacy. Unfortunately, the disability park thrives on essentialism and the well meaning but perhaps somewhat misguided efforts of professional activity that capture and retain a bolus of people in fiscally and emotionally dependent positions.

Although infrequent, the social worker focusing professional activity on large systems might be involved in disability legitimacy legislation, policy, and response at the local, state, and federal levels. Considering the social justice mission of social work and its mandate "to [attend to] the environmental forces that create, contribute to, and address problems in living" (National Association of Social Workers, 2010), one would expect that social work would have taken a progressive leading furlong in disability rights. Yet, according to Mackelprang and Salsgiver (2009), Yuen, Cohen, and Tower (2007), Murphy and Pardeck (2005), May and Raske (2004) and Rothman (2002), social work has not attended to disability as a category of oppression, but rather, as we noted above, has ministered to those who are legitimately qualified through clientizing (Cowger, 1998) the atypical body. Whatever legitimate response is followed to address the category of people with atypical bodies and minds, social work along with its professional counterparts perpetuates the disability park.

The mission of social work itself stages a potential direction for the profession to take a leading role in theater of the disability park. Because of its ostensible holistic stance and articulated charge to eradicate social injustice, social work is well positioned to analyze the disability park and work toward its elimination. However, long-range, progressive, explanatory theoretical development and implementation would be indicated, such that social work could move toward creating person-environment juncture. An initial step would involve "looking in the mirror" to examine and change the role of social work in perpetuating the disability park through clientizing.

Psychology

As we mentioned above, psychology has a central and demanding role in disability legitimacy, both in determination and response through two primary roles, assessment and counseling. While psychologists can subscribe to multiple explanatory frameworks of human thinking, feeling, and behavior, disability legitimacy determination follows the medical lead in that it is located in the interior as a medical diagnostic condition, even if a psychologist subscribes to exterior environment explanations of behavior. Recent trends have intermingled psychology and neurology, creating the field of neuropsychology, a specialization that addresses the mapping and functioning of the human brain. This field along with neurology has been active in foregrounding diagnostic categories such as *autism spectrum disorders* in the disability park. Similar to other nonmedical professions, however, medically-based disability determination does not drive psychological praxis. Rather, psychologists capitalize on medical-diagnostic legitimacy to secure clients and payment for services to clients and then proceed to inform legitimate responses through multiple and diverse longitudinal, interior, and exterior environment approaches. The desired practice response outcome is psychological stability.

Given the purposive use of multiple explanatory theories, the credibility and agreement of psychiatric diagnoses are more subject to scrutiny than those that are clearly observable and consistent with the legitimate medical disability criteria of specificity and universality. Moreover, because desired psychological responses are diverse and outcome is inferable, the accountability of responses for a category of questionable and low-pedigree disability status renders psychology less understood and less effective than medicine and, to some extent, rehabilitation professions in determining and responding to disability legitimacy in some domains but not all. Consider the debate regarding the credibility of mental retardation as an important example.

As we indicated previously, in our discussion of reportables, the literature reveals skepticism about the nature of mental retardation. Because cognition and intelligence are reportables, some have theorized that what has been considered cognition is actually behavior or communication (Allen & Allen, 1995). To complicate matters, intelligence testing relies on behavioral and communication indicators of the underlying, reportable, and inferable construct of intelligence and most recently has been subject to questioning on the basis of cultural differences in knowledge and performance.

Psychology has significant potential to upend the disability park, since its legitimate professional responses are diverse and are often informed by complex explanatory theories. However, the role of psychology in legitimating disability in educational settings poses an economic dilemma for this profession in that abolishing the disability park would threaten the centrality of psychology in determining and affirming legitimate disability in educational and psychiatric settings. Moreover, how psychology would engage in the 21st century post-postmodern challenge to reconstitute the body remains to be developed. We see these two quandaries as the 21st century work of psychology within the domain of disability legitimacy and juncture.

Architecture and Engineering

Architecture and product design are among the most vilified exterior environment disablers. When using the term *engineering*, we are referring mostly to product design standards and practices. We discuss these two professions together, not to imply that they are the same but rather because they share similar design responses to disability and to the maintenance of the disability park. Standards for product design and architecture are well accepted as legitimate causes of disability and thus changes in standards are considered to be legitimate responses. However, architecture and engineering alone do not legitimate disability determination. The atypical body must be present and experience ill-fit in order to legitimate architecture and engineering as disabling.

As we have discussed in previous chapters, until recently, the majority of architectural standards responded to the embodied male ideal proportions of Leonardo da Vinci's *Vitruvian Man* institutionalized by Le Corbusier, the father of modern architecture (Gilson & DePoy, 2007). Atypical bodies, those that are too big, small, or move in a nonstandard manner, experience ill fit in geographies and spaces built according to Vitruvian bodies. Product design is also based on a standard body. As example, computer keyboards assume two hands that move and react dexterously, dancing with vision as they capture screen images. But the body with a medical label that legitimates the corpus as disabled remains as the secret element of architectural and engineering disability. A mere glance at building accessibility standards and product design responses illuminates this point and the contribution of design standards to the disability park. For the most part, disability rights legislation across the globe mandates wheelchair, visual, and auditory access as major responses to the broad category of disability. Ramps, expanded door widths, elevators, automatic door openers, captioning, and Braille signage are some of more popular responses, each designed for an atypical body part. Thus, rather than being designed for a larger range of human diversity, legitimate architectural and engineering responses governed by policies and legislation guiding new construction, retrofitting of existing built environments, structure of virtual environments and design of some products provide guidance for partitioned and clearly labeled spaces and objects that comprise the disability park and hold it intact. Thus, architectural and engineering practices carve up space, geography, and gizmos and then mark this response with the iconic wheelchair symbol that denotes its artistry as exclusive for disabled bodies whether or not those bodies use wheeled mobility.

As we have discussed, universal design was in part a progressive ideology to counter architectural, engineering, and other accommodations, which resulted in segregation of disabled and nondisabled bodies. Unfortunately, this ideology did not live up to its promise, in part because it was doomed by three inherent flaws. First, universal design emerged from disability design and thus was perceived as just another set of a compliance mandates for disabled bodies. Second, universal responses, especially retrofitting, were branded as expensive. And third and perhaps most profound, the interpretation of universal design as a single response to the full range of diverse bodies is not possible.

We are not suggesting that architects and product engineers are intentionally discriminatory. Rather, we see current responses as positive intermediate steps in fashioning built environments and useful objects that can accommodate diversity. However, medical explanations for disability continue to lurk in the shadows of legitimate design responses and thus create spaces and items which still fit only some bodies, albeit an expanded set of corpuses. Full juncture requires careful analysis, planning, and a paradigm shift away from disability park thinking and action.

Business

As we have detailed, we see business as one of the linchpins in creating full juncture. Because business is a profession with profit as its primary aim, business professionals respond to changes in exterior environment context. While business still crafts and brands its responses to medical-diagnostic disability legitimacy and derives significant profit from the disability park, business practice has also provoked new markets that have brought products and services previously considered as disability-specific into the mainstream of the market economy. In the context of a global market economy, professional business must befriend and legitimate disability as a viable market if full juncture is to be created and sustained.

Chapter Conclusion

Our analysis of professional legitimacy suggests some important themes. First, each profession views human activity, appearance, and experience through its own set of explanatory lenses. However, medical-diagnostic explanations inhere in each profession as legitimate disability criteria despite the professional response. Second, while we see medicine as an important profession in responding to disability, we suggest that medical diagnostic legitimacy does not serve other professional masters whose responses are nonmedical. In order for the disability park to be identified, dismantled, and replaced with full juncture, each profession has its tasks laid out. In the next chapter, we detail and illustrate our model for professional thinking and action.

PART IV

Fashioning Communities

16

Integrative Academic-Professional Stance Through Disjuncture Theory

A s promised, this chapter advances synthetic theory and illustrates its application to informed and integrated multiple academic and professional masters.

Until now, the majority of our discussion has indulged in analysis of diverse explanatory approaches that precede legitimate determination and response to disability. Perhaps one major advantage of "the good ole days" of monism is that answers from a single perspective can be more easily found, rather than searching for them within a yet to be assembled mosaic of ideas that are awaiting ordering and logical application. However, as we discussed, our universe is in flux and in desperate need of contemporary ideas to guide complex issues of disability legitimacy as well as to counter the disability park. In large part, the virtual and technological advances, which bring immediacy and global variation into daily lives, elevate the need for relevant and purposive knowledge and response beyond patina to diversity depth. Clearly, disability legitimacy demands change in knowledge development, transmission, and application, as explanatory theory and emerging new models of legitimacy have, to some extent, severed their tether to pathology. Yet, as we illustrated, medical hegemony still reigns supreme in legitimacy of determination, despite its limited or absent guidance for legitimate responses in so many fields that touch disability.

Flexible and synthetic thinking and action can meet the tall orders of the 21st century to reconstitute the body and eliminate the disability park while improving our globe for the full diversity depth of humans.

As discussed throughout the book, Disability Studies has synthesized interdisciplinary thinking from multiple academic and professional arenas, including humanities, arts, social science, natural sciences, and professions to inform definition, analysis, and response to disability. Yet, despite spates of intellectual richness, too many academic debates still bifurcate disability as either medical-diagnostic or socially constructed (DePoy & Gilson, 2004). In order to advance intellectually and teleologically, we suggest that the field not only can but also must serve multiple academic and professional masters. Disjuncture theory as explanatory of disability creates the perimeter of lines and shapes awaiting substantive theoretical color. What intellectual colors are selected, how disjuncture is substantiated, and how it is applied are flexible with purpose as the major guiding principle.

Figure 16.1 depicts disjuncture theory and its opposite, juncture. As we noted previously, the word *disjuncture* is defined as a disconnected relationship between at least two entities, and *juncture* refers to a relationship of connection and goodness-of-fit. Thus, advancing beyond the binary debate about the correctness of disability as either embodied or environmental, disjuncture holds neither element as solely responsible but rather highlights the relationship between the two as the explanatory locus. This relational gaze furthers the pluralistic opportunity for dialog and cooperative thinking and action among diverse fields. Considering disability as a function of both bodies and of environments, therefore, can bring multiple fields of knowledge to bear on healing disjuncture without dismissing the contribution of either the body or the environment to the explanatory repertoire. In addition, the term disjuncture does not demean the atypical body but rather looks to a less than satisfactory relationship between individuals and one or more types of environments as the target of change.

Particularly potent to advance full juncture are the fields of human factors and design. As we noted in Chapter 10, human factors integrates multiple fields of inquiry

> to understand interactions between people and everything that surrounds us, and based on such knowledge, [seeks] to optimize human well-being and overall systems performance. (Salvendy, 2006, p. 5)

The field of human factors is substantive in addressing embodied diversity and environmental response. As a collaboration among many professionals, scholars, and laypersons, human factors provides adequacy of depth

Figure 16.1 Levels of Juncture-Disjuncture

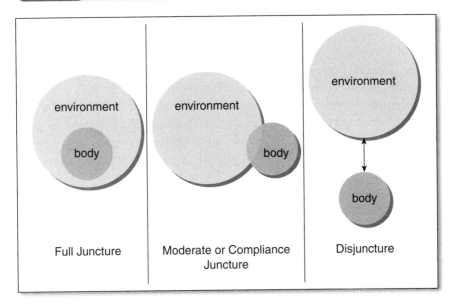

Full Juncture   Moderate or Compliance Juncture   Disjuncture

and complexity to understanding both the corporeal and the environmental elements of disability. Embodied knowledge is obtained through drawing on fields such as physiology, anatomy, kinesiology, psychology, neurology, sensory function, human communication, work, and social functioning.

Informed by multiple fields, analysis of the environment is substantive as well. Of particular value is the incorporation of detailed task analysis in all problem resolution thinking. Task analysis answers two major questions: (1) What are the steps of a task? (2) How can they be accomplished in diverse ways depending on one's embodied characteristics and processes within the given environment? Task analysis is the clandestine gem in human factors in that this thinking tool holds the power to parse human description into multiple and, if needed, miniscule parts necessary for complex analysis. Detailed analysis thus meets diversity depth pluralistically. By engaging in task analysis, universal design principles are left in the 20th century, replaced by precision, pluralism, and the acceptance that juncture can only occur if embodied diversity is met with creative environmental diversity.

We agree with Salvendy (2006), who asserts that human factors should drive technology, broadly defined as "the entire system of people and organizations, knowledge, processes and devices that go into creating and operating technological artifacts as well as artifacts themselves" (p. 5). Thus, within the human factors theoretical rubric, technology itself is interactive and engages human intellect and skills from many areas of expertise in resolving problems that interfere with human activity and actualization.

While Salvendy (2006) includes design within human factors, we make the distinction between design as engineering and design as we have previously discussed in Chapters 10 and 15. We reiterate this definition here for clarity. *Design* is comprised of activities of conceptualizing, planning, creating, and claiming credit for one's ideas, products, and entities as well as the inherent intentional or patterned characteristics of bodies, spaces, and ideas (Margolin, 2002; Munari et al., 2003). Of particular note is the contemporary commonality in all definitions of design as purposive and intentional. That is to say, design is not frivolous but rather is powerful, political, and is both shaped by and shapes notions of standards, acceptability, membership, and desirability (Foster, 2003; Munari et al.). This broad definition of design extends beyond science to include political, artistic, and axiological considerations.

Because of its breadth and depth, human factors is not a field for singular expertise. It demands the integrative thinking and action of multiple schools of thought and people and thus is a democratic foundation in which analysis, debate, and pluralistic legitimacy responses can be advanced. Furthermore, given that the two fields of design and human factors in themselves are interdisciplinary, they bring expansive and substantive human thinking and action to bear on legitimate response to disability. Together they are the Ruby Slippers for full juncture, the creation of goodness of fit between diverse bodies and environments.

Figure 16.2 provides a graphic representation of problem mapping (DePoy & Gilson, 2007), an expansive, multidimensional, powerful thinking tool to depict the contribution and relationships of diverse academic and professional fields to healing disjuncture. The problem mapping process is a democratic, complex thinking method to expand a problem beyond its original conceptualization. The process involves a multidirectional approach, mapping upstream to theorize causes, and mapping downstream to identify consequences. The value of this conceptual map is its movement beyond first impression to the creation of an integrative, substantive, yet flexible systemic approach to analyzing problems as multidimensional, nonlinear, and complex.

The two text boxes on the top of Figure 16.2 represent the two prevailing and often conflicting causal models of disability: embodied and environmentally constructed. Note that they are connected with a broken arrow to depict their current limited interaction but future potential within human factors to articulate complex analyses. As we have noted in previous chapters, the term *embodied* broadly refers to the organic and experiential

Figure 16.2 Problem Map #1—Disjuncture Conceptualized as Embodied

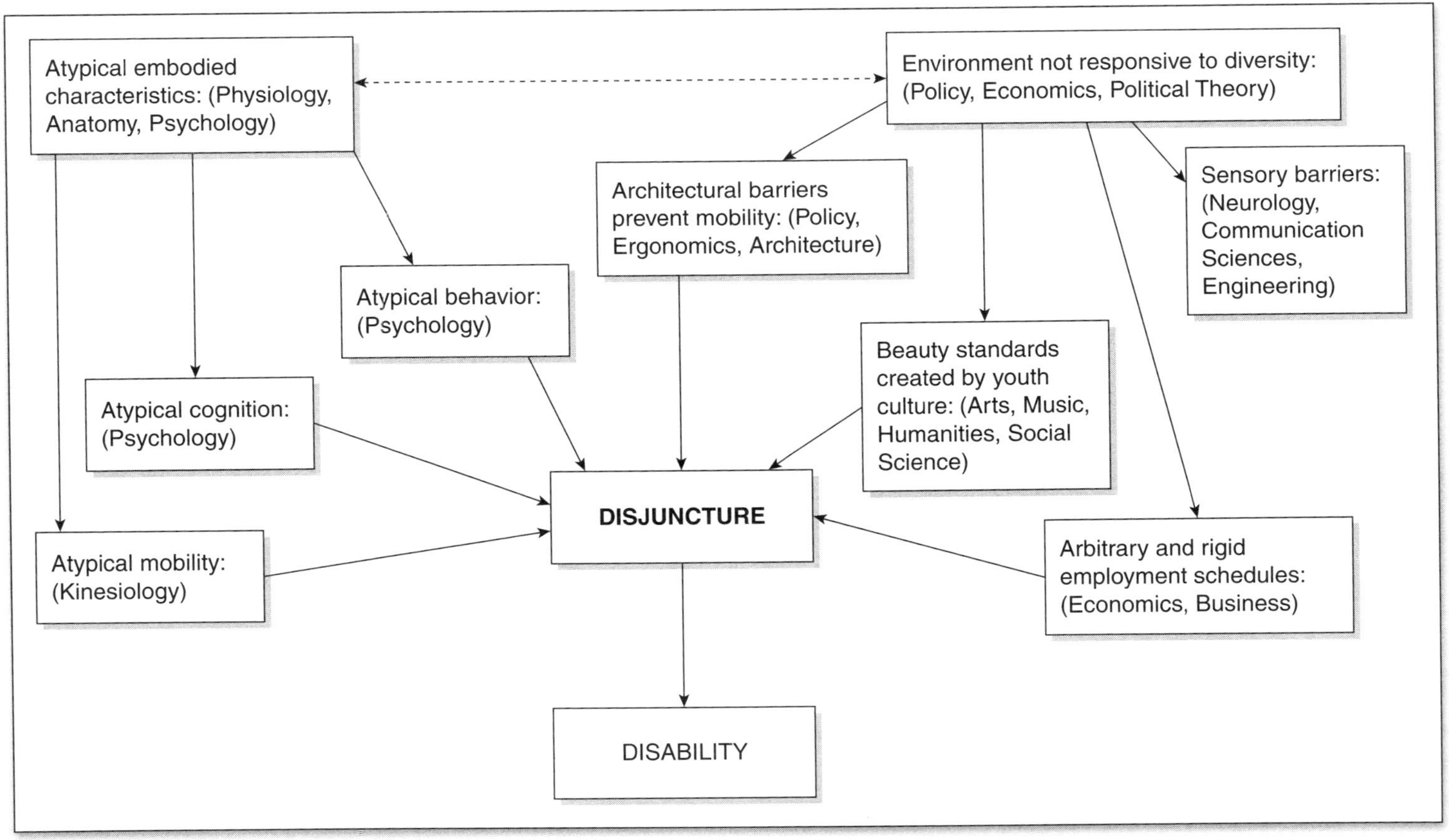

Sensory barriers: (Neurology, Communication Sciences, Engineering)

Environment not responsive to diversity: (Policy, Economics, Political Theory)

Arbitrary and rigid employment schedules: (Economics, Business)

Beauty standards created by youth culture: (Arts, Music, Humanities, Social Science)

Architectural barriers prevent mobility: (Policy, Ergonomics, Architecture)

DISJUNCTURE

DISABILITY

Atypical behavior: (Psychology)

Atypical embodied characteristics: (Physiology, Anatomy, Psychology)

Atypical cognition: (Psychology)

Atypical mobility: (Kinesiology)

human corpus. And *environment* refers to sets of conditions external to bodies, including but not limited to physical, sensory, social, virtual, expressive, economic, policy, cultural, national, linguistic, global elements, and so forth. As depicted in Figure 16.2, included in this analysis of disjuncture are the sensory body, the cognitive body, the social-emotional body, the spiritual body, the economic body, the productive body, the body of ideas and meanings, and the body in multiple garb and spaces (Gilson & DePoy, 2007).

Figure 16.3 presents the same problem map depicted in Figure 16.2 but with the professional fields of concern noted in each text box.

Turning to professional education and practice, fields such as medicine, rehabilitation, education, psychology, social work, and so forth conceptualize and teach healing disjuncture as remediating embodied deficits or making accommodations to permanently impaired bodies so that they can function in unchanged environments. Conversely, engineering and architectural design focus on the exterior environment. And to a large extent, public health addresses disjuncture through attempting to prevent it.

As depicted in Figure 16.3, while each field has a specialty, it has potential to work interdisciplinarily and democratically with others to deepen analysis and legitimate responses to disjuncture. Adding humanities and business to human factors and design has great potential to move beyond partial compliance juncture to create full juncture, since understanding and creating environmental conditions and change in the 21st century requires 21st century thinking.

By accepting the explanation for disability as relational, that is to say, an ill fit between embodied phenomena and the environments in which bodies act, the opportunities for multiple fields, in collaboration with one another, to posit the complexity of disability and thus enlarge the range of legitimate responses boundless. Figure 16.4 represents this theoretical state of juncture.

Disjuncture theory creates a scaffold for multiple fields to educate students and produce practice that expands analysis of disability beyond atypical embodied phenomena to the creation of juncture through the reciprocal relationship of diverse bodies and environments. Moreover, as we discuss in the next chapter, within this theoretical perimeter, juncture refers to equality, human rights, and justice that can be advanced through multiple, creative, response avenues.

Thus, in addition to transcending the binary medical-social model debate that is focused on impaired bodies and their treatment in environmental milieus, disjuncture theory guides purposive, legitimate human rights responses that have the potential to engage the interests, values, knowledge, and expertise of multiple fields in healing disjuncture for all populations. Disability, while possibly being related to atypical bodies, may also indicate a broader state of ill fit,

Figure 16.3 Problem Map #2—Disjuncture Conceptualized as Disciplinary

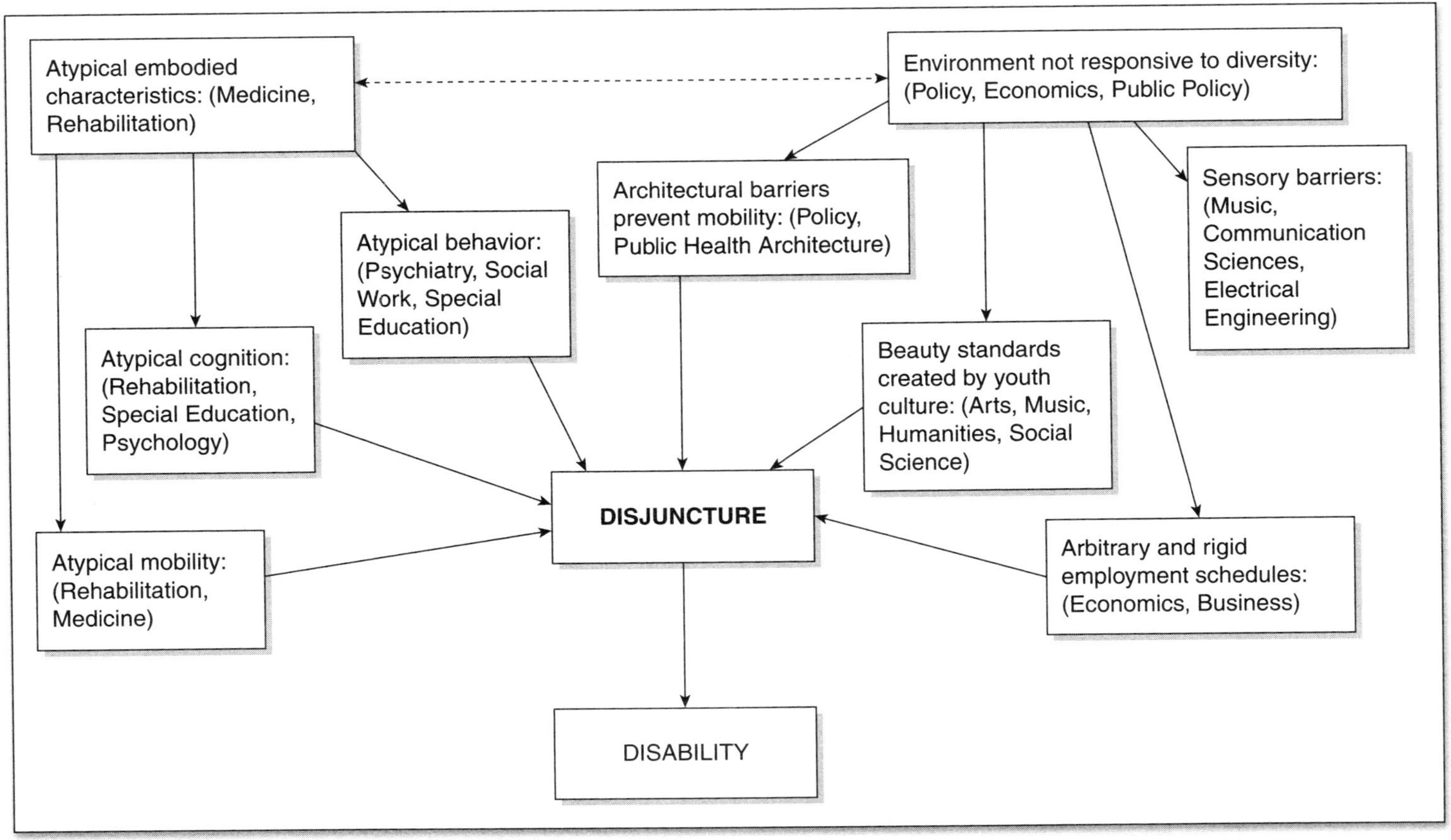

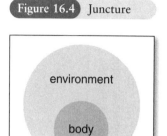

Figure 16.4 Juncture

locating disability squarely within theory, examination, teaching, learning, and social action aimed at social justice, rather than restricting it to remediation of an embodied condition through bodily treatment or environmental revision.

Resolution

We now illustrate the implementation of our synthetic theory to healing disjuncture. This project that we present involves an *ill fit* between the information environment and the way in which diverse individuals can receive knowledge. When applying disjuncture theory to the project, barriers to information access are analyzed through problem mapping (DePoy & Gilson, 2007). These violations of human rights to information (and in this case health information) are serious, complex, and cannot be resolved by monistic approaches such as legislation or policy promulgation that perpetuate the disability park but are ineffectual in their stated aims. While the explicit access barriers are located at the intersection of bodies and the virtual, textual environment, problem map analysis of the disjuncture, as depicted in Figure 16.5 reveals the unpacked complexity of the initial problem statement and its resolution.

Illustration

Building on these problem maps, the past several years have been spent in an ongoing project to promote equality of access to web-based health information. This project involves human factors, design, humanities, and professional knowledge to actualize the design, development, testing, and dissemination of a website that translates existing health information into alternative literacy and accessible formats, regardless of the features on the original website. Experts from the fields of design, health, and human service professions, education, art, computer science, English, and marketing are collaborating in diverse roles on this work.

The initial step of the project focused on preferred website design. Research was conducted by an artist and a social worker to elicit color, navigation, imagery, and preferred general appearances of diverse web users. Note that despite the project aim of healing disjuncture for two specified populations—those with cognitive impairments and those with low English literacy—*design* formed the entrance to action, thereby dismantling the disability and illiteracy parks at the outset.

Figure 16.5 Disjuncture Analysis

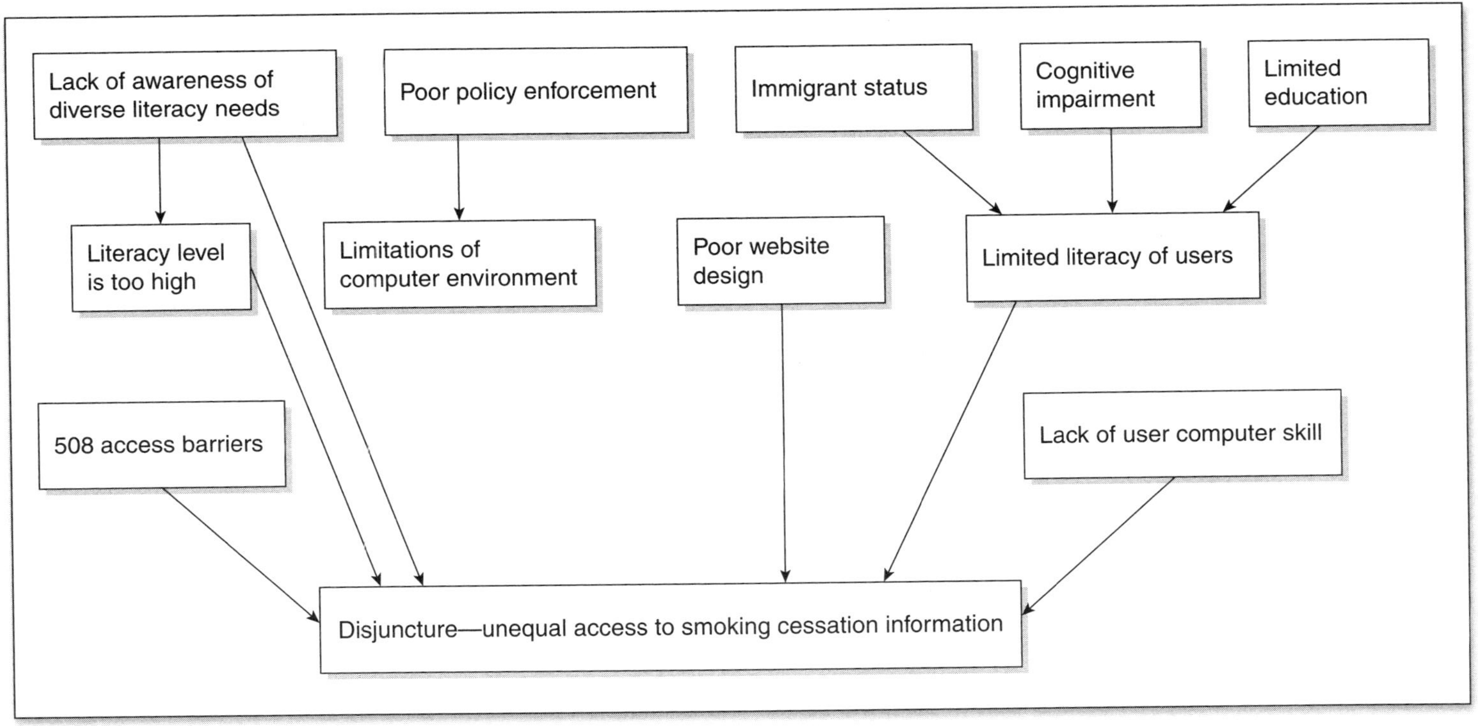

Limited education

Cognitive impairment

Immigrant status

Limited literacy of users

Lack of user computer skill

Poor policy enforcement

Poor website design

Limitations of computer environment

Lack of awareness of diverse literacy needs

Literacy level is too high

508 access barriers

Disjuncture—unequal access to smoking cessation information

199

Figure 16.6 Juncture Response

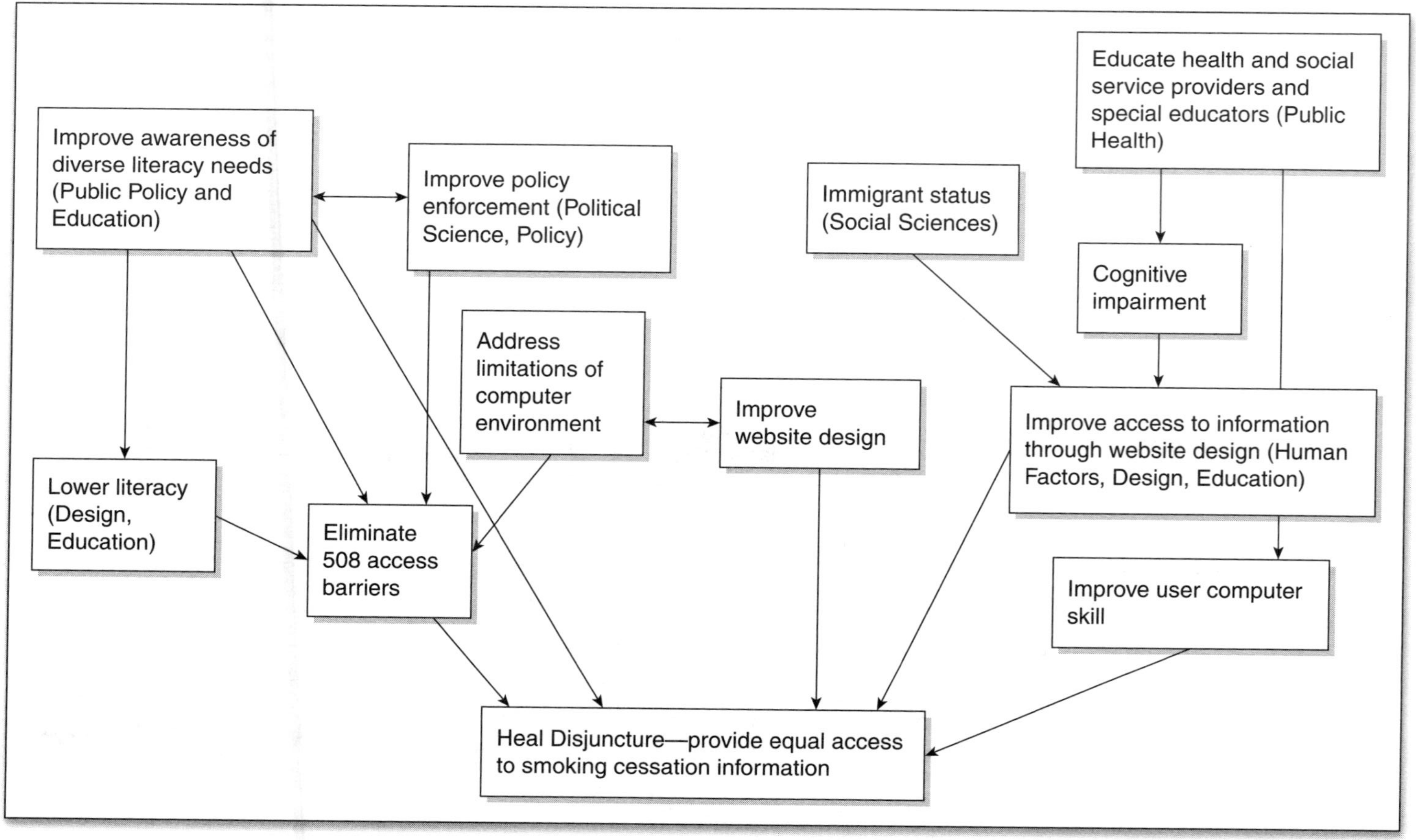
Improve awareness of diverse literacy needs (Public Policy and Education)
Improve policy enforcement (Political Science, Policy)
Immigrant status (Social Sciences)
Educate health and social service providers and special educators (Public Health)
Cognitive impairment
Address limitations of computer environment
Improve website design
Improve access to information through website design (Human Factors, Design, Education)
Lower literacy (Design, Education)
Eliminate 508 access barriers
Improve user computer skill
Heal Disjuncture—provide equal access to smoking cessation information

We then applied for funding to support the website development. Because the project was initially funded by the American Legacy Foundation (2007–2009), the web portal was developed to translate electronic smoking cessation information. See Figures 16.7 and 16.8: screen captures

Figure 16.7 Original Site

Source: Printed with permission. http://www.ccids.umain.edu/projects/tap/ default.htm

Figure 16.8 Easy-to-Read Site

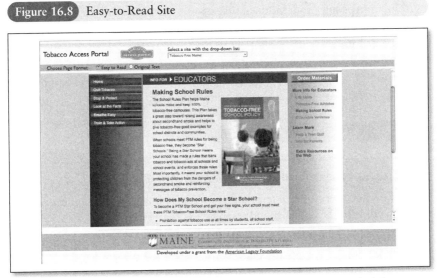

Source: Printed with permission. http://www.ccids.umain.edu/projects/tap/ default.htm

of untranslated and translated pages. Note that anyone can use them as there are no brands denoting *special* accommodations.

Due to the limitations of the funding source, new web design was not initiated at this point. However, consistent with the tenets of disjuncture theory, which posit the synthesis of design, human factors, and business, we have established a corporate structure, Astos, for the further development of this access solution and intend to bring it into the mainstream of commerce. Note that the word *astos* means civil in Greek and thus was chosen as a corporate name and logo to a company devoted to the advancement of civilized environments. We discuss this point in more detail in the final chapter. The addition of marketing, branding, and commercialization illustrate the progressive integration of diverse fields in order to heal disjuncture without instituting a restrictive park environment for either disability or low literacy.

Figure 16.6 illustrates how disjuncture was mapped and addressed in interdisciplinary analysis and response.

Note that in Figure 16.6 the embodied condition of cognitive impairment and diversity patina immigrant status are not changed, but attention to these embodied and diversity phenomena, as well as to the environment, is a function of the intersection and collaboration of the multiple fields that informed this work.

Table 16.1 summarizes the principles that emerge from our synthetic approach to healing disjuncture.

As the 21st century proceeds, we envision the future in which thinking and action transcend the rigid disciplinary boundaries that produce unfruitful debates about which theory best legitimates disability and response. Within a purposive context, disability can be reconceptualized and met with socially just responses that do not require a village of like-minded people but an informed universe of varied perspectives and responses. In the final chapter, we unveil our vision of community legitimacy, a model that eliminates the disability park or any categorical park that is restrictive and responds to diversity depth though enacting equality of human rights.

Table 16.1   Principles for Healing Disjuncture

- Rethink disability as the fit of bodies and environments.
- Promote informed action through the democratic collaboration of multiple fields, thinking, and response approaches.
- Marry disciplines in a purposive framework.
- Broaden the disability discourse beyond bodies to purposive and informed thinking and action to advance equality of access and rights.
- Locate thinking and action within the mission, human rights, and social justice.

17

A Model of
Community Legitimacy

Creating
Human-Environment Juncture

The final chapter of the book presents an ideal in which disjuncture theory is used to provoke conversation, debate and propose socially just synthetic thinking, and initiate action to disability categorization and response.

In our last book on disability, we referred to Robin Kelley, a biographer of social activists. Since this wisdom is timeless, once again we return to Kelley's sage advice to be critical for the sake of learning while keeping our vision of what should be (Kelley, in DePoy & Gilson, 2004). Throughout this book, we have presented issues and debates about disability from the perspective of Explanatory Legitimacy. We critically discussed diverse explanatory theories of disability and linked them to legitimate categorization and response. As we moved through history, we saw the diverse contextual limits of typical and atypical, of explanations for the atypical, and of value determinations for worthiness and response criteria. We then looked at legitimacy through the lens of diverse professional and academic fields as the basis for advancing synthetic collaborative theory and action to dissolve the disability park.

In this chapter, we follow Kelley's guidance and present our vision of community as one that heals disjuncture within a larger agenda of equality of *human rights* and *social justice*. Similar to our approach to linguistic challenges throughout the book, we clarify these two terms before proceeding to suggest how they can reframe disability legitimacy and response as legitimacy (Ishay, 2008) of diversity depth.

Human Rights

Because histories and current meanings of human rights are so diverse, there is significant debate about their origin and current actualization. Glancing back to ancient civilizations, references to human rights, while not lexically named as such, were contained not only in agreements among governing bodies and subordinates but also in writings of philosophy, myth, and religion as well (Campbell, 1990; Ishay, 2008). Considering that these three arenas, among many more, were documented birthplaces of contemporary human rights conceptualizations, it is not surprising that debate is voracious in human rights rhetoric and praxis. For example, some argued that human rights were innate, moral principles derived from inherent human goodness while others countered that human rights laws had to be imposed in order to create and maintain a civil society. Still others asserted that rights were earned or won and thus were not universal (Donelly, 2003).

Ishay paints a large but scant portrait of human rights by stating,

> Human rights are rights held by individuals simply because they are part of the human species. They are rights shared by everyone regardless of sex, race, nationality, and economic background. (2008, p. 3)

Because Ishay's aim is to position human rights as chronologically and contextually relative, who determines the substantive content and limits of rights and decision processes and how rights are actualized in a civil society are not part of this definition. And without that level of detail, specifically the methods that will be used to decide the nature of rights, their scope of ownership, and insurance that human rights are fairly and equally applied to all, some scholars suggest that the very term is nothing but simulacra, or empty, lexical symbolism (Heard, 1997). We disagree with the simulacra perspective while acknowledging the difficulty of conceptualizing and implementing a universal human rights vision. We suggest that disjuncture cannot be healed without human rights thinking and action, even if a universal definition is never attained and only tolerance is proposed. We return to this point later in the chapter.

Clearly, human rights is a global concern (Turmusani, 2003) as evidenced by the United Nations' efforts over the past 60 years in this area. Adopted by the UN General Assembly, Resolution 217A (III) of December 10, 1948, is a nonbinding vision that in part was a response to discrimination, oppression, torture, and genocide that occurred in World War II (Ishay, 2008). Figure 17.1 presents the full text of the resolution. A surface reading reveals its value on equality of application to all humans without qualification. However, inherent in the specific rights is the majoritarian assumption of *standard adult*. For example, children do not vote and thus would not be fully included in this document. For this reason, along with political jockeying and economic advantage, the future division of the 1948 document was laid out. It was first bifurcated and then subjected to further bodies and backgrounds segmentation.

While we acknowledge the importance of redressing categorical abrogation of rights as we have asserted, we see such an approach to human rights as a strategy that cannot eliminate divisions and confer equality of rights in the long term. Thus, in large part, the 1948 version of the resolution is consistent with our thinking about human rights because it defines substantive areas of rights and participation that, for us, form the basis for democratic conversation within ongoing attention to context. Moreover, it does not parse rights into identity bodies and backgrounds categories, which create parkscapes. However, because it is nonbinding and harbors clandestine norms, the document fails to denote its scope, how rights are to be agreed upon, and how they will be ensured. Nonetheless, dissimilar from its successors, the 1948 resolution advances an ideology, which does not unintentionally segregate populations and fence them as *special*, a euphemism for excludable (Titchkosky, 2007).

Synthesized with the capabilities approach (Nussbaum, 2006; Sen, 2007), which levels the human rights playing field so to speak, we see great potential for a productive human rights dialogue among multiple individuals and interest groups that can heal disjuncture within local geographies and start the process globally. As we noted previously, Nussbaum posited ten rights or entitlements for human dignity that should belong to all regardless of the dowry of skills, personal agency, and resources that one brings to the marriage of rights and existence. Thus, to some extent, while Nussbaum explains disability as embodied, she collocates it within an interactive context in which capabilities should be guaranteed through humanitarian means regardless of embodied insufficiency or ill fit with the typical array brought by others to this important exchange. In our model of human rights, the substance of rights is well laid out as the basis for informed negotiation with the

(Text continued on page 210)

Figure 17.1   U.N. General Assembly Resolution, 217A (III)

Human rights are basic rights and freedoms that all people are entitled to regardless of nationality, sex, national or ethnic origin, race, religion, language, or other status.

Human rights include civil and political rights, such as the right to life, liberty, and freedom of expression; and social, cultural, and economic rights, including the right to participate in culture, the right to food, and the right to work and receive an education. Human rights are protected and upheld by international and national laws and treaties.

1. All human beings are born free and equal in dignity and rights. They are endowed with reason and conscience and should act toward one another in a spirit of brotherhood.

2. Everyone is entitled to all the rights and freedoms set forth in this Declaration without distinction of any kind, such as race, color, sex, language, religion, political or other opinion, national or social origin, property, or birth or other status. Furthermore, no distinction shall be made on the basis of the political, jurisdictional, or international status of the country or territory to which a person belongs, whether it be independent, trust, non-self-governing, or under any other limitation of sovereignty.

3. Everyone has the right to life, liberty, and security of person.

4. No one shall be held in slavery or servitude; slavery and the slave trade shall be prohibited in all their forms.

5. No one shall be subjected to torture or to cruel, inhuman, or degrading treatment or punishment.

6. Everyone has the right to recognition everywhere as a person before the law.

7. All are equal before the law and are entitled without any discrimination to equal protection of the law. All are entitled to equal protection against any discrimination in violation of the Declaration and against any incitement to such discrimination.

8. Everyone has the right to an effective remedy by the competent national tribunals for acts violating the fundamental rights granted him by the constitution or by law.

9. No one shall be subjected to arbitrary arrest, detention, or exile.

10. Everyone is entitled in full equality to a fair and public hearing by an independent and impartial tribunal in the determination of his rights and obligations and of any criminal charge against him.

11.

1. Everyone charged with a penal offense has the right to be presumed innocent until proved guilty according to law in a public trial at which he has had all the guarantees necessary for his defense.
2. No one shall be held guilty of any penal offense on account of any act or omission that did not constitute a penal offense, under national or international law, at the time it was committed. A heavier penalty shall not be imposed other than the one that was applicable at the time the penal offense was committed.

12. No one shall be subjected to arbitrary interference with his privacy, family, home, or correspondence, or to attacks upon his honor and reputation. Everyone has the right to the protection of the law against such interference or attacks.

13.

1. Everyone has the right to freedom of movement and residence within the borders of each state.
2. Everyone has the right to leave any country, including his own, and to return to his country.

14.

1. Everyone has the right to seek and to enjoy asylum from persecution in other countries.
2. This right may not be invoked in the case of prosecutions genuinely arising from nonpolitical crimes or from acts contrary to the purposes and principles of the United Nations.

15.

1. Everyone has the right to a nationality.
2. No one shall be arbitrarily deprived of his nationality nor denied the right to change his nationality.

16.

1. Men and women of full age, without any limitation due to race, nationality, or religion, have the right to marry and to found a family. They are entitled to equal rights as to marriage, during marriage, and at its dissolution.
2. Marriage shall be entered into only with the free and full consent of the intending spouses.
3. The family is the natural and fundamental group unit of society and is entitled to protection by society and the State.

(Continued)

Figure 17.1 (Continued)

17.

    1. Everyone has the right to own property alone as well as in association with others.

    2. No one shall be arbitrarily deprived of his property.

18. Everyone has the right to freedom of thought, conscience, and religion; this right includes freedom to change his religion or belief and freedom, either alone or in community with others and in public or private, to manifest his religion or belief in teaching, practice, worship, and observance.

19. Everyone has the right to freedom of opinion and expression; this right includes freedom to hold opinions without interference and to seek, receive, and impart information and ideas through any media and regardless of frontiers.

20.

    1. Everyone has the right to freedom of peaceful assembly and association.

    2. No one may be compelled to belong to an association.

21.

    1. Everyone has the right to take part in the government of his country, directly or through freely chosen representatives.

    2. Everyone has the right of equal access to public service in his country.

    3. The will of the people shall be the basis of the authority of government; this shall be expressed in periodic and genuine elections, which shall be by universal and equal suffrage and shall be held by secret vote or by equivalent free-voting procedures.

22. Everyone, as a member of society, has the right to social security and is entitled to realization, through national effort and international cooperation and in accordance with the organization and resources of each State, of the economic, social, and cultural rights indispensable for his dignity and the free development of his personality.

23.

    1. Everyone has the right to work, to free choice of employment, to just and favorable conditions of work, and to protection against unemployment.

    2. Everyone, without any discrimination, has the right to equal pay for equal work.

3. Everyone who works has the right to just and favorable remuneration, ensuring for himself and his family an existence worthy of human dignity, and supplemented, if necessary, by other means of social protection.

4. Everyone has the right to form and to join trade unions for the protection of his interests.

24. Everyone has the right to rest and leisure, including reasonable limitation of working hours and periodic holidays with pay.

25.

1. Everyone has the right to a standard of living adequate for the health and well-being of himself and of his family, including food, clothing, housing, medical care and necessary social services, and the right to security in the event of unemployment, sickness, disability, widowhood, old age, or other lack of livelihood in circumstances beyond his control.

2. Motherhood and childhood are entitled to special care and assistance. All children, whether born in or out of wedlock, shall enjoy the same social protection.

26.

1. Everyone has the right to education. Education shall be free, at least in the elementary and fundamental stages. Elementary education shall be compulsory. Technical and professional education shall be made generally available, and higher education shall be equally accessible to all on the basis of merit.

2. Education shall be directed to the full development of the human personality and to the strengthening of respect for human rights and fundamental freedoms. It shall promote understanding, tolerance, and friendship among all nations, racial, or religious groups, and shall further the activities of the United Nations for the maintenance of peace.

3. Parents have a prior right to choose the kind of education that shall be given to their children.

27.

1. Everyone has the right to participate freely in the cultural life of the community, to enjoy the arts, and to share in scientific advancement and its benefits.

2. Everyone has the right to the protection of the moral and material interests resulting from any scientific, literary, or artistic production of which he is the author.

(Continued)

Figure 17.1 (Continued)

> 28. Everyone is entitled to a social and international order in which the rights and freedoms set forth in this Declaration can be fully realized.
>
> 29.
>
>   1. Everyone has duties to the community in which, alone, the free and full development of his personality is possible.
>
>   2. In the exercise of his rights and freedoms, everyone shall be subject only to such limitations as are determined by law solely for the purpose of securing due recognition and respect for the rights and freedoms of others and of meeting the just requirements of morality, public order, and the general welfare in a democratic society.
>
>   3. These rights and freedoms may in no case be exercised contrary to the purposes and principles of the United Nations.
>
> 30. Nothing in this Declaration may be interpreted as implying, for any state, group, or person, any right to engage in any activity or to perform any act aimed at the destruction of any of the rights and freedoms set forth herein.

Source: Millennium Development Goals Report 2008 © United Nations, 2009. Reproduced with permission.

"An Inuit Reality," Duane Smith, in *UN Chronicle* © United Nations, November 2007 (Volume XLIV). Reproduced with permission.

understanding that response to ensure rights will be made on the basis of need rather than category membership. Who meets the needs and how needs and responses are democratically discussed, debated, decided, and enacted is a local process with the power of multiple intellectual and professional perspectives brought into the mix. Currently, policy is the legitimate avenue through which to propose and enforce human rights. However, healing the disjuncture requires more complex and complete responses with involvement beyond mandated compliance. We introduced commerce as a major venue for change and will discuss this point more later in the chapter.

Social Justice

A close relative of human rights is social justice. As might be expected, there are many definitions of social justice, with a major debate between those who see social justice as opportunity and those who view it as outcome. Substantively, the term refers to fairness related to opportunity or outcome depending on one's view of distribution of rights, privileges, and resources throughout a social context. Because social justice is both an ideology and distributive formula, social justice debates are often vague with the proverbial apples and oranges talking in parallel rather than intersecting conversations.

Rawls (1999) has been in the forefront of contemporary social justice theory. As we discussed previously, his basic principle, notwithstanding the complexities of political power, asymmetrical personal resources, and distributive dilemmas, suggests that in exchange for benefits and advantage, individuals and groups entrust legitimate power to governing institutions. Consensus of those who are subject to policy and regulation, not ideology, according to Rawls is the legitimate test of a socially just society. Again challenged by Nussbaum (2006) and Sen (2009), Rawls' theory does not account for asymmetry of power in the legitimating process, and thus we have espoused the capabilities framework along with noncategorical human rights as the ideological guidance for healing disjuncture.

In concert with Kymlicka (2009)—who suggested that global human rights policy is plagued by the failure of current, categorical frameworks to do viable work in carving up humanity into useful categories—we advance a vision of juncture in which legitimate response to *ill fit* is determined by need rather than bodies and backgrounds patina categories. Moving from need to response, without the middlemen of essentialism and identity politics, creates contexts in which action nails its human rights target by implementing socially just solutions of goodness of fit.

Disjuncture theory, within a larger context of human rights and social justice, provides the lens through which we envision and suggest actions to advance our ideal community. We have named this ideal *community legitimacy*, denoting its theoretical and ideological foundation.

We defined *community* as local entities comprised of physical, social, spiritual, and environmental elements in which individuals engage in family interaction, self-care, work, leisure, education, commerce, citizenship, and the host of other activity categories that we have included in human description.

Legitimate communities are environments in which the following values and principles inhere:

1. Human rights and social justice frame all legitimate responses to disjuncture.

2. Binary and bodies and backgrounds categories are reframed as categories of direct need.

3. Need, not identity politics category membership, informs responses.

4. Explanations for human description are well-informed, explicit, and verified.

5. Analysis and dismantling of the disability park are ongoing initiatives.

6. Values are articulated, continuously examined, negotiated, and decided on in a democratic fashion.

7. Response to need is informed by a wealth of pluralistic knowledge.

8. Response creates opportunity for fit but does not prescribe it.

9. The responsibility for dismantling the disability park and creating full juncture belongs to the community, including those who benefit from it as well as those who are victimized by it.

10. Progressive economics, business, and commerce are valued and essential to the creation of juncture, locally, nationally, and globally.

Seminal values inhere in these principles. First, as we have professed throughout the book, we value pluralism of perspective as well as roles. Diversity of thinking and action is critical in order to analyze disjuncture and develop and implement responsive resolutions. Because of its intellectual power, interdisciplinarity is far more desirable than monism. Monism can only proffer strategies within delimited theory and praxis. Considering the complexity of disjuncture, contemporary post-postmodernism provides guidance for integrative theorizing and critical action outcomes.

Second, we value logic and internal consistency. As we have noted, it makes sense to craft full juncture strategies that address problems and fulfill needs logically and directly. Considering that bodies and backgrounds characteristics are relatively stable, inviting and sanctioning the middlemen of identity politics and medical diagnosis to specify and then craft solutions within areas that they have limited expertise, and by definition cannot change, seems ill-advised. As we have discussed in Chapter 10 and our legitimacy chapters, disjuncture theory has the intellectual and logical potential to expand the binaries that maintain segregation. Joining bodies and environments in ongoing analysis and praxis provides the structure, timing, and processes for complex understandings, negotiation, development, and implementation of contemporary, relevant, junctured communities devoid of disability and other identity politic parks. Recognizing the intermediate value of categorical response does not warrant its continuation in the long term. Too many segregating and marginalizing consequences have resulted from the creation of the disability park.

Third, community legitimacy thinking and action are not prescriptive. As we have discussed, prescription relies on nomothetic approaches to inquiry.

These groups-based approaches, while purposive in many efforts, do not do justice to diversity depth. They, thus, perpetuate essentialism and look for commonality within the very groups that are named as diverse. Multiple approaches to full juncture provide a host of options and opportunities rather than channeling category members into singular access mazes that cannot respond to diversity depth. We value pluralism and multiplicity of negotiation and production as keys to create relevant and useful opportunity and juncture.

The principles for community legitimacy are based on a synthesis of explanatory theory and axiological models, which hold each community member responsible for contributing to juncture as well as entitled to it. A civil society that conforms to community legitimacy respects citizen need while seeing each as accountable for the resolution of community problems. Thus, there needs to be a balance between receiving help and participating in the development of juncture. Change cannot belong to others.

Finally, in addition to health and so-called helping professions, commerce and business have a valued and essential role in community legitimacy. Without business strategies that eliminate the disability park, it will remain intact, stigmatizing, and segregating. In a global economy, business practices such as marketing branding and mainstream commercialization are critical for equalizing value and worth of individuals and groups. For example, Astos, a nonprofit corporation, has the logo and mission in Figure 17.2.

This mission addresses full juncture, while eliminating parkesque language, references to categorical services and products, and methods to achieve its aims. The mission and logo mentioned below are similarly contemporary and contrasted to other disability park logos.

Figure 17.2   Astos

astos

Mission Statement:

The purposive application of systematic thinking and action processes to the definition and clarification of social, health, and access problems, to the identification of what is needed to resolve them, and to the way in which and extent to which problems have been resolved.

Source: Astos.org, 2008–2010. Used with permission.

Consider these two exemplars related to sports access. As indicated in its name, Disabled Sports USA is an organization that focuses its mission on sporting activity for the disabled population. In the mission statement and logo of this not-for-profit organization, the term disabled is foregrounded as the population segment of concern. Thus, while historically intended to provide the opportunity for sports participation to individuals excluded from typical sports due to disability, the perpetuation of separate sports activities and venues is not useful for eliminating segregated disability parks. Images on the website reflect atypical bodies using equipment that is recognized as adaptive. Both logo and mission project an inspirational sentiment and resortative purpose. Implicit within these images and messages are that the disabled person enters the sports arena to develop the absent or insufficient qualities of independence, confidence, and a well-lived life. Moreover, requests for donations are made on the homepage of the website, further reifying disability sport as a charity park for unfortunates. (Disabled Sports USA, 2009).

In contrast, the logo and narrative for Renegade Wheelchairs exemplifies full juncture. As indicated on their website and stated in the logo, these mobility devices are considered to be all terrain sports equipment in which the design and functionality fit with a "busy life" (http://www.renegade-wheelchairs.com/about.htm). The term "disability" does not appear on any part of the website, eliminating the bifurcation of populations into disabled and non-disabled segments and thereby locating their product selection and its use outside of the disability park. This point is further illuminated by the claim that Renegade Wheelchairs are designed for full access to the outdoors without the need for parkesque constructions such as ramps and lifts.

Conclusion

The time for change is upon us. The global economy, despite its many criticisms, has created a forum and opportunity for progressive thinking and social change. No single discipline should perpetuate and own the disability park, nor is a single discipline responsible for dismantling it. Full juncture is a democratic, creative, post-postmodern, interdisciplinary, ongoing process that can be attained.

References

Abrams, J. (1998). *Judaism and disability: Portrayals in ancient texts from the Tanach through the Bavli.* Washington, DC: Gallaudet University Press.

Ackland Art Museum. (n.d.). *Glossary.* Retrieved February 24, 2010, from Ackland www.ackland.org/tours/classes/glossary.html

Adair, V. (2002). *Branded with infamy: Inscriptions of poverty and class in the United States.* Chicago: University of Chicago Press.

Adolph, K. E., Eppler, M. A., Marin, L., Weise, I. B., & Clearfield, M. W. (2000). Exploration in the service of prospective control. *Infant Behavior and Development, 23*: 441–460.

Adolph, K. E., Weise, I., & Marin, L. (2003). Motor development. In L. Nadel (Ed.), *Encyclopedia of cognitive science* (pp. 134–137). London: Macmillan Reference Ltd.

Albrecht, G. L. (1992). *The disability business: Rehabilitation in America.* Newbury Park, CA: Sage.

Albrecht, G. L. (Ed.). (2005). *Encyclopedia of disability.* Thousand Oaks, CA: Sage.

Albrecht, G. L., Seelman, K. D., & Bury, M. (Eds.). (2001). *Handbook of disability studies.* Thousand Oaks, CA: Sage.

Allan, J. (Ed.). (2003). *Inclusion, participation, and democracy: What is the purpose?* Dordrecht, the Netherlands: Kluwer Academic.

Allen, B., & Allen, S. (1995). The process of socially constructing mental retardation: Toward value-based interaction. *JASH, 20*(2), 158–160.

Altman, B., & Gulley, S. (2007, August 10). *Unraveling disability measurement: An examination of methodological and conceptual differences in estimates of the population with disability using four varieties of disability questions.* Paper presented at the annual meeting of the American Sociological Association. Retrieved May 8, 2009, from http://www.allacademic.com/meta/p183646_index.html

American Association on Intellectual and Developmental Disabilities (AAIDD). (2009). *Definition of intellectual disability.* Retrieved March 1, 2010, from http://www.aaidd.org/index.cfm

American Institute of Architects. (2010). *The architects knowledge resource.* Retrieved March 15, 2010, from http://www.aia.org/index.htm

American Physical Therapy Association. (2010). *About APTA. Mission statement.* Retrieved March 1, 2010, from http://www.apta.org/AM/Template.cfm?Section=About_APTA&Template=/TaggedPage/TaggedPageDisplay.cfm&TPLID=41&ContentID=18579

American Psychiatric Association. (1968). *Diagnostic and statistical manual-II.* Washington, DC: Author.

American Psychiatric Association. (2000). *Diagnostic and statistical manual-VI-TR* (4th ed., Text Rev.). Arlington, VA: Author.

Amnesty International USA. (2009). *Amnesty International.* Universal Declaration of Human Rights. Retrieved August 17, 2009, from http://www.amnestyusa.org/human-rights/page.do?id=1031002

Anderson, S. K., & Middleton, V. A. (2005). *Explorations in privilege, oppression and diversity.* Pacific Grove, CA: Wadsworth.

Anker, S., & Talasek, J. (2009). *Visual culture and bioscience issues in cultural theory, no. 12.* Vancouver, BC: Center for Art, Design and Visual Culture, UMBC.

Antonetta, S. (2007). *A mind apart: Travels in a neurodiverse world.* New York: Penguin.

Apgar, V. (1953). A proposal for a new method of evaluation of the newborn infant. *Current Researches in Anesthesia and Analgesia,* July–August. Retrieved March 1, 2010, from http://www.apgar.net/virginia/Apgar_Paper.html

Appleby, G. A., Colon, E., & Hamilton, J. (2007). *Diversity, oppression, and social functioning: Person-in-environment assessment and intervention.* Boston: Pearson/Allyn & Bacon.

Armstrong, D. (2002). *A new history of identity: A sociology of medical knowledge.* Hampshire, UK: Palgrave Macmillan.

Axinn, J., & Stern, M. J. (2000). *Social welfare: A history of the American response to need* (7th ed.). Needham Heights, MA: Allyn & Bacon.

Aylward, G. P. (1994). *Practitioner's guide to developing and psychological testing (Critical issues in developmental and behavioral pediatrics).* New York: Springer.

Backett-Milburn, K., & McKie, L. (2001). *Constructing gendered bodies.* New York: Palgrave Macmillan.

Bacon, F. (2009). *The advancement of learning, divine and human.* Sioux Falls, SD: NuVision.

Badinter, E. (2006). *Dead end feminism.* Cambridge, UK: Polity Press.

Bandura, A. (1977). *Social learning theory.* New York: General Learning Press.

Bandura, A. (1986). *Social foundations of thought and action.* Englewood Cliffs, NJ: Prentice-Hall.

Barnes, C., Mercer, G., & Shakespeare, T. (1999). *Exploring disability: A sociological introduction.* Cambridge, UK: Polity Press.

Barney, D. (2004). *The networked society.* Malden, MA: Polity.

Barrett, J. (n.d.). *History of discriminaton against disabled people.* Retrieved March 1, 2010, from http://www.jackiebarrett.ca/DisabledDiscrimination2.htm

Bassnett, I. (2001). Health care professionals and their attitudes towards decisions affecting disabled people. In G. Albrecht, K. D. Seelman, & M. Bury (Eds.), *Handbook of disability studies* (pp. 450–467). Thousand Oaks, CA: Sage.

Basson, L. (2004). Blurring the boundaries of diversity: Racial mixture, ethnic ambiguity and indigenous citizenship in settler states. *International Journal of Diversity in Organisations, Communities and Nations. 4.* Retrieved February 13, 2010, from http://laurenlbasson.cgpublisher.com/product/pub.29/prod.62

Baudrillard, J. (1995). *Simulacra and simulation: The body in theory: Histories of cultural materialism* (S. F. Glaser, Trans.). Ann Arbor: University of Michigan Press.

Baum, W. M. (2004). *Understanding behaviorism: Behavior, culture, and evolution* (2nd ed.). Hoboken, NJ: Wiley-Blackwell.

Baxter, P. (2007, June 19). *Combining cognits.* Retrieved March 1, 2009, from http://paul-baxter.blogspot.com/search?q=embodiment+history

Belsey, C. (2002). *Poststructuralism: A very short introduction.* New York: Oxford University Press.

Berger, S. E., & Adolph, K. E. (2003). Infants use of handrails as tools in a locomotor task. *Developmental Psychology, 39,* 594–605.

Berube, M. (2009, May 7). *Disability as a complex cultural construction.* Retrieved June 9, 2009, from http://badcripple.blogspot.com/2009/05/disability-as-complex-cultural.html

Betta, M. (2006). *The moral, social, and commercial imperatives of genetic testing and screening: The Australian case.* Dordecht, the Netherlands: Springer.

Boas, F. (1940). *Race, language, and culture.* Chicago: University of Chicago Press.

Bock, R. (2009, April 24). *New centers begin recruiting for national children's study.* Retrieved April 24, 2009, from http://www.nih.gov/news/health/apr2009/nichd-24.htm

Bonilla-Silva, E. (2003). *Racism without racists: Color-blind racism and the persistence of racial inequality in the United States.* Lanham, MD: Rowman & Littlefield.

Boyles, D. (2007, May 1). *Enforcing the ugly laws.* Retrieved April 7, 2009, from http://urbansemiotic.com/2007/05/01/enforcing-the-ugly-laws/

Braddock, D. L., & Parish, S. L. (2001). An institutional history of disability. In G. L. Albrecht, K. D. Seelman, and M. Bury (Eds.), *Handbook of disability studies,* (pp. 145–157). Thousand Oaks, CA: Sage.

Bronfenbrenner, U., (Ed.). (2005). *Making human beings human: Bioecological perspectives on human development.* Thousand Oaks, CA: Sage.

Bronfenbrenner, U., & Morris, P. A. (2006). The ecology of human developmental processes. In W. Damon (Series Ed.) & R. M. Lerner (Vol. Ed.), *Theoretical models of human development, vol. 1 of handbook of child psychology* (6th ed., pp. 793–828). New York: Wiley.

Brown, S. (n.d.). *Institute on disability culture.* Retrieved March 2, 2010, from http://www.instituteondisabilityculture.org/

Brown, S. (1998–1999). *Institute on disability culture.* Retrieved March 2, 2010, from http://www.dimenet.com/disculture/

Bruininks, R. H., & Bruininks, B. D. (2009). *Bruininks-Oseretsky test of motor proficiency* (2nd ed.). San Antonio, TX: Pearson.

Bryman, A. (2008). *Social research methods.* Cambridge, MA: Oxford University Press.

Bugeja, M. (2005). *Interpersonal divide: The search for community in a technological age.* New York: Oxford University Press.

Butler, R., & Parr, H. (1999). *Mind and body spaces: Geographies of illness, impairment and disability.* New York: Routledge.

Cahoone, L. (2003). *From modernism to postmodernism: An anthology.* Oxford: Blackwell.

Campbell, J. (1990). *The power of myth.* New York: Anchor Books.

Campbell, R. L. (2006). *Jean Piaget's genetic epistemology: Appreciation and critique.* Retrieved March 2, 2010, from http://hubcap.clemson.edu/~campber/piaget .html

Carmen, I. H. (2004). *Politics in the laboratory.* Madison: University of Wisconsin Press.

Chahira, K. (2006). Dwarfs in ancient Egypt. *American Journal of Medical Genetics, 140*(4), 303–311.

Changeaux, J.-P. (2004). *The physiology of truth: Neuroscience and human knowledge* (M. B. De-Bevoise, Trans.). Cambridge, MA: Belknap Press of Harvard University Press.

Charlton, J. (2000). *Nothing about us without us: Disability oppression and empowerment.* Los Angeles: University of California Press.

Clapton, J., & Fitzgerald, J. (1997). The history of disability: A history of 'otherness.' *New Renaissance Magazine.* 7(1). Retrieved March 2, 2010, from www.ru.org/index2.php?option=com_content&do_pdf=1&id=180

Cockerham, W. C. (2003). *Medical sociology.* (9th ed.). Englewood Cliffs, NJ: Prentice-Hall.

Cognitive Evolution Laboratory. (2009). *Moral sense test.* Retrieved June 11, 2009, from http://moral.wjh.harvard.edu/index2.html

Cohen, J., & Weiss, G. (Eds.). (2003). *Thinking the limits of the body.* New York: State University of New York Press.

Connor, D. (2007). Cripping school curricula: 20 ways to re-teach disability. *Review of Disability Studies, 3*(3). Retrieved March 2, 2010, from www.rds.hawaii .edu/counter/count.php?id=20

Conrad, P. (2007). *The medicalization of society: On the transformation of human conditions into treatable disorders.* Baltimore: Johns Hopkins University Press.

Conservation Online. (2010, February 12). *Cool.* Retrieved March 23, 2010, from http://cool.conservation-us.org/index.shtml

Corwin, M. (2002). *Brief treatment in clinical social work practice.* Pacific Grove, CA: Brooks/Cole.

Couser, G. T. (1997). *Recovering bodies: Illness, disability, and life-writing.* Au Claire: University of Wisconsin Press.

Cowger, C. D. (1998). Clientism and clientification: Impediments to strengths-based social practice. *Journal of Sociology and Social Welfare, 25*, 25–37.

Cranz, G. (2000). *The chair: Rethinking culture, body, and design.* New York: W. W. Norton.

Cross, N. (2001). Designerly ways of knowing: Design discipline versus design science. *Design Issues, 17*(3), 49–55. Retrieved August 28, 2007, from MIT Press (PDF).

Dalai Lama XIV. (2005). *The universe in a single atom: The controversy of science and spirituality.* New York: Morgan Road Books.

David, R. (2005). *Child and adolescent neurology.* Hoboken, NJ: Wiley-Blackwell.

Davidson, M. (2008). *Concerto for the left hand.* Ann Arbor: University of Michigan Press.

Davis, L. J. (1995). *Enforcing normalcy: Disability, deafness, and the body.* London: Verso.

Davis, L. J. (Ed.). (1997). Constructing normalcy. *The disability studies reader.* New York: Routledge.

Davis, L. J. (2002). *Bending over backwards: Disability, dismodernism, and other difficult positions.* New York: New York University Press.

Davis, L. J. (2006). *Disability studies reader* (Rev. 2nd ed.). New York: Routledge.

Death with Dignity Act. Retrieved December 2, 2009, from http://www.oregon .gov/DHS/ph/pas/

Deitz, J. C., Kartin, D., Kopp, K. (2007). Review of the Bruininks-Oseretsky Test of Motor Proficiency (2nd ed.). *Physical and Occupational Therapy in Pediatrics, 27*(4), 87–102.

DePoy, E., Gilmer, D., & Martzial, E. (2000). Adolescents with disabilities and chronic illnesses in transition: A community action assessment. *Disability Studies Quarterly, 20,* 4–10.

DePoy, E., & Gilson, S. F. (2004). *Rethinking disability: Principles for professional and social change.* Pacific Grove, CA: Wadsworth.

DePoy, E., & Gilson, S. F. (2005/2006). Reinventing atypical bodies in art, literature and technology. *International Journal of Technology, Knowledge and Society, 3,* 7. Retrieved March 2, 2010, from http://www.Technology-Journal.com

DePoy, E., & Gilson, S. F. (2007). *The human experience: Description, explanation, and judgment.* Lanham, MD: Rowman & Littlefield.

DePoy, E., & Gilson, S. F. (2008). Healing the disjuncture: Social work disability practice. In K. M. Sowers & C. N. Dulmus (Series Eds.) & B. W. White (Vol. Ed.), *Comprehensive handbook of social work and social welfare: Vol. 1. The profession of social work* (pp. 267–282). Hoboken, NJ: Wiley.

DePoy, E., & Gilson, S. F. (2009, June 20). *Designer disability.* Retrieved March 3, 2010 from http://www.astos.org

DePoy, E., & Gilson, S. F. (in press). Disability design and branding: Rethinking disability within the 21st century. *Disability Studies Quarterly.*

DePoy, E., & Gitlin, L. N. (2010). *Introduction to research: Understanding and applying multiple strategies* (4th ed.). St. Louis, MO: Elsevier.

DePoy, E., & MacDuffie, H. (2004). Force field analysis: A model for promoting adolescent involvement in their own health care. *Journal of Health Promotion Practice, 5*(3), 306–313.

Developmental Disabilities Assistance and Bill of Rights Act of 2000. 42 USC 15001 (2000).

Dimitriu, L. (n.d.). *Livio Dimitriu–Pratt Institute.* Retrieved March 17, 2010, from http://www.pratt.edu/academics/architecture/grad_dept_architecture/faculty_ and_staff/bio/?id=ldimitri

Disabled Sports USA. (2009). Retrieved March 1, 2010, from http://www.dsusa.org.

Doig, K. B., Macias, M. M., Saylor, C. F., Craver, J. R., & Ingram, P. E. (1999). The child development inventory: A developmental outcome measure for follow-up of the high-risk infant. *Journal of Pediatrics. 135*(3): 358–362.

Donelly, J. (2003). *Universal human rights in theory and practice* (3rd ed.). Ithaca New York: Cornell University Press.

Durant, W. (1991). *Story of philosophy: The lives and opinions of the world's greatest philosophers.* New York: Pocket Books.

EcoSurvey. (n.d.). *Value.* Retrieved March 5, 2010, from ecosurvey.gmu.edu/glossary.htm

Education of All Handicapped Children Act (Individuals with Disabilities Education Act) of 1975. Pub. L. No. 94-142, Title 20 U.S.C. Section 1400 et. seq. (1997).

Ember, C. R., & Ember, M. (2002). *Anthropology: A brief introduction* (5th ed.). Englewood, NJ: Prentice-Hall.

Farlex. (2010a). Diversity. *The free dictionary by Farlex.* Retrieved February 20, 2010, from http://thefreedictionary.com/diversity

Farlex. (2010b). Ethics. *The free dictionary by Farlex.* Retrieved February 20, 2010, from http://thefreedictionary.com/ethics

Farlex. (2010c). Humanities. *The free dictionary by Farlex.* Retrieved March 6, 2010, from http://www.thefreedictionary.com/humanities

Farlex. (2010d). Patina. *The free dictionary by Farlex.* Retrieved February 28, 2010, from http://www.thefreedictionary.com/patina

Farlex. (2010e). Social Science. *The free dictionary by Farlex.* Retrieved February 28, 2010, from http://www.thefreedictionary.com/social+science

Farmer, S. (2002). *Surviving poverty in medieval Paris: Gender, ideology, and the daily lives of the poor.* Ithaca, NY: Cornell University Press.

Faust, J. (n.d.). *Handout 1: Design theory.* Retrieved March 8, 2010, from http://jfaust.com/newsite/pages/teaching/documents/designdefinitions.pdf

FeelGood Store. (2009). *The FeelGood store.* Retrieved July 31, 2009, from http://www.feelgoodstore.com/cgi-bin/feelgood/index_home.html

Finucane, R. C. (1995). *Miracles and pilgrims.* New York: Macmillan.

Fischer, F., Miller, G., & Sidney, M. S. (2006). *Handbook of public policy analysis.* Boca Raton, FL: CRC Press.

Foster, H. (2003). *Design and crime (and other diatribes).* New York: Verso.

Foundation Aiding the Elderly. (n.d.). *History of nursing homes.* Retrieved March 29, 2009, from http://www.4fate.org/history.html

Frankenburg, W. K., Dodds, J., Archer, P., Shapiro, H., & Bresnick, B. (1992). The Denver II: A major revision and restandardization of the Denver Developmental Screening Test. *Pediatrics, 89,* 91–97.

Freud, S. (1938). *The basic writings of Sigmund Freud* (A. A. Brill, Trans.). New York: Modern Library.

Friedson, E. (1980). *Doctoring together: A study of professional social control.* Chicago: Chicago University Press.

Fries, K. (Ed.). (1997). *Staring back.* New York: Plume.

Fries, K. (2007). *The history of my shoes and the evolution of Darwin's theory.* Cambridge, MA: Da Capo Press.

Fuchs, S. (2005). *Against essentialism: A theory of culture and society*. Cambridge, MA: Harvard University Press.

Fussell, P. (1992). *Class: A guide through the American status system*. New York: Touchstone.

Galician, M.-L. (2004). *Handbook of product placement in the mass media: New strategies in marketing theory, practice, trends, and ethics*. New York: Routledge.

Gardner, H. (2000). *Intelligence reframed: Multiple intelligences for the 21st century*. New York: Basic Books.

Garland-Thomson, R. M. (1996). *Extraordinary bodies: Figuring physical disability in American culture and literature*. New York: Columbia University Press.

Garland-Thomson, R. M. (2009). *Staring: How we look*. New York: Oxford University Press.

Garland-Thomson, R. M., & Longmore, P. (2009). Statement of principles. *Disability Studies Quarterly*. Retrieved March 15, 2010, from http://www.dsq-sds.org/about/editorialPolicies

Geertz, C. (1973). *The interpretation of cultures: Selected essays*. New York: Basic Books.

Gill, C. (1992, November). Who gets the profits? Workplace oppression devalues the disability experience. *Mainstream, 12,* 14–17.

Gilson, S. F., & DePoy, E. (2003). *Rethinking disability: Principles for professional and social change*. Belmont, CA: Brooks-Cole.

Gilson, S. F., & DePoy, E. (2004). Disability, identity, and cultural diversity. *Review of Disability Studies, 1*(1), 16–23.

Gilson, S. F., & DePoy, E. (2005). Universal access technology: Advancing the civil right to information literacy. *International Journal of Technology, Knowledge and Society, 1*. Retrieved March 3, 2010, from http://www.Technology-Journal.com.

Gilson, S. F., & DePoy, E. (2007). Da Vinci's ill fated design legacy: Homogenization and standardization. *The International Journal of the Humanities, 5*(7), 145–154. Retrieved March 3, 2010, from http://ijh.cgpublisher.com/product/pub.26/prod.1150

Gilson, S. F., & DePoy, E. (2008). Designer diversity: Constructing bodies and backgrounds through contemporary design theory. *International Journal of the Humanities, 6*(4), 177–188.

Gilson, S. F., & DePoy, E. (2009a). Disjuncture theory: Expanding beyond universal design for the 21st century. *Ono research institute conference*. Kiyrat Ono, Israel. Ono Academic Institute.

Gilson, S. F., & DePoy, E. (2009b). *New ways of thinking and doing business: Advancing full participation through design and marketing*. Presented at the Association of University Centers on Disabilities 2009 Annual Meeting and Conference.

Gleeson, B. J. (1997). Disability studies: A historical materialist view. *Disability and Society, 12*(2), 179–202.

Gleeson, B. J. (1999). *Geographies of disability.* London: Taylor & Francis.

Goffman, E. (1961). *Asylums. Essays on the social situation of mental patients and other inmates.* Garden City, NY: Doubleday Anchor.

Goffman, E. (1963). *Stigma: Notes on the management of spoiled identity.* Englewood Cliffs, NJ: Prentice-Hall.

Goldberg, D. T. (1994). *Multiculturalism: A critical reader.* Oxford, UK: Blackwell.

Google. (n.d.). *Definitions of value on the web,* Retrieved March 3, 2010, from http://www.google.com/search?hl=en&lr=&client=safari&rls=en&oi=defmore&defl=en&q=define:value

Gould, S. J. (1996). *The mismeasure of man.* New York: W. W. Norton & Co.

Grandquist, L. (2009). 'Ugly laws' were a very ugly way to discriminate. *Minnesota's Disability Community Newsletter.* Garland, TX: Access Press.

Green, M. (2006). Disability in medieval Europe: Physical impairment in the high Middle Ages, c. 1100–c. 1400. *Social History of Medicine, 19,* 539–540. Retrieved March 1, 2010, from http://www.ingentaconnect.com/content/oup/sochis/2006/00000019/00000003/art00539;jsessionid=7c9t3m4gv4bjb.victoria

Groopman, J. (2007). *How doctors think.* New York: Houghton Mifflin.

Gubrium, J., & Holstein, J. (2009). *Analyzing narrative reality.* Thousand Oaks, CA: Sage.

Habermas, J. (2003). *The future of human nature* (H. Beister & W. Rehg, Trans.). New York: Polity Press.

Hagley Museum and Library. (n.d.). *Universal design digital exhibit.* Retrieved July 28, 2009, from http://www.hagley.lib.de.us/library/exhibits/univdesign exhibit/Harrison.htm

Hahn, H. (1991). Alternative views of empowerment: Social services and civil rights. *Journal of Rehabilitation, 57,* 17–19.

Hahn, H. (1993). The politics of physical differences: Disability and discrimination. In M. Nagler (Ed.), *Perspectives on disability* (2nd ed., pp. 37–42). Palo Alto, CA: Health Markets Research.

Haller, B. (2000). How the news frames disability: Print media coverage of the ADA. *Research in Social Science and Disability, 1,* 55–83.

Hanson, B. (2002). Inequalities created in bio-medicine as the body business. In J. J. Kronenfeld (Ed.), *Social inequalities, health and health care delivery* (pp. 22–44). Oxford, UK: Elsevier Press.

Harris, L., & Associates. (2000). *2000 N.O.D./Harris survey of Americans with disabilities.* Washington, DC: National Organization on Disability.

Harrison, J. E. (2006). *Mythology.* Boston: Marshall Jones.

Harrison, L. E., & Huntington, S. (2000). *Culture matters: How values shape human progress.* New York: Basic Books.

Hays, A. (2006). *Shaping disability rights through international exchange* (Japan). Retrieved April 5, 2009, from http://www.miusa.org/ncde/stories/hays

Healy, J. (2004). *Diversity and society.* Thousand Oaks, CA: Pine Forge Press.

Heard, A. (1997). *Human rights: Chimeras in sheep's clothing?* Retrieved August 18, 2009, from http://www.sfu.ca/~aheard/intro.html

Heiferman, M., & Kismaric, C. (Organizers). (2005). *Paradise now: Picturing the genetic revolution.* [Art exhibit, September 16th 2001–January 6th 2002]. Retrieved March 6, 2010, from http://tang.skidmore.edu/index.php/posts/view/30/

Henderson, B. (2006). Impairment. In G. Albrecht (Ed.), *Encyclopedia of disability* (Vol. 2, pp. 920–922). Thousand Oaks, CA: Sage.

Herek, G. M. (2009). *Facts about homosexuality and mental health.* Retrieved July 23, 2009, from http://psychology.ucdavis.edu/rainbow/html/facts_mental_health.html

Herrington. (2000–2009). *Herrington.* Retrieved July 21, 2009, from http://www.herringtoncatalog.com/

Hickman, L. (2007). *Pragmatism as post-postmodernism: Lessons from John Dewey.* New York: Fordham University Press.

Holmes, M. S. (2004). *Fictions of affliction.* Ann Arbor: University of Michigan Press.

Holstein, M. S., & Cole, T. R. (1996). The evolution of long-term care in America. In R. H. Binstock, L. E. Cluff, & O. Von Mering (Eds.), *The future of long-term care: Social and policy issues* (pp. 19–47). Baltimore: Johns Hopkins University Press.

Holt, D. (2004). *How brands become icons: The principles of cultural branding.* Cambridge, MA: Harvard Business School Press.

Horkheimer, M., Adorono, T., Noerr, G. S., & Jepgcott, E. (2002). *Dialectic of enlightenment.* Palo Alto, CA: Stanford University Press.

Howson, A. (2004). *The body in society.* Cambridge, UK: Polity.

Huitt, W., & Hummel, J. (2003). Piaget's theory of cognitive development. *Educational Psychology Interactive,* Retrieved March 6, 2010, from http://www.edpsycinteractive.org/topics/cogsys/piaget.html

Hutchison, E. D. (2007). *Dimensions of human behavior: Bundle* (3rd ed.). Thousand Oaks, CA: Pine Forge Press.

Imrie, R. (1996). *The disabling city.* New York: St. Martin's Press.

Imrie, R., & Hall, P. (2001). *Inclusive design: Designing and developing accessible environments.* New York: Spon Press.

Ingstad, B., & Whyte, S. R. (1995). *Disability and culture.* Berkeley: University of California Press.

Institute on Community Integration, University of Minnesota. (2005). *Impact: Feature issue on enhancing quality and coordination of health care for persons with chronic illness and/or disabilities 18(1).* Retrieved July 23, 2009, from http://ici.umn.edu/products/impact/181/default.html

Ione, A. (2008). Introduction: Visual images and visualization in the neurosciences. *Journal of the History of the Neurosciences, 17*(3), 1–6.

Ishay, M. (2008). *The history of human rights: From ancient times to the globalization era* (2nd ed.). Los Angeles: University of California Press.

Jianli, Y. (2009, July 27). *Attended harvard event: Witness—arts, humanities, and human rights.* Retrieved July 27, 2007, from http://www.initiativesforchina.org/2009/03/16/dr-yang-jianli-attended-harvard-event-witness%E2%80%94arts-humanities-and-human-rights/

Johnson, M. (2008). *The meaning of the body*. Chicago: University of Chicago Press.

Jost, T., & Major, B. (2002). *The psychology of legitimacy: Emerging perspectives on ideology, justice, and intergroup relations*. Cambridge, UK: Cambridge University Press.

Kac, E. (2006). *Signs of life: Bio art and beyond*. Boston: MIT Press.

Kagan, J. (2002). Empowerment and education: Civil rights, expert-advocates, and parent politics in Head Start, 1964–1980. *Teachers College Record, 104*(3), 516–562.

Kail, R., & Cavanaugh, J. (2004). *Human development: A life-span view* (3rd ed.). Belmont, CA: Wadsworth.

Kane, R. A., & Kane, R. L. (1998). *The heart of long term care*. New York: Oxford.

Kanigel, R. (1999). *The one best way: Frederick Winslow Taylor and the enigma of efficiency (Sloan Technology Series)*. New York, NY: Viking Press.

Kaul, N. (2008). *Imagining economics otherwise*. New York: Routledge.

Keenan, M., Henderson, M., Kerr, K. P., & Green, G. (2006). *Applied behaviour analysis and autism: Building a future together*. London: Jessica Kingsley.

Kelley, R. (2003). *Freedom dreams: The black radical imagination*. Boston: Beacon Press.

Kendrick, M. J., Jones, D. L., Bezanson, L., & Petty, R. E. (2006, January). *Independent living research utilization key components of systems change: First of three papers on unlocking the code of effective systems change*. Retrieved April 24, 2009, from http://communitylivingbc.ca/what_we_do/innovation/pdf/Key_Components_ of_Systems_Change.pdf+systems+change&cd=2&hl=en&ct=clnk&gl=us&client =firefox-a

Kertzer, D., & Arel, D. (2002). *Census and identity*. Cambridge: Cambridge University Press.

Kielhofner, G. (2002). *A model of human occupation: Theory and application* (3rd ed.). Baltimore: Lippincott, Williams, & Wilkins.

Kielhofner, G. (2004). *Conceptual foundation for occupational therapy* (3rd ed.). Philadelphia: F. A. Davis.

Kim, B. (2001). Social constructivism. In M. Orey (Ed.), *Emerging perspectives on learning, teaching, and technology*. Retrieved March 6, 2010, from http://www .coe.uga.edu/epltt/SocialConstructivism.htm

Kleege, G. (2005). Blindness and visual culture: An eyewitness account. *Journal of Visual Culture, 4*(2), 179–190.

Klein, N. (2003). *No logo: Taking aim at the brand bullies*. New York: HarperCollins.

Koch, T. (2006). Response to Peter Singer. *Journal of Disability Policy Studies, 17*(1), 57–58.

Kongstvedt, P. (2003). *Managed care* (2nd ed.). Sudbury, MA: Jones and Bartlett.

Kotler, P., Roberto, N., & Lee, N. (2002). *Social marketing: Improving the quality of life*. Thousand Oaks, CA: Sage.

Kukathas, C. (2003). *The liberal archipelago: A theory of diversity and freedom*. Oxford: Oxford University Press.

Kuppers, P. (2003). *Disability and contemporary performance: Bodies on the edge.* New York: Routledge.

Kymlicka, W. (2007). *Multicultural odysseys: Navigating the new international politics of diversity.* New York: Oxford University Press.

Lane, C. (2007). *Shyness: How normal behavior became a sickness.* New Haven, CT: Yale University Press.

Lee, K., Buse, K., & Fustukia, S. (2002). *Health policy in a globalising world.* Cambridge, UK: Cambridge University Press.

Lefebvre, H. (1991). *The production of space.* Oxford, UK: Blackwell.

Lefebvre, H. (2001). Comments on a new state form. *Antipode, 33*(5), 769–782. Published Online: Dec 16 2002. Retrieved March 8, 2010, from http://prxy4.ursus .maine.edu:2070/auth/EZProxy/test/authej.asp?url=http://prxy4.ursus.maine .edu:2059/login.aspx?direct=true&db=aph&AN=5854565&site=ehost-live

Lewis, H. (2000). *A question of values: Six ways we make the personal choices that shape our lives.* Crozet, VA: Axios Press.

Liamputtong, P. (2008). *Doing cross-cultural research: Ethical and methodological perspectives.* New York: Springer.

Licht, A., & O'Rourke, J. (2007). *Sound art: Beyond music, between categories.* New York: Rizzoli.

Linton, S. (1998). *Claiming disability: Knowledge and identity.* New York: New York University Press.

Linton, S. (2005). *My body politic.* Ann Arbor: University of Michigan Press.

Livingston, J. (2005). *Debility and the moral imagination in Botswana: Disability, chronic illness, and aging.* Bloomington: Indiana University Press.

Livingston, J. (2006). Insights from an African history of disability. *Radical History Review Issue 94* (Winter 2006) *94,* 111–126.

Livneh, H., & Parker, R. (2005). Psychological adaptation to disability. *Rehabilitation Counseling Bulletin, 49*(1), 17–28.

Longmore, P. K. (2003). *Why I burned my book and other essays on disability.* Philadelphia, PA: Temple University Press.

Longmore, P. K., & Umansky, L. (Eds.). (2001a). *The new disability history: American perspectives (history of disability).* New York: New York University Press.

Longmore, P. K., & Umansky, L. (2001b). Screening stereotypes. In A. Enns, & C. Smit, *Screening disability* (pp. 65–78). Lanham, MD: University Press of America.

Machan, T. (1998). *Generosity.* Washington DC: Cato Institute.

Mackelprang, R., & Salsgiver, R. (2009). *Disability: A diversity model approach in human service practice.* Chicago: Lyceum Press.

Margolin, V. (2002). *The politics of the artificial: Essays on design and design studies.* Chicago: Chicago University Press.

Martin, A., & Lynch, M. (2009). Counting things and people: The practices and politics of counting. *Social Problems, 56*(2), 243–266.

Martin, A., & Volkmar, F. (2007). *Lewis's child and adolescent psychiatry: A comprehensive textbook* (4th ed.). Philadelphia: Lippincott.

May, G., & Raske, M. (2004). *Ending disability discrimination: Strategies for social workers.* New York: Allyn & Bacon.

McClellan, J. E., & Dorn, H. (2006). *Science and technology in world history* (2nd ed.). Baltimore: Johns Hopkins University Press.

McClennen, S. (2007). The humanities, human rights, and the comparative imagination. *Comparative Literature and Culture 9.1, 9*(1), 1–13.

McClintock, A. (1995). *Imperial leather.* New York: Routledge.

McLuhan, M., & Fiore, Q. (2005). *The medium is the massage.* New York: Ginko Press.

McRuer, R. (2006). *Crip theory.* New York: New York University Press.

Mead, M. (2001). *Coming of age in Samoa: A psychological study of primitive youth for Western civilisation.* New York: HarperCollins.

Medina, J. (2000). *The genetic inferno: Inside the seven deadly sins.* Cambridge: Cambridge University Press.

Memodata Corporation. (2009). *Sensagent:* Culture. Retrieved March 8, 2010, from http://dictionary.sensagent.com/culture/en-en/

Merleau-Ponti, M. (2008). *The world of perception.* New York: Routledge.

Merriam-Webster. (2010a). Design. *Merriam-Webster Online.* Retrieved March 7, 2010, from http://www.merriam-webster.com/dictionary/design

Merriam-Webster. (2010b). Fashion. *Merriam-Webster Online.* Retrieved March 7, 2010, from http://www.merriam-webster.com/dictionary/fashion

Merriam-Webster. (2010c). Foundation. *Merriam-Webster Online.* Retrieved February 18, 2010, from http://www.merriam-webster.com/dictionary/foundations

Merriam-Webster. (2010d). Inclusion. *Merriam-Webster Online.* Retrieved February 18, 2010, from http://www.merriam-webster.com/dictionary/include

Metzler, I. (2006). *Disability in medieval Europe.* New York: Routledge.

Michaels, W. B. (2006). *The trouble with diversity: How we learned to love identity and ignore inequality.* New York: Metropolitan.

Michailakis, D. (2003). The systems theory concept of disability: One is not born a disabled person, one is observed to be one. *Disability & Society, 18*(2), 209–229.

Michalko, R. (2002). *The difference disability makes.* Philadelphia: Temple University Press.

Mink, G., Solinger, R., & Piven, F. C. (2003). *Welfare: A documentary history of America's policies and politics.* New York: New York University Press.

Minkler, M., & Fadem, P. (2002). "Successful aging": A disability perspective. *Journal of Disability Policy Studies 12*(4), 229–236.

Mitchell, D., & Snyder, S. (2000). *Narrative prosthesis.* Ann Arbor: University of Michigan Press.

Moller Okin, S., Al-Hibri, A. Y., Gilman, S. L., & Raz, J. (1999). *Is multiculturalism bad for women?* Princeton, NJ: Princeton University Press.

Morra, M., & Smith, J. (2005). *The prosthetic impulse.* Boston: MIT Press.

Munari, B., Eames, C., Eames, R., Guixe, M., & Bey, J. (2003). *Bright minds, beautiful ideas.* Amsterdam, NE: Bis.

Murphy, J. W., & Pardeck, J. T. (2005). *Disability issues for social workers and human services professionals in the 21st century.* London, UK: Haworth Press.

Murray, C. (1994). Quantifying the burden of disease: The technical basis for disability-adjusted life years. *Bulletin of the World Health Organization, 72,* 429–445.

Mussen, P. H. (Ed.). (1983). *Handbook of child psychology.* 4 vols. New York: Wiley.

Nakamura, K. (2006). *Deaf in Japan.* Ithaca, NY: Cornell University Press.

Nancy, J. L. (2008). *Corpus.* New York: Fordham University Press.

Nathan.com. (n.d.a). *An evolving glossary of experience Design: Design.* Retrieved March 8, 2010, from http://www.nathan.com/ed/glossary/

Nathan.com. (n.d.b). *An evolving glossary of experience design: Value.* Retrieved March 8, 2010, from http://www.nathan.com/ed/glossary

National Association of Social Workers. (2010). *Code of ethics of the National Association of Social Workers* (Revised 2008). Retrieved March 8, 2010, from http://www.socialworkers.org/pubs/code/code.asp

National Library of Medicine. (2009, February). *The visible human project.* Retrieved June 21, 2009, from http://www.nlm.nih.gov/research/visible/visible_human.html

Nauert, C. (2006). *Humanism and the culture of renaissance Europe.* Cambridge, UK: Cambridge University Press.

NCBuy. (2009). *Financial terms and acronyms glossary data lookup & reference services:* Value. Retrieved March 3, 2009, from http://www.ncbuy.com/credit/glossary.html?action=SEARCH&dictionary=lingo&data=business&term=value

Negrin, L. (2008). *Appearance and identity: Fashioning the body in postmodernity.* New York: Palgrave MacMillan.

New York Real Estate. (n.d.). *New York real estate glossary v:* Value. Retrieved March 8, 2010, from http://www.new-york-new-york-real-estate.com/v1.html

Nussbaum, M. C. (2001). *Women and human development.* New York: Cambridge University Press.

Nussbaum, M. C. (2006). *Frontiers of justice: Disability, nationality, species membership.* Cambridge, MA: Belknap.

O'Brien, R. (2004). Introduction. In R. O'Brien, *Voices from the edge* (pp. 3–25). New York: Oxford University Press.

OfficeFinder. (1995–2010). *Glossary of real estate terms:* Value. Retrieved March 8, 2010, from http://www.officefinder.com/gloss2.html

Oliver, M. (1997). *The politics of disablement.* New York: Palgrave MacMillan.

Oliver, M. (2009). *Understanding disability, from theory to practice* (2nd cd.). London: Macmillan.

Olsen, K. (2008, May 4). *Culture, chaos theory and choice.* Retrieved June 2, 2009, from http://thegimpparade.blogspot.com/2008/05/chaos-theory-and-choice.html

Olyan, S. M. (2008). *Disability in the Hebrew Bible: Interpreting mental and physical difference*s. New York: Cambridge University Press.

Onians, J. (2008). *Neuroarthistory.* New Haven, CT: Yale University Press.

Parillo, V. (2005). *Diversity in America* (2nd ed.). Thousand Oaks, CA: Pine Forge Press.

Parker, R., Schaller, J., & Hansmann, S. (2003). Catastrophe, chaos, and complexity models and psychosocial adjustment to disability. *Rehabilitation Counseling Bulletin, 46*(4), 234–241.

Parsons, T. (1937). *Structure of social action.* New York: McGraw-Hill.

Parsons, T. (1954). *Essays in sociological theory.* New York: Free Press.

Parsons, T. (1956). *Economy and society: A study in the integration of economic and social theory.* Glencoe, IL: Free Press.

Pasquinelli, M. (2005). *An assault on neurospace.* Retrieved March 8, 2010, from http://osdir.com/ml/culture.internet.nettime/2005-07/msg00031.html

Paul, A. (2001). Organizing Husserl: On the phenomenological foundations of Luhmann's systems theory. *Journal of Classical Sociology 1*(3), 371–394.

Pauwels, L. (2005). *Visual cultures of science: Rethinking representational practices in knowledge building and science communication.* Hanover, NH: Dartmouth University Press.

Pavlov, I. P. (1928–1941). *Lectures on conditioned reflexes.* 2 vols. New York: International.

Pavlov, I. P. (1957). *Experimental psychology, and other essays.* New York: Philosophical Library.

Perry, K. (2005). Theory of child cognitive development. *Child development guide,* Retrieved March 8, 2010, from http://www.child-development-guide.com/cognitive_child_development.html

Pfeiffer, D. (2002). Philosophical foundations of disability. *Disability Studies Quarterly, 22*(2), 3–22.

Phillips, S. (2008). *Out from under: Disability, history and things to remember—dressing.* Royal Ontario Museum. Retrieved March 9, 2010, from http://www.rom.on.ca/media/podcasts/out_from_under_audio.php?id=5

Piaget, J. (1955). *The child's construction of reality.* London: Routledge & Kegan Paul.

Piaget, J. (1959). *Language and thought of the child.* London: Routledge & Kegan Paul.

Piaget, J. (1962). *Play, dreams and imitation in childhood.* New York: Norton.

Piaget, J. (1970). *Structuralism.* New York: Harper & Row.

Piaget, J. (1985). *The equilibration of cognitive structures: The central problem of intellectual development.* Chicago: University of Chicago Press.

POETS at Kyoto Notre Dame University. (2009, March 3). *WordNet 3.0 vocabulary helper:* design. Retrieved March 8, 2010, from http://poets.notredame.ac.jp/cgi-bin/wn?cmd=wn&word=design

Powell, J. (1998). *Postmodernism for beginners.* New York: Writers and Readers Publishers.

Premier Exhibitions. (n.d.). *Bodies: The exhibition.* Retrieved June 2, 2009, from http://www.bodiestheexhibition.com/

Pullin, G. (2009). *Design meets disability.* Boston: MIT Press.

Quetelet. A. (1969). *A treatise on man and the development of his faculties. A facsimile reproduction of the English translation of 1842.* Gainesville, FL: Scholars' Facsimiles & Reprints.

Rampley, M. (2005). *Exploring visual culture: Definitions, concepts, contexts.* Edinburgh, Scotland: Edinburgh University Press.

Rawls, J. (1999). *A theory of justice* (Rev. ed.). Cambridge: Belnap Press.

Resnick, D. (1997). *Some definitions of key ethics concepts.* Retrieved June 3, 2009, from https://uwacadweb.uwyo.edu/fcsc4112/Ethics.htm

Riley, C. (2005). *Disability and the media: Prescriptions for change.* Lebanon, NH: University Press of New England.

Riley, C. (2006). *Disability and business.* Lebanon, NH: New England University Press.

Rimmer, J. (2009). Health promotion for persons with disabilities. Paper presented at the Annual Exposition and Meeting for the American Public Health Association, Philadelphia, PA, No. v 10.

Rimmer, J. H., Chen, M. D., McCubbin, J. A., Drum, C., & Peterson, J. (2010, March). Exercise intervention research on persons with disabilities: What we know and where we need to go. *American Journal of Physical Medicine and Rehabilitation, 89*(3), 249–263.

Rispler-Chiam, V. (2007). *Disability in Islamic law.* Dordrecht, the Netherlands: Springer.

Rivoli, P. (2009). *The travels of a t-shirt in the global economy: An economist examines the markets, power, and politics of world trade.* Hoboken, NJ: Wiley.

Robinson, H. (2007, October 10). *Dualism.* Retrieved May 2, 2009, from http://plato.stanford.edu/entries/dualism/

Rodas, J. M. (2009). On blindness. *Journal of Literary and Cultural Studies, 3*(2), 115–130.

Rodriguez, R. (2002). *Brown: The last discovery of America.* New York: Viking.

Roland, J. (n.d.). *Reflections on the revolution in France by Edmund Burke 1790.* Retrieved August 17, 2009, from http://www.constitution.org/eb/rev_fran.htm

Rose, M. (2003). *The staff of Oedipus.* Ann Arbor: University of Michigan Press.

Rosenfeld, D., & Faircloth, C. (2006). *Medicalized masculinities: The missing link?* Philadelphia: Temple University Press.

Rothbart, D. (2007). *Philosophical instruments.* Chicago: University of Chicago Press.

Rothman, J. (2002). *Social work practice across disability.* Saddle River, NJ: Allyn-Bacon

Rothschild, J. (2005). *The dream of the perfect child.* Bloomington: Indiana University Press.

Rowland, C., & Mariger, H. (2005). *Web accessibility system change: The myths, realities, and what we can learn from two large scale efforts.* Retrieved 2009, from http://www.ncdae.org/policy/systemchange.cfm

Rowland, J. L., White, G. W., & Wyatt, D. A. (2006). Analysis of an intervention to reduce or prevent secondary conditions among people with newly-diagnosed spinal cord injuries. *Journal of Clinical Psychology in Medical Settings, 13*(3), 261–269.

Running Subway Productions. (2008). *Bodies: The exhibition.* Retrieved June 21, 2009, from http://www.bodiesny.com/?gclid=CLyk04v-m5sCFRFWagod_B7Bpg

Salvendy, G. (2006). *Handbook of human factors and ergonomics.* Hoboken, NJ: Wiley.

Sandahl, C. A. (2005). *Bodies in commotion.* Ann Arbor: University of Michigan Press.

Sandor, J. (2003). *Society and genetic information*. Budapest, Hungary: Central European University Press.

Sardar, Z., & Abrams, I. (2009). *Introducing chaos: A graphic guide*. London, UK: Totem.

Scanlon, T. (2008). *Moral dimensions*. Cambridge: Belknap Press.

Schmidt, R. A., & Wrisberg, M. A. (2004). *Motor learning and performance*. Champaign, IL: Human Kinetics.

Schneider, D. J. (2004). *The psychology of stereotyping*. New York: Guilford.

Scotch, R. K. (2001). *From good will to civil rights: Transforming federal disability policy* (2nd ed.). Philadelphia: Temple University Press.

Scotch, R. K., & Schriner, K. F. (1997). Disability as human variation: Implications for policy. *The Annals of the American Academy of Political and Social Science, 549*, 148–160.

Scott, A. O. (2008, June 9). Metropolis now. *New York Times Magazine Section*.

Scully, J. L. (2008). *Disability bioethics*. Lanham, MD: Rowman & Littlefield.

Seidel, K. (2004–2009). *Neurodiversity weblog*. Retrieved July 4, 2009, from http://www.neurodiversity.com/main.html

Seifert, K. L., Hoffnung, R. J., & Hoffnung, M. (2000). *Lifespan development*. (2nd ed.). Boston: Houghton Mifflin.

Seldon, A., Bartholomew, J., & Myddelton, D. R. (2007). *Capitalism: A condensed version*. London: Institute of Economic Affairs.

Seligman, M., & Darling, R. B. (2007). *Ordinary families, special children*. New York: Guilford.

Sen, A. (2007). *Identity and violence: The illusion of destiny*. New York: Penguin.

Sen, A. (2009). *The idea of justice*. Cambridge, MA: Cambridge University Press.

Seymour, S. (2008). *Fashionable technology: The intersection of design, fashion, science, and technology*. New York: Springer.

Shakespeare, T. (2006). *Disability rights and wrongs*. New York: Routledge.

Shane, S., & Venkataraman, S. (2001). *Entrepreneurship as a field of research: A response to Zahra and Dess, Singh, and Erikson*. Retrieved from Academy of Management Web site: http://www.jstor.org/action/showPublisher?publisherCode=aom

Sherry, J. (2000). Place, technology and representation. *Journal of Consumer Research, 27* (4). Retrieved August 29, 2008 from http://www.journals.uchicago.edu/doi/abs/10.1086/314325

Shiao, J. L. (2004). *Identifying talent, institutionalizing diversity*. Durham, N.C.: Duke University Press.

Shilling, C. (2008). *Changing bodies: Habit, crisis, and creativity*. Thousand Oaks, CA: Sage.

Siebers, T. (2000). *The body aesthetic: From fine art to body modification*. Ann Arbor: University of Michigan Press.

Siebers, T. (2008). *Disability theory*. Ann Arbor: University of Michigan Press.

Silvers, A., Wasserman, D., & Mahowald, M. B. (1998). *Disability, difference, discrimination: Perspectives on justice in bioethics*. Lanham, MD: Rowman & Littlefield

Simmons, A. J. (2001). *Justification and legitimacy* (1st ed.). Cambridge: Cambridge University Press.

Skinner, B. F. (1977). The experimental analysis of operant behavior. In R. W. Rieber & K. Salzinger (Eds.), *The roots of American psychology: Historical influences and implications for the future. Annals of the New York Academy of Sciences (29)*1, 374–385. New York: New York Academy of Sciences.

Skymall, Inc. (2009). *Skymall.* Retrieved July 31, 2009, from http://www.skymall .com/shopping/homepage.htm?pnr=59K&cm_mmc=Google-_-Brand_Brand-_- skymall_Exact-_-2960250883l-l1000000000000000003301&cm_guid=1-_- 1000000000000000003301-_-2960250883

Smith, M., & Morra, J. (2007). *The prosthetic impulse: From a posthuman present to a biocultural future.* Cambridge: MIT Press.

Society for Disability Studies. (2009). *Disability studies quarterly editorial policies.* Retrieved Dec. 3, 2009, from http://www.dsq-sds.org/about/editorialPolicies

Standard Dictionary of the English Language. (2010). In *Encyclopædia Britannica.* Retrieved March 07, 2010, from Encyclopædia Britannica Online: http://www.britannica.com/EBchecked/topic/562942/A-Standard-Dictionary- of-the-English-Language

Stein, M. D. (2006). *Distributive justice and disability: Utilitarianism against egalitarianism.* New Haven, CT: Yale University Press.

Steinberg, S. (2001). *The ethnic myth* (3rd ed.). Boston, MA: Beacon Press.

Stiker, H.-J. (2000). A history of disability (W. Sayers, Trans.). *Corporealities: Discourses of disability.* Ann Arbor: University of Michigan Press.

Stocking, G. (1998). *After Tylor: British social anthropology, 1888–1951.* Madison, WI: University of Wisconsin Press.

Stone, D. A. (1986). *The disabled state.* Philadelphia: Temple University Press.

Stone, D. A. (2001). *Policy paradox: The art of political decision making* (Rev. ed.). New York: W. W. Norton.

Strasser, D., Falconer, J., Herrin, J., Bowen, S., Stevens, A., & Uomoto, J. (2005). Team functioning and patient outcomes in stroke rehabilitation. *Archives of Physical Medicine and Rehabilitation, 86*(3), 403–409.

Strzelecki, M. (2009). An uphill climb. *OT Practice, 14*(11), 7.

Sunami, C. (2009, July 4). *Reconstructivist art.* Retrieved July 4, 2009, from http://kitoba.com/pedia/Reconstructivist+Art.html

Takala, T. (2009). Gender, disability and personal identity. In K. K. Vehmas & T. Shakespeare, *Arguing about disability* (pp. 124–136). New York: Routledge.

Tashakkori, A., & Teddlie, C. (2002). *Handbook of mixed methods social and behavioral research.* Thousand Oaks, CA: Sage.

Tate Museum. (n.d.). *History of mass production.* Retrieved March 29, 2009, from http://www.infobritain.co.uk/Mass_Production.htm

Teghtsoonian, K. A., Moss, P., & Teghtsoonian, K. (2008). *Contesting illness: Processes and practices.* Toronto, Ontario, Canada: University of Toronto Press.

Ten Step. (2003–2005). *Portfolio Step*. Retrieved on September 2, 2009, from http://portfoliostep.com/390.1TerminologyDefinitions.htm

Thelen, E., & Smith, L. B. (2006). Dynamic systems theories. In W. Damon (Ed.). & R. M. Lerner (Vol. Ed.), *Handbook of child psychology, volume 1, theoretical models of human development* (6th ed., pp. 258–312). Hoboken, NJ: Wiley.

Thiher, A. (2002). *Revels in madness*. Ann Arbor: University of Michigan Press.

Thomas, R. M. (2001). *Recent theories of human development*. Thousand Oaks, CA: Sage.

Titchkosky, T. (2007). *Reading and writing disability differently*. Toronto, Ontario, Canada: University of Toronto Press.

Toddle Dredge. (2009, April 29). *Toddle dredge*. Retrieved May 5, 2009, from http://toddleddredge.com/the-usual-blather/western-beauty-standards

Tomahawk Products. (n.d.). Retrieved on December 2, 2009, from http://www .tomahawkproducts.com/terms/index.html

Tooby, J., & Cosmides, L. (2000). Toward mapping the evolved functional organization of mind and brain. In M. S. Gazzaniga (Ed.), *The new cognitive neurosciences* (2nd ed., pp. 1167–1178.). Cambridge: MIT Press.

Tregaskis, C. (2004). *Constructions of disability: Researching the interface between disabled and nondisabled people*. London: Routledge.

Triano, S. (2003). *Cultural expressions of pride*. Retrieved May 27, 2009, from http://www.disabledandproud.com/prideart.htm

Tufte, E. (1990). *Envisioning information*. Cheshire, CT: Graphics Press.

Tufte, E. (2006). *Beautiful evidence*. Cheshire, CT: Graphics Press.

Turmusani, M. (2003). *Disabled people and economic needs in the developing world*. Burlington, VT: Ashgate.

University of Pittsburgh Office of Child Development. (2005). *Children, youth, and family background*. Retrieved on March 3, 2010 from http://www.education.pitt .edu/ocd/family/backgrounders.aspx

US Census Bureau. (2005, April 25). *Housing vacancies and homeownership (CPS/HVS)*. Retrieved March 2, 2010 from http://www.census.gov/hhes/www/ housing/hvs/qtr105/q105def.html

US Department of Education, Office of Special Education and Rehabilitative Services, National Institute on Disability and Rehabilitation Research. (2000). *Long-range plan 1999–2003, Executive summary*. Washington, DC: GPO, 2000. Retrieved March 8, 2010 from http://www2.ed.gov/rschstat/ research/pubs/nidrr-lrp-99-03-exec-summ.pdf

US Department of Education, Office of Special Education and Rehabilitative Services, National Institute on Disability and Rehabilitation Research. (2007). *NIDRR long-range plan for fiscal years 2005–09: Executive summary*. United States Department of Education, Office of Special Education and Rehabilitative Services, National Institute on Disability and Rehabilitation Research. Washington, DC: United States Department of Education.

Ustun, T. B., Catterji, S., Rehm, J., Shekhar, S., Bickenbach, J. E., Trotter, R. T., & Room, R. (2002). *Disability and culture: Universalism and diversity.* Seattle, WA: Hogrefe & Huber.

Valadez, J. (2001). *Deliberative democracy, political legitimacy, and self-determination in multicultural societies.* Boulder, CO: Westview Press.

Vincenti, V. (2002). *Some definitions of key ethics concepts.* Retrieved on March 3, 2010, from University of Wyoming Web site: http://uwacadweb.uwyo.edu/fcsc4112/Ethics.htm

Volkmar F. (Ed.) (2007). *Autism and pervasive developmental disorders.* (2nd ed.). New York: Cambridge University Press.

Von Bertalanffy, L. (1969). *General systems theory: Foundations, development, applications* (Rev. ed.). New York: G. Braziller.

Von Bertalanffy. (1976). *General system theory: Foundations, development, applications.* New York, NY: George Braziller.

Wagner, D. (2005). *The poorhouse.* Lanham, MD: Rowman & Littlefield.

Walker, J. (2008, June 8). The silence generation: Quiet comfort headphones. *New York Times Magazine.* Retrieved March 8, 2010 from http://www.nytimes.com/2008/06/08/magazine/08wwln-consumed-t.html

Ware, L. (2003). Locating the field of humanities-based disability studies. In J. Allan, *Inclusion, participation, and democracy* (pp. 118–120). New York: Springer.

Warschauer, M. (2004). *Technology and social inclusion.* Cambridge: MIT Press.

Watson, J. B. (Au.), & Kimble, G. (Intro.). (1997). *Behaviorism* (New ed.). Piscataway: Rutgers–The State University of New Jersey, Transaction Press.

Watson, R., & Schwartz, L. (2004). *Transforming through occupation: Human occupation in context.* Hoboken, NJ: Wiley.

Weber, M. (1958). *The protestant ethic and the spirit of capitalism.* New York: Scribner.

Webster's Revised Unabridged Dictionary of the English Language (N. Porter, Ed.). (1913). *Diversity.* Springfield, MA: G. & C. Merriam.

Weitz, R. (2000). *The sociology of health, illness, and health care: A critical approach* (2nd ed.). Belmont, CA: Wadsworth.

Weller, M., & Wolff, S. (2005). *Autonomy, self-governance and conflict resolution.* New York: Routledge.

WETA. LDOnline. (2008). Learning Disabilities Association of America. (1999). *Early identification: Motor skills milestones.* Retrieved March 7, 2010, from http://www.ldonline.org/article/6045

Wikipedia. (2010a). *Culture.* Retrieved on March 7, 2010, from http://en.wikipedia.org/wiki/Culture

Wikipedia. (2010b). *Value (Semiotics).* Retrieved on January 28, 2010, from http://en.wikipedia.org/wiki/Value_%28semiotics%29

Wilson, J. C., & Lewiecki-Wilson, C. (Eds.). (1999). *Embodied rhetorics: Disability language and culture.* Carbondale, IL: SUI Press.

Wingate. (n.d.). *Dennis Ashbaugh*. Retrieved March 17, 2010, from http://www .wingatestudio.com/Ashbaugh.html

Winzer, M. (1993). *The history of special education*. Washington, DC: Gallaudet University Press.

Wiseman, B. (2000). *Introducing Levi-Strauss and structural anthropology*. Lanham, MD: Totem Books USA.

Wolfensberger, W. (1972). *The principle of normalization in human services*. Toronto, Ontario, Canada: National Institute on Mental Retardation.

Wolfensberger, W. (1980). The definition of normalization: Update, problems, disagreements, and misunderstandings. In R. J. Flynn, & K. E. Nitsch (Eds.), *Normalization, social integration. and community services* (pp.71–115). Baltimore, MD: University Park Press.

Wolfensberger, W. (1983). Social role valorization: A proposed new term for the principle of normalization. *Mental Retardation, 21*(6), 234–239.

Wolfensberger, W. (1984). A reconceptualization of normalization as social role valorization. *Mental Retardation* (Canada), *34*(7), 22–26.

Wolfensberger, W. (1985). An overview of social role valorization and some reflections on elderly mentally retarded persons. In M. Janiki & H. Wisniewski, *Aging and developmental disabilities: Issues and approaches* (pp. 61–76). Baltimore, MD: Paul Brookes.

Wolfensberger, W., & Thomas, S. (2007). *Passing a tool for analyzing service quality according to social role valorization criteria*. Syracuse, NY: Training Institute for Human Service Planning.

Wolfram, S. (2002, May 14). *A new kind of science*. Champaign, IL: Wolfram Media, Inc.

World Health Organization. (2010). *International classification of functioning, disability and health* (ICF). Retrieved March 9, 2010, from http://www.who .int/classifications/icf/en/

World Images. (n.d.). *Art glossary*. Retrieved March 2, 2010, from http://world images.com/ArtGlossary.php

Wright, D. (2001). *Mental disability in Victorian England: The Earlswood Asylum 1847–1901*. Oxford, UK: Oxford University Press.

Yong, A. (2007). *Theology and Down syndrome*. Waco, TX: Baylor University Press.

Yuen, F. K. O., Cohen, C. B., & Tower, K. (2007). *Disability and social work education: Practice and policy issues*. New York: Routledge.

Yzerbyt, V. Y., & Rogier, A. (2001). Blame it on the group. In J. Jost & B. Major, *Psychology of legitimacy* (pp. 133–134). New York: Cambridge University Press.

Zelditch, M. (2001). Theories of legitimacy. In J. Jost & B. Major, *Psychology of legitimacy* (pp. 33–53). New York: Cambridge University Press.

Index

Able-embodied explanations, 62
Abortion, selective, 82–83
"Access symbols" for public venues, 38 (figure)
Acquired disability, as legal term, 67
Activity, in Explanatory Legitimacy Theory, 45
Advancement of Learning, Divine and Human, The (Bacon), 18, 21 (table)
African American aid/support systems, 33
Aging, 74–75, 76
Albrecht, G. L., 172–173
AlphaVille (film), 132, 162
American Association on Intellectual and Developmental Disability, 150–151, 158
American Public Health Association, Disability Section, 110, 176–177
Americans with Disabilities Act, 132, 133, 136, 182
Anthropology, 49–50
Anthropometrics, 136
Apgar scale, 72
Appearance, 45, 52
Applied behavioral analysis, 58, 88, 154
Architectural design, 89
Architectural standards, 130–131, 131 (figure), 186
Architecture, 186–187
Aristotle, 12, 13 (table), 105
Armstrong, D., 92
Art, 122, 125, 166–168

Arts, performing, 162–163
As Good As It Gets (film), 132
Ashbaugh, Dennis, 71–72
Assistive technology, 89, 134
Astos, 202, 213, 213 (figure)
Attire, 129–130
Atypical body as estranged, 35–36
    See also Typical/atypical axis
Authority, professional, 26–29, 86–87
Autism, 57, 154
Autism Spectrum Disorders, 76

Bacon, Francis, 18, 21 (table)
Badinter, E., 134
"Bake sale to commodity" phenomenon, 173
Baldness, 12
Bandura, A., 58
Baudrillard, J., 118
Beauty, 80–81
Beggars, 10, 16–17
Behavioral analysis, applied, 58, 88, 154
Behavioral and learning theory, 85–88
    See also Exterior environment theories
Behaviorism, 58, 85–88
Behavior modification, 87–88
Bell-shaped curve. *See* Normal curve
Berube, M., 112
Bible, Hebrew, 14
Biology, 83
Biopsychosocial humans, 107
Blade Runner (film), 132, 162
Blindness, in film, 132

Blogs, 105
Bodies, The Exhibition, 123
Bodies and backgrounds diversity.
    See Diversity patina
Bodily disadvantage, 98
Body:
    atypical, as estranged, 35–36
    defined, 7, 32, 80
    euphemistic disabled, 37–38,
        38 (figure)
    included, as excluded, 37
    linguistic, 39–40
    as measured, 80–83
    medicalizing, 81
    normal, emergence of concept of, 92
    performing, 40
    political, 36–37
    prescriptive, 36
    See also Reconstituting the
        fragmented body
Body embellishments, 108, 109–110
Body objects, 98
Botswana, 19
Braddock, D. L., 16
Brain developmental disorder causes
    of autism, 154
Branding:
    contemporary and emerging
        explanations, 126–128,
        128–135, 129 (figure),
        130 (figure), 131 (figure),
        132 (figure)
    cultural, 127
    exterior categorical theories, 101
    humanities responses, legitimate,
        167–168
Brandscape, 128
Bronfenbrenner, U., 107, 110, 111
Brown, S., 100
Buddhism, 15, 16
Business, 187, 213, 213 (figure)

Caregiving, 30, 108
Carmen, I. H., 124
Categorical legitimacy, 154–157
Categorical theories:
    Explanatory Legitimacy Theory,
        descriptive element of, 50–51

Explanatory Legitimacy Theory,
    explanation in, 59–60
    exterior, 91, 98–101
    heuristics of, 92, 92 (table)
    interior, 91, 96–98
    See also Categorical legitimacy;
        Diversity
Catholic Church, 17 (table)
Central tendency measures, 22–23
Chair design, 167
Chaos theory, 51, 60, 106, 112
    See also Systems theories
Chemical sensitivity, multiple, 64–65
Christianity, 14, 16
Civil rights movements, 59–60
Classical systems theories, 51
Closed systems, 60, 106
    See also Systems theories
Cognition, role of technology in
    measuring, 82
Cognitive development theory, 48, 56,
    70–71
Communications, electronic, 28–29
Communities, legitimate, 211–213
Community, defined, 211
Community integration, as term, 37
Community legitimacy model,
    211–214, 213 (figure)
    human rights and, 204–205, 210
    social justice and, 210–211
Community living sites, 37
Complex systems, 112–114
    See also Systems theories
Compliance juncture, 193 (figure)
Computers, 29, 109, 119
Confucianism, early, 15
Congenital genetic disability, 123
Consistency, internal, 212
Constructed explanations, 41, 62,
    63–65, 78, 98–101
Contemporary and emerging
    legitimacy, 158–159, 159 (table)
Contemporary and emerging theories:
    branding, 126–128
    design definitions, 125–126,
        126 (figure)
    disability as disjuncture, 135–138,
        138 (figure)

diversity depth, 116–117
Explanatory Legitimacy Theory,
    descriptive element of,
    51–52
Explanatory Legitimacy Theory,
    explanation in, 61
heuristics of, 116–117, 117 (table)
observables in, 53 (table)
postmodernism, 117–120
product design and branding,
    128–135, 129 (figure),
    130 (figure), 131 (figure),
    132 (figure)
reportables in, 53 (table)
social constructivism, 120–122
trends affecting, 115–116
values in, 158, 159 (table)
visual culture, 122–124
See also Postmodernism;
    Post-postmodernism
Contextual factors:
    ancient Greeces, 13 (table)
    Enlightenment era, 21 (table)
    Middle Ages, 17 (table)
    20th century, 26–40
    Victorian era, 24 (table)
Cultural branding, 127
Culturally-friendly atmosphere, 156
Cultural productions,
    high-brow, 100
Cultural theories, 49–50
Culture, defined, 49, 99
Cybernetics, 106

Dalai Lama, 119
DALYs. See Disability-adjusted life
    years
Data, sense, 46–47
da Vinci, Leonardo, 18, 89
    See also Vitruvian Man
Davis, L. J., 137
Deinstitutionalization, 31
DePoy, E., 36, 120, 132–133
Description:
    physical, 71–72, 73–74 (table),
        74–75
    verifiable, in interior categorical
        theory, 96

Descriptive element of Explanatory
    Legitimacy Theory:
    categorical theories, 50–51
    contemporary and emerging
        theories, 51–52, 53 (table)
    cultural theories, 49–50
    elements of, 45
    environmental theories, 48–49
    foundations of, 46
    longitudinal theory, 47–48
    observable-reportable axis, 46–47
    overview, 5, 6
    systems theories, 51
    See also Explanatory Legitimacy
        Theory
Design:
    architectural, 89
    defined, 125–126, 126 (figure), 194
    exterior categorical theories
        and, 101
    humanities responses, legitimate,
        166–168
    scientization of, 136–137
    universal, 166–167, 186–187
Developmental disability, as legal
    term, 67
Developmental milestones,
    72, 73–74 (table)
Developmental theories. See
    Longitudinal theories
Deviance, defined, 48
DIS (prefix), 11–12
DIS (ruler of Hades), 10
Disability:
    acquired, 67
    congenital genetic, 123
    developmental, 67
    impairment versus, 35
    intellectual, 149–151, 185
    as oppression, 99–100
    political construction of, 101
    as term, 10–11, 24
    World Health Organization
        definition of, 81
Disability-adjusted life years (DALYs),
    175–176
Disability culture explanations, 98–100
Disability-embedded policy, 113

Disability-exclusive policy, 113
Disability identity, 36, 87, 97–98, 156
Disability-implicit policy, 113
Disability industry, 27, 31, 132–133,
    172–173
Disability language, 163
Disability park, 109, 132–133, 157–158
Disability products, 172–173
Disabled-embodied explanations, 62
Disabled Sports USA, 214
Disabling forces, in constructed
    explanations, 63
Disabling microsystems, 108
Discrimination, 35–36
Disjuncture, defined, 192
Disjuncture theory:
    disability and, 194, 195 (figure),
        196, 197 (figure), 198
    health information, web-based, and,
        198, 199 (figure), 200 (figure)
        201–202, 201 (figure)
    illustration of, 193 (figure)
    intellectual foundation of, 136–138,
        138 (figure)
    overview, 192
    principles for healing disjuncture,
        202 (table)
Distributive justice, 113, 164–165
Diversity, 32–34, 63, 93
    See also Categorical theories
Diversity depth:
    contemporary and emerging
        explanations and, 116–117
    lack of, 33–34
    membership as principle of, 95
    postmodernism and, 119
    symmetry as principle of, 95
Diversity patina:
    categorical legitimacy and, 154–155
    cultural theories and, 50
    described, 5
    Explanatory Legitimacy Theory,
        descriptive element of, 50–51
    history of, 33–34
    oppression and, 93–94
Diversity patina/diversity depth axis:
    categorical theories and, 50–51, 59–60
    described, 5
    longitudinal theories and, 56

Down syndrome, 34
Dramaturgy, 87
Dualism, 80

Economic context:
    ancient Greeces, 13 (table)
    Enlightenment era, 19, 20,
        21 (table)
    Middle Ages, 16–17, 17 (table)
    Victorian era, 24 (table)
Economic exterior explanations, 101
Economics of disability legitimacy,
    172–173
Education, 35–36, 180–183
Egypt, early, 15
Electronic communications/media,
    28–29
Embellishments, body, 108, 109–110
Embodied, defined, 194, 196
Embodied systems theories, 61
Embodiment, slivers of.
    See Reconstituting the
    fragmented body
Emergent and Contemporary Theory.
    See Contemporary and emerging
    theories
Employment discrimination, 36
End of life issues, 83
Engineering, 186–187
England. See United Kingdom
Enlightenment era, 18–20,
    21 (table), 77
Environment, defined, 77, 152, 196
Environmental legitimacy, 152–154,
    153 (table)
Environmental simulacra, 133
Environmental theories:
    Explanatory Legitimacy Theory,
        descriptive element of, 48–49
    Explanatory Legitimacy Theory,
        explanation element of, 57–59
    heuristics of, 78 (table)
    longitudinal theories and, 75
    values in, 152–153, 153 (table)
    See also Environmental legitimacy;
        Exterior environment theories;
        Interior environment theories
Environments, inadequate, 108–109
Ergonomics, 136

Erikson, Erik, 69, 70
Essentialist diversity patina
    thinking, 51
Ethics, 143, 164–165
Ethnography, 49–50, 99
Euphemistic disabled body, 37–38,
    38 (figure)
Europe, Western:
    Enlightenment era, 18–20,
        21 (table)
    Middle Ages, 15–17, 17 (table)
Exclusion, as term, 95
Exosystems, 107 (table), 110
    See also Systems theories
Experience, in Explanatory Legitimacy
    Theory, 45
Experts, 26–29, 86–87
Explanations element of Explanatory
    Legitimacy Theory:
    categorical theories, 59–60
    constructed explanations, 62, 63–65
    contemporary and emerging
        explanations, 61
    described, 5–6, 6–7
    environmental explanations, 57–59
    longitudinal theories, 55–57
    medical-diagnostic explanations,
        61–63
    systems theories, 60–61
Explanatory Legitimacy Theory, 3–7
    about, 4
    elements of, 5–7
    legitimacy theory and, 3
    See also Descriptive element of
        Explanatory Legitimacy
        Theory; Explanations element
        of Explanatory Legitimacy
        Theory
Exterior categorical theory,
    91, 98–101
    See also Categorical theories
Exterior environment theories:
    behavioral and learning theory,
        85–88
    described, 78
    Explanatory Legitimacy Theory,
        descriptive element of, 49
    Explanatory Legitimacy Theory,
        explanation element of, 58–59

heuristics of, 85 (table)
legitimacy in, 154
longitudinal legitimacy and,
    148–149
longitudinal theories and, 75
social models, 90
social role theory and, 58–59,
    86–87
technology and, 88
usable/nonusable environmental
    theories, 88–89
See also Environmental theories

Faith healing, 16
Family systems, 108
Fashion, 130
Fashionable technology, 129, 134
Feminist research, 50
Film analysis, 131–132, 162
Finding Nemo (film), 132, 162
Fine motor development milestones,
    73–74 (table)
Flattening the curve, 94–95,
    94 (figure)
    See also Normal curve
Forrest Gump (film), 132
Foundations, defined, 3
Fragmented body. See Reconstituting
    the fragmented body
Francis, of Assisi, Saint, 16
Freud, Sigmund, 47–48, 69–70
Fries, K., 111, 135
Full juncture, 34, 193 (figure)
Function:
    health versus, 176
    in rehabilitation professions,
        178–179
Functional adequacy, in interior
    categorical theory, 96–97

Garland-Thomson, R. M.,
    170–171
Gender, and competitive sports, 50
Gender equality, 134
Gender role in caregiving, 30
Genetics, 71–72, 82, 123, 124
Geographic/natural context:
    ancient Greeces, 13 (table)
    Enlightenment era, 21 (table)

Middle Ages, 17 (table)
Victorian era, 24 (table)
Gesell, Arnold, 72
Gilson, S. F., 36, 120, 132–133
Goffman, E., 87
Gould, S. J., 50
Greece, Ancient, 11–13, 13 (table),
    80, 82
Gross motor development milestones,
    73–74 (table)

Haller, B., 132
Handicap, as term, 10
Headphones, 129
Head Start, 108
Health information, web-based,
    198, 199 (figure), 200 (figure)
    201–202, 201 (figure)
Health professions, development of,
    27–28
    See also specific professions
Health versus function, 176
Hearing impairment, 37–38,
    38 (figure)
Hebrew Bible, 14
Hephaestus (Greek god of fire), 12
Herek, G. M., 155
High-brow cultural productions, 100
High-brow products, 129
Higher education, 182
Hippocrates, 12–13, 13 (table)
Holmes, M. S., 20–21
Holt, D., 127, 167–168
Homosexuality, 155
Hospitals, faith-based, 16
Human factors, 136–137, 192–194
Humanities legitimacy, 161–168
    art and design, 166–168
    ethics, 164–165
    humanities definition, 161–162
Human rights:
    community legitimacy model,
        204–205, 210
    global policy, 133–134, 205,
        206–210 (figure)
    humanities responses, legitimate, 163
Human rights legitimacy, 171–172
Human rights theories, 63

Icon, disability, 131, 131 (figure),
    132 (figure), 186
Identity, 36, 87, 97–98, 156
Immigrants, 21–22, 33, 50
Impairment, 35, 96
Impairment/disability binary, 35
Included body as excluded, 37
Inclusion, as term, 37, 40, 95
Independence, 121
Industrialization, 23, 29
Infant deformity, 12, 82
Institutions:
    Enlightenment era, 20
    20th and 21st centuries,
        30, 31, 37
    Victorian era, 21, 22
Intellectual context:
    ancient Greeces, 13 (table)
    Enlightenment era, 21 (table)
    Middle Ages, 17 (table)
    Victorian era, 24 (table)
Intellectual disability, 149–151, 185
Intelligence, 12, 50
Intelligence tests, 149, 150, 185
Interaction, identity as function of, 87
Interactional theories, 75–76
Interior categorical theory, 91, 96–98
    See also Categorical theories
Interior environment theories:
    body as measured, 80–83
    criticism of, 84–85
    described, 78
    Explanatory Legitimacy Theory,
        descriptive element of, 48–49
    Explanatory Legitimacy Theory,
        explanation element of, 57–58
    heuristics of, 79, 79 (table)
    legitimacy in, 153, 154
    longitudinal legitimacy and,
        148–149
    longitudinal theories and, 75, 76
    medical-diagnostic explanations
        and, 78, 84
    technology and, 82–83, 83–84
    theoretical underpinnings of, 83
    See also Environmental theories;
        Medical-diagnostic
        explanations

International Classification of
    Functioning, 52
International Classification of
    Functioning, Disability and
    Health, 81
International Classification of
    Functioning and Disability, 52
Interpreters, 156
Intersubjectivity, 121
IQ tests, 149, 150, 185
Ishay, M., 204
Islam, 14, 16

Japan, 15, 36
Jewish aid/support systems, 33
Johnson, Harriet McBryde, 164, 165
Judaism, early, 14–15
Judgment, as legitimacy subelement, 6
Juncture:
    defined, 192
    full, 34, 193 (figure)
    illustration of, 193 (figure),
        198 (figure)
    moderate/compliance, 193 (figure)
    See also Disjuncture theory
Justice:
    distributive, 113, 164–165
    social, 210–211

Kelley, Robin, 203
Knowledge:
    descriptors in professional fields, 52
    longitudinal legitimacy and, 149
    postmodernist view of, 119–120
    social constructivist view of,
        121–122
Kymlicka, W., 133–134

Language:
    disability, 163
    person-first, 38–39
Learning and behavioral theory, 85–88
    See also Exterior environment
        theories
Le Corbusier, 89, 136, 186
Leech child (metaphoric story), 15
Legislation, 93, 180–181, 182
    See also specific laws

Legitimacy:
    categorical, 154–157
    contemporary and emerging,
        158–159, 159 (table)
    environmental, 152–154, 153 (table)
    in Explanatory Legitimacy Theory,
        6, 7
    from within, 146
    from without, 145, 146
    humanities, 161–168
    longitudinal, 147–152, 148 (table)
    medical, 177–178
    political theory and human rights,
        171–172
    professional, 175–187
    quasi-, 97
    responses in, 145
    social science, 169–174
    sociological, 170–171
    systems, 157–158, 157 (table)
    values in, 141–142,
        142–143 (table), 143–144
Legitimacy theory, 3–4
    See also Explanatory Legitimacy
        Theory
Legitimate communities, 211–213
Life stage theories. See Longitudinal
    theories
Linguistic body, 39–40
Logic, 212
Longitudinal clues, in interior
    categorical theory, 96
Longitudinal-exterior environment
    theories, 75
Longitudinal-interactional
    explanations, 75–76
Longitudinal-interior environment
    explanations, 75, 76
Longitudinal legitimacy, 147–152,
    148 (table)
Longitudinal theories:
    behavior and age-appropriate tasks,
        69, 70
    cognitive development, 70–71
    Explanatory Legitimacy Theory,
        descriptive element of, 47–48
    Explanatory Legitimacy Theory,
        explanation in, 55–57

exterior environment theories and, 75
heuristics of, 68 (table)
interactional theories and, 75–76
interior environment explanations and, 75, 76
introduction, 67
nomothetic inquiry and, 69
physical description, 71–72, 73–74 (table), 74–75
psychosexual development, 69–70
values in, 147–148, 148 (table), 149
See also Longitudinal legitimacy
Longmore, P., 170–171
Low vision, 37–38, 38 (figure)

Macrosystems, 107 (table), 110–111, 112
See also Systems theories
"Madness," 17, 18, 20, 21 (table)
Mainstreaming, as term, 37
Managed care, 28
Market economy, 29–32
Marketing, 88, 101
Mass production, 23, 31–32
Measured, body as, 80–83
Measures of central tendency, 22–23
Media, electronic, 28–29
Medical-diagnostic explanations:
body as measured, 80–83
environmental explanations and, 57
eschewing of, 40–41
Explanatory Legitimacy Theory, explanation element of, 61–63
interior categorical theory and, 96–97
interior environment theories and, 78, 84
longitudinal theories and, 56–57, 67
psychology professions and, 184–185
rehabilitation professions and, 179
See also Interior environment theories; Longitudinal theories
Medicalization, 81, 178
Medical legitimacy, 177–178
Medicine, descriptors in, 52
Medina, J., 84

Membership, as principle of diversity depth, 95
Mental illness, neurological basis of, 83–84
Mental retardation, as term, 149, 158
Mesosystems, 107 (table), 110
See also Systems theories
Metzler, I., 15, 16
Michaels, Benn, 172
Micro-observables, 97
Microsystems, 107–110, 107 (table)
See also Systems theories
Middle Ages, 15–17, 17 (table)
Milestone theories, 72, 73–74 (table)
Million Dollar Baby (film), 132
Mismeasure of Man, The (Gould), 50
Moderate juncture, 193 (figure)
Monists, 51–52
Moral man, 69
Motor development milestones, 73–74 (table)
Multicultural theories, 59–60
Multiple chemical sensitivity, 64–65

National Institute on Disability and Rehabilitation Research (U.S.), 137
National Institutes of Health (U.S.), 58
National Library of Medicine (U.S.), 124
Neonates, deformed, 12, 82
Neurodiversity, 65, 135
Neuro-imaging, 123–124
Neurology, 83–84, 185
News media portrayals, 132
Nomothetic inquiry, 56–57, 69
Nondiscrimination, as term, 40
Normal:
as term in longitudinal theories, 69
in visual culture, 124
Normal body, emergence of concept of, 92
Normal curve, 22–23, 40, 69, 72, 80–81
See also Flattening the curve
Normalization (Wolfensberger), 36
Normalization theory, 59

"Not normal":
  diversity as euphemism for, 93
  as term in longitudinal theories, 69
  in visual culture, 124
Nursing, 52
Nursing homes, 30
Nussbaum, M. C., 171–172, 205

Objects, body, 98
Observable/reportable axis, 5, 46–47
  See also Reportables
Observables, 5, 46–47, 53 (table),
  96–97
Occupational therapy, 52, 179
  See also Rehabilitation professions
Olsen, K., 105
Open systems, 60, 64, 106
Oppression, 93–94, 99–100
Oregon, physician-assisted suicide
  in, 83

Parish, S. L., 16
Parking symbols, 131, 131 (figure)
Parsons, Talcott, 59, 86–87, 105
Participation, as term, 40
Patina, defined, 5
  See also Diversity patina
Pavlov, I. P., 58
Performing arts, 162–163
Performing body, 40
Person-first language, 38–39
Phase theories. See Longitudinal
  theories
Phillips, S., 129–130
Physical microenvironments, 108–109
Physical spaces, meaning of, 109, 128
Physical therapy, 179, 180
  See also Rehabilitation professions
Physicians, 26–27
Physiology, 83
Piaget, J., 48, 56, 70–71
Pluralism, 212, 213
Policy analysis, 111–113, 133–134
Political body, 36–37
Political construction of disability, 101
Political context:
  ancient Greeces, 13 (table)
  Enlightenment era, 21 (table)

Middle Ages, 17 (table)
  Victorian era, 24 (table)
Politically correct body as
  subcategory, 38–39
Political theory and human rights
  legitimacy, 171–172
Poorhouses, 20, 22
  See also Poverty
Poor Laws (England), 19, 21 (table)
Positivism, 93
Postmodernism, 77, 93, 117–120
  See also Contemporary and
  emerging theories
Postpositivism, 93
Post-postmodernism:
  contemporary and emerging
  explanations, 124–125
  definitions of environment, 77
  influence on disability
  explanations, 65
  legitimate humanities responses
  and, 163
  longitudinal-interactional theories
  and, 75–76
  postmodernism and, 120
  product design and branding
  and, 135
  See also Contemporary and
  emerging theories
Poverty:
  Enlightenment era, 19, 20
  Middle Ages, 16–17
  20th century, 29–30
  Victorian era, 21–22, 23
  See also Poorhouses
Powell, J., 118–119
Pragmatism, 120
Predeterministic theories. See
  Longitudinal theories
Prenatal practices, 82–83, 113
Prescriptive body, 36
Present Difference (conference), 100
Problem mapping:
  of disability, 194, 195 (figure),
  196, 197 (figure)
  of health information, web-based,
  199 (figure), 200 (figure)
  overview, 194

Product design:
  contemporary and emerging
    explanations, 128–135,
    129 (figure), 130 (figure),
    131 (figure), 132 (figure)
  professional legitimacy in, 186–187
  sports innovations, 167
Products:
  disability, 172–173
  high-brow, 129
Professional authority, 26–29, 86–87
Professional fields, and problem
    mapping, 196, 197 (figure)
Professional legitimacy, 175–187
  architecture and engineering,
    186–187
  business, 187
  education, 180–183
  medicine, 177–178
  psychology, 184–185
  public health, 175–177
  rehabilitation professions, 178–180
  social work, 183–184
Prostheses, racing, 130, 131 (figure)
Psychology, 83, 86, 184–185
Psychosexual theory, 47–48, 69–70
Public health, 175–177
Public venues, "access symbols" for,
    38 (figure)
Pullin, G., 167, 168

Quality of life, 121, 176
Quasi-legitimacy, 97
Queer theories, 113–114
Quetelet, A., 22–23, 24 (table), 69

Rampley, M., 130
Rational model of policy analysis,
    111–112
Rawls, J., 211
"Reality," social constructivist view
    of, 120
Reconstituting the fragmented body,
    34–40
  atypical body as estranged, 35–36
  euphemistic disabled body, 37–38,
    38 (figure)
  impairment/disability binary, 35
  included body as excluded, 37

linguistic body, 39–40
performing body, 40
political body, 36–37
politically correct body as
    subcategory, 38–39
prescriptive body, 36
Reconstructivist art, 125
Rehabilitation professions,
    178–180
Religious context:
  ancient Greeces, 13 (table)
  Enlightenment era, 19–20,
    21 (table)
  Middle Ages, 17 (table)
  Victorian era, 24 (table)
Renaissance, 18
Renegade Wheelchairs, 214
Reportables, 5, 47, 53 (table)
  See also Observable/reportable
    axis
Resnick, D., 143
Response, as legitimacy subelement, 6
Riley, C., 173
Rimmer, J. H., 176–177
Rispler-Chiam, V., 14, 16
Rose, M., 10–11, 12
Rothschild, J., 82

Salvendy, G., 136
Scent of a Woman (film), 132
Schneider, D. J., 51
Science, 26–29, 118, 122
Scientization of design, 136–137
Scott, A. O., 131–132
Scully, J. L., 165
Sen, A., 171–172
Sense data, 46–47
Severity, in interior categorical
    theory, 96
Shaping, 88
Shintoism, 15
Shower seats, 128, 129 (figure)
Shrek (film), 132, 162
Shyness, 155
Sick role concept, 86–87
Sightist assertions, 122
Simulacra, 118, 131, 133
Singer, Peter, 164–165
Skinner, B. F., 58

Slivers of embodiment. *See*
    Reconstituting the fragmented
    body
Social action, 105
Social constructivism, 120–122
Social contract theory, 172
Social exchange theory, 59
Social justice, 210–211
Social marketing, 88
Social models, 90, 101, 105,
    120, 170
    See also Exterior environment
        theories
Social role theory, 58–59,
    86–87
Social role valorization, 36, 87
Social science legitimacy,
    169–174
    economics of disability legitimacy,
        172–173
    political theory and human rights
        legitimacy, 171–172
    social science definition, 169
    sociological legitimacy, 170–171
Social Security policy, 111
Social work, 183–184
Society for Disability Studies, 110,
    170–171
Sociological legitimacy, 170–171
Spaces, meaning of, 109, 128
"Special," as euphemism for
    excludable, 205
Sports access, 50, 214
Sports innovations, 167
Stage theories. *See* Longitudinal
    theories
Standardization, 23, 31–32
Standards, architectural, 130–131,
    131 (figure), 186
Starees, 96
Subgroups, 155
Suicide, physician-assisted, 83
Sunami, C., 125
Support, as term, 151
Symbols:
    "access," 38 (figure)
    parking, 131, 131 (figure)
    wheelchair, 131, 131 (figure),
        132 (figure), 186

Symmetry, as principle of diversity
    depth, 95
Systems:
    closed, 60, 106
    complex, 112–114
    exosystems, 107 (table), 110
    family, 108
    macrosystems, 107 (table),
        110–111, 112
    mesosystems, 107 (table), 110
    microsystems, 107–110, 107 (table)
    open, 60, 64, 106
Systems change, 61, 104
Systems legitimacy, 157–158,
    157 (table)
Systems theories:
    classical, 51
    complex systems, 112–114
    constructed explanations and, 64
    embodied, 61
    Explanatory Legitimacy Theory,
        descriptive element of, 51
    Explanatory Legitimacy Theory,
        explanation in, 60–61
    heuristics of, 103 (table), 104
    history of, 104–106
    system levels and exemplars,
        107–112, 107 (table)
    values in, 157, 157 (table)
    See also Systems legitimacy

Tangential-influential policies, 110
Task analysis, 193
Tasks, behavior and age-appropriate,
    69, 70
Technology:
    assistive, 89, 134
    defined, 193
    exterior environment theories
        and, 88
    fashionable, 129, 134
    human factors as driver of,
        193–194
    interior environment theories and,
        82–83, 83–84
    postmodernism and, 119
    role in measurement, 82–83
    as 20th century contextual factor,
        26–29

Thompson, Garland, 96
Titchkosky, T., 37
Typical/atypical axis, 5, 52, 56

Ugly Laws, 32
UN Convention on the Rights of
    Persons with Disabilities, 134
UN General Assembly Resolution
    217A (III), 205, 206–210 (figure)
United Kingdom:
    handicap, origin of term, 10
    impairment/disability binary, 35
    person-first language, 39
    Poor Laws, 19, 21 (table)
United States:
    colonial era, 20, 21 (table)
    education, 35–36, 180–182
    immigrants, 21–22, 33
    person-first language, 39
    prenatal screening policies, 113
    suicide, physician-assisted, 83
    Victorian era, 21–22
Universal design, 166–167, 186–187
Usable/nonusable environmental
    theories, 88–89
    See also Exterior environment
        theories

Value, adding, 127
Values:
    ancient Greeces, 13 (table)
    in contemporary and
        emerging theories, 158,
        159 (table)
    defined, 142, 142–143 (table), 143
    Enlightenment era, 21 (table)
    in environmental theories, 152–153,
        153 (table)
    importance of, 141, 143–144

in longitudinal theories, 147–148,
    148 (table), 149
Middle Ages, 17 (table)
in systems theories, 157, 157 (table)
Victorian era, 24 (table)
Victorian era, 20–23, 24 (table)
Visible Human Project, 124
Vision, low, 37–38, 38 (figure)
Visual culture, 122–124
Vital Signs (film), 100
Vitruvian Man, 18, 89, 130–131,
    136, 186
Volkmar, F., 57
von Bertalanffy, L., 60, 106

Walking, 5, 6–7, 96–97
War injury, 10, 13
Watson, J. B., 86
Weber, M., 4
Wheelchairs, 37–38, 38 (figure), 130,
    130 (figure)
Wheelchair symbol, 131, 131 (figure),
    132 (figure), 186
WHO. See World Health
    Organization
Within, legitimacy from, 146
"Within normal limits," as
    concept, 84
Without, legitimacy from, 145, 146
Witness: Arts, Humanities, and
    Human Rights (event), 163
Wolfensberger, W., 36, 59, 87
Womb to tomb theories, 76
Women, exclusion from men's
    competitive sports, 50
Work, 30
Workplace regulations, 113
World Health Organization
    (WHO), 81

About the Authors

Elizabeth DePoy is professor of social work and interdisciplinary disability studies and also holds an appointment as Senior Research Fellow at Ono Academic College, Research Institute for Health and Medical Professions in Kiryat Ono, Israel. Dr. DePoy is a nationally and internationally recognized scholar in research and evaluation methods and original theory in the fields of disability, diversity, and design. With coauthor, Stephen Gilson, DePoy developed Explanatory Legitimacy Theory, which analyzes how population group membership is assigned, is based on political purpose, and is met with formal responses that serve both intentionally and unintentionally to perpetuate segregation, economic status quo, and intergroup tension.

DePoy has applied legitimacy theory to the analysis of diversity and human rights. Along with Gilson, DePoy has implemented her vision of socially just policy and praxis, based on principles of full participation and access through the creation of a web portal that renders existing illness prevention information accessible to individuals across diversity category boundaries.

Her work has created an important theoretical advancement in disability and diversity studies and has been acknowledged as a new paradigm for Disability Studies by many scholars in the field. Most recently, DePoy, with coauthor Gilson, applies design theory and practice to the analysis of diversity categories, their membership and their maintenance.

DePoy's most recent research interests and publications have focused on epistemology and research methodology, disability as designed, human rights, and advancement of equality of access to environments and resources. Dr. DePoy is currently working on her tenth book, has contributed many chapters to edited collections, and has over 100 articles published in peer-reviewed journals. She has earned over seven million dollars in extramural research grants at the University of Maine. Dr. DePoy presents her work locally, regionally, nationally, and internationally and has collaborative relationships with international scholars. In the service arena, Dr. DePoy provides evaluation, research, and grant writing consultation to agencies and organizations.

Dr. DePoy's awards for scholarship include:

- Senior Scholar Award. Society for Disability Studies, June 2009.
- Elected to The Honor Society of Phi Kappa Phi. University of Maine, April 2009.
- Distinguished Lifetime Achievement Award. American Public Health Association, October 2008.
- Faculty Fellowship Summer Institute in Israel. Society for Peace in the Middle East; Sponsored by Bar-Ilan University, Hebrew University of Jerusalem, Ben Gurion University, Tel Aviv University, Haifa University, Technion–Israel Institute of Technology, Jewish National Fund, Media Watch International, Scholars for Peace in the Middle East. Summer 2008.
- Presidential Research and Creative Achievement Award. University of Maine, May 2007.
- Outstanding Achievement Award. Association of University Centers on Disability, November 2006.
- Allan Meyers Award for Scholarship in Disability. American Public Health Association, September 2005.
- Fulbright Senior Specialist Scholar. Grant awarded to Assuit University, March 2003.
- Feminist Scholarship Award. Council on Social Work Education, March 2000.

In *Rethinking Disability* (2004), and in her most recent writing on disability, DePoy, with coauthor Gilson, takes on the essentialist nature of current diversity categories with a particular focus on disability, laying bare the value foundation and political and economic purpose of *disability category* assignment and social, professional, and community response. Her additional works, coauthored with Gilson, include *The Human Experience* (2007) and selected essays and papers. This scholarship applies legitimacy theory to understanding theories of human description and explanation and their purposive, political use in diverse helping-professional worlds.

Stephen French Gilson is professor of social work and interdisciplinary disability studies and also holds an appointment as Senior Research Fellow at Ono Academic College, Research Institute for Health and Medical Professions in Kiryat Ono, Israel. He is a theorist and policy analyst who is best known for his work in disability, diversity, and health policy through the lens of legitimacy theory. With coauthor Elizabeth DePoy, Gilson developed Explanatory Legitimacy Theory, which analyzes how population group membership is assigned, is based on political purpose, and is met with formal responses that serve both intentionally and unintentionally to perpetuate segregation, economic status quo, and intergroup tension.

Gilson has applied legitimacy theory to the analysis and enactment of health policy related to access to illness prevention information. Along with DePoy, Gilson has implemented his vision of socially just policy based on principles of full participation and access through the creation of a web portal that renders existing illness prevention information accessible to individuals across diversity category boundaries. His work has created an important theoretical advancement in disability and diversity studies and has been acknowledged as a new paradigm for Disability Studies by many scholars in the field. Most recently, Gilson, with coauthor DePoy, applies design theory and practice to the analysis of diversity categories, their membership, and their maintenance.

His research interests and publications have focused on disability identity, experiences of domestic violence and women with disabilities, disability theory, disability as diversity, social justice, and health and disability policy and advocacy. Dr. Gilson is currently working on his ninth book, has contributed many chapters to edited collections, and has over 60 articles published in peer-reviewed journals. He is currently pursuing a collaborative research agenda to develop and test software that will provide full access to web and electronic information. Dr. Gilson presents his work locally, regionally, nationally, and internationally and has collaborative relationships with international scholars. In the service arena, Dr. Gilson is extremely active on university, local, national, and international committees, organizations, and concerns. His commitment to universal ideology as a means to promote social justice and equal opportunity guides his service work.

His awards for scholarship include:

- Senior Scholar Award. Society for Disability Studies (SDS), 2009.
- Stanley Sue Distinguished Lecture Series, Diversity Lecture—"Now guess who is coming to the diversity dinner: Disability and beyond bodies and backgrounds." University of Maine, Department of Psychology, 2009.
- Multicultural Council Award for Leadership in Diversity. Association of University Centers on Disabilities (AUCD), 2008.
- Faculty Fellowship Summer Institute in Israel. Society for Peace in the Middle East, Summer, 2008.
- Allan Meyers Award for Scholarship in Disability, American Public Health Association, September, 2005.
- Commission on the Role and Status of Women; Feminist Scholarship Award for 2000; E. P. Cramer, S. F. Gilson, and E. DePoy—"Experiences of Abuse and Service Needs of Abused Women with Disabilities." Council on Social Work Education (CSWE), 2000.

In *Rethinking Disability* (2004), and in his most recent work, Gilson, with coauthor DePoy, takes on the essentialist nature of current diversity categories with a particular focus on disability, laying bare the value foundation and political and economic purpose of *disability category* assignment and social, professional, and community response. His additional works, coauthored with DePoy, include *The Human Experience* (2007) and selected essays and papers. This scholarship applies legitimacy theory to understanding theories of human description and explanation and their purposive, political use in diverse helping-professional worlds. Dr. Gilson was elected Chair for the Disability Section for the American Public Health Association (2 year term to begin November 2009).

Supporting researchers for more than 40 years

Research methods have always been at the core of SAGE's publishing program. Founder Sara Miller McCune published SAGE's first methods book, *Public Policy Evaluation*, in 1970. Soon after, she launched the *Quantitative Applications in the Social Sciences* series—affectionately known as the "little green books."

Always at the forefront of developing and supporting new approaches in methods, SAGE published early groundbreaking texts and journals in the fields of qualitative methods and evaluation.

Today, more than 40 years and two million little green books later, SAGE continues to push the boundaries with a growing list of more than 1,200 research methods books, journals, and reference works across the social, behavioral, and health sciences. Its imprints—Pine Forge Press, home of innovative textbooks in sociology, and Corwin, publisher of PreK–12 resources for teachers and administrators—broaden SAGE's range of offerings in methods. SAGE further extended its impact in 2008 when it acquired CQ Press and its best-selling and highly respected political science research methods list.

From qualitative, quantitative, and mixed methods to evaluation, SAGE is the essential resource for academics and practitioners looking for the latest methods by leading scholars.

For more information, visit **www.sagepub.com**.